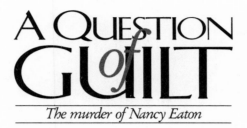

A QUESTION of GUILT

The murder of Nancy Eaton

by WILLIAM SCOULAR & VIVIAN GREEN

A QUESTION of GUILT

The murder of Nancy Eaton

by WILLIAM SCOULAR & VIVIAN GREEN

Stoddart

First published in 1989 by
Stoddart Publishing Co. Limited
34 Lesmill Road
Toronto, Canada
M3B 2T6

Canadian Cataloguing in Publication Data
Scoular, William
   A question of guilt: the murder of Nancy Eaton
ISBN 0-7737-2216-5
1. Leyshon-Hughes, Andrew. 2. Eaton, Nancy. 3. Murder — Ontario
— Toronto. 4. Trials (Murder) — Ontario — Toronto. 5. Insanity —
Jurisprudence — Canada. 6. Crime and criminals — Ontario —
Toronto.
I. Green, Vivian. II. Title.
HV6248.L49S35 1989   364.1'523'0924   C88-094322-X

"You and Me Against the World"
   Lyrics and music by Paul Williams and Ken Ascher
   © 1974 Almo Music Corp. (ASCAP)
   All rights reserved — International Copyright Secured

Printed in the United States of America

For K. M.

Hard questions must have hard answers.
PLUTARCH, *LIVES: ALEXANDER*

CONTENTS

PREFACE

THIS HAS BEEN AN unsettling book to write and many readers may well find it a disturbing one to read. Andrew Leyshon-Hughes, at the age of seventeen, stabbed his closest friend, Nancy Eaton, twenty-one times with a butcher's knife and then raped her dead body. This book attempts to explain how such a tragedy could occur.

We regret that in recounting these dire events we are bound to cause some degree of pain to those who have been personally involved in them. For their part they may well prefer, insofar as it is possible, to drink from the springs of Lethe and to consign the past to oblivion. But the dramatic increase in this type of murder, in all countries of the world, purposeful yet apparently motiveless, which brought Nancy Eaton's short life to so precipitate and undeserved an end, demands attention, no matter how discomforting, for if we can identify the cause of such atrocities we may be better able to detect such a deviant personality before it does harm and causes suffering.

Andrew Leyshon-Hughes is not a stranger in our midst. He is no scion of the slums driven by desperation to crime, but one of us, son and heir to a respected and respectable family. He could be the boy next door. What, we ask, turned a seemingly harmless adolescent into a brutal and sadistic killer? How valid was the plea of insanity put forward in his defense? Was he a responsible agent, the product of his upbringing and social environment or, as was argued at the trial, the impotent victim of a particular brain dysfunction? What weight should be attached to the evidence proffered by the psychiatrists? Why was the crime so sadistic in its nature? How adequate are both the psychiatric classification of mental disorders and the legal concepts relating to them? And how effective is the after-care of such offenders?

These are some of the questions which we seek to ventilate. In doing so we have been led to investigate not merely the course of events which led to the murder, but the different views which were voiced at the trial. The defense argued that Andrew was insane, that behavior conditioned by his infancy and family background exempted him from moral responsibility. The Crown, on the other hand, believed that there must be no excuse for Andrew's moral defects; though psychopathic, he was not insane. He killed Nancy Eaton in cold blood with full awareness and deliberation and should, therefore, have been found guilty of murder in the first degree.

It is impossible to say for certain which of these views is the more authentic. They both give voice to the thoughts of a disturbed youth who created his own hell and then dragged other human beings into it. In the end, we will probably never know why, but it is because we need to ask why that this book has been written.

─── *ACKNOWLEDGMENTS* ───

THIS BOOK HAS BEEN COMPILED, in the main, from the records of the preliminary hearing and of the trial, and from the massive evidence at the disposal of the court. Where published material has been used, we have tried to indicate the source in the notes.

We have had the benefit of interviews with so many people that it is impossible to acknowledge them all and, if we have failed to mention any by name, we hope they will accept our apologies. We are grateful to Susan Bardsley, Harry Beer, Cicely Bell, Paul Farberman, Diane Ferguson, Belinda Gallant, Stephen Harper, Burton Kellock, Deb and Wyn Kennedy, Brenda McCarthy, Michael McConnell, Susanne Milnes, Tami Mori, Norman Nault, Stephen Niblett, Patti Sifton and Paul Speck.

We would also like to thank Bert Bruser, Jackie Burroughs, Michael Carver, Edward Gilbert, Jacqueline Masson, Gardner McKay, Jon Pearce, Irene Perro, Carol Roup, Mary Beth Schofield, Mr. and Mrs. A. Scoular, Elizabeth Shepherd, Andrew Simms and Pam Wilmot.

More particularly, our thanks are due to Sergeant Joe Cziraky, Staff Sergeant Ed Stewart, Kristi Morrison and, most especially, Mrs. Nancy Leigh Eaton, without whose cooperation this book could not have been written.

We have been very fortunate to have as our editor Sandra Tooze, whose astute judgment inspired many improvements.

1

-MONDAY, 21 JANUARY 1985-

Murder, though it have no tongue, will speak
With most miraculous organ

SHAKESPEARE, *HAMLET*

TWILIGHT IS SHORT AND DARKNESS comes early in January in
Toronto, shedding a black cloak over the icy city. For Mrs. Nancy
Eaton that January day, Monday the twenty-first, 1985, had been one of
increasing concern. Her daughter phoned every morning as soon as she
woke up. Punctually. On the dot. And while she made tea, they would
talk. Mother and daughter. Every morning.

But today was unlike other days. There was no call. When Mrs.
Eaton rang at ten o'clock, Tiger's answering machine was on, echoing
into the void: "I'm sorry I can't come to the phone right now but if you
leave your name and number I'll get back to you as soon as I can."

The hours inched past. No call.

That whole day Mrs. Eaton felt on edge, a nagging, sinking feeling. At a quarter to five she phoned Tiger's office. The receptionist said that she hadn't been seen or heard from all day. Did anyone know where she was? No. Did she wish to leave a message? Yes. To please tell Tiger to call her mother as soon as possible — it was urgent.

At last in desperation, at half-past seven in the evening, Mrs. Eaton tried her daughter's number once more. Again no answer. "I am absolutely frantic," she said into the answering machine. "I'm taking the dog for a walk, and I'm coming right up."

It was snowing heavily. She got in her car and, shaking uncontrollably, drove the mile and a half to Tiger's apartment at 4 Farnham Avenue, in her agitation parking the car on the wrong side of the street, leaving its lights on.

The apartment was in darkness. Soundless. Illuminated only by a single bulb in the hallway outside. She did not go immediately into the bedroom, fearing that she might stumble in the darkness. But as she turned right into the dining room and kitchen, she noticed a black stain on the bedroom carpet and a tall plant sitting on top of the bed. The living room was in complete chaos.

"Tiger, where are you?" very softly. No answer. "Tiger!" The flashing red light of the answering machine signaled a backlog of unanswered calls.

She moved through the darkness towards the bedroom. Inside the open doorway she stumbled over something which should not have been there. A leg. Sticking out from under the bedclothes. Her hand touched the carpet. It was soaked with blood.

She lifted the bedclothes. The body was nude, smeared with blood, a torn nightshirt pulled up to the neck. Ten stabs? Twenty stabs? Thirty? She felt the leg. It was cold.

"Oh, Tiger," the stricken mother whispered.

A knife, its blade bent out of shape, jutted out from under the bed.

The scene scorched her senses.

She fumbled in the dark for the telephone and dialed 911. "Please!" she gasped. She tried to continue but she couldn't. The words wouldn't come out, her limbs were trembling, she lost control of her bowels. The receiver fell to the floor.

She pulled off her soiled clothes and flung them into the bathtub. Then she groped for the phone and blurted out her story.

When the sirens came she ran out into the hallway. Then, realizing that she didn't have any clothes on, she grabbed her fur coat and scrambled downstairs in the dark.

When the police arrived they were flagged down by a woman wrapped in a mink coat. "My daughter's been murdered, she's dead. I know who did it. It was Andrew." She was standing barefoot in the snow.

Across the road, at a popular radio station, the disc jockey could hear the wail of approaching sirens. He looked out the window of the studio where his nightly radio spot was just getting underway.

Turmoil and confusion. Lights were flashing. Police cars blocked off the entrance to Farnham Avenue. A crowd was gathering outside number four, staring. Somebody came out of the front door. Fur coat and bare feet. He couldn't make out who it was. But he knew the apartment building. His friend Tiger lived there.

Less than a block away, the Metro Homicide teletype stirred to life:

PROVINCIAL ALERT #40

THE BODY OF 23-YEAR-OLD NANCY EATON, GREAT-GREAT-GRANDDAUGHTER OF THE DEPARTMENT STORE FOUNDER TIMOTHY EATON, HAS BEEN FOUND STABBED TO DEATH IN HER APARTMENT AT 4 FARNHAM AVENUE, TORONTO.

THE VICTIM'S MOTHER ADVISED THAT NANCY EATON HAD BEEN WITH A SEVENTEEN-YEAR-OLD BOY NAMED ANDREW LEYSHON-HUGHES OF 109 ALCORN AVENUE, TORONTO, THE PREVIOUS EVENING.

THE VICTIM'S VEHICLE, A 1979 BUICK SKYHAWK, WHITE IN COLOR, BEARING THE ONTARIO MARKERS 'TYGER' (THE NICK-NAME OF THE DECEASED GIRL) IS MISSING FROM ITS PARKING SPOT.

APPREHEND THE VEHICLE AND DRIVER ON SIGHT.

END OF MESSAGE.

Into the wintry night, going north, on slippery roads, Andrew Leyshon-Hughes drove Nancy Eaton's white Buick up Highway 400, destination unknown.

But as he approached Major Mackenzie Drive the engine began to rattle suggesting to Andrew, who knew something about the working of cars, that TYGER was about to seize up. It was no wonder. Nancy didn't believe in putting oil in her car. "No, no, just put the gas in," she would say. "It'll run fine." But it wasn't running fine for Andrew. The last thing he wanted to do was stop. But he had no choice.

At 9:50 he drove up to the Petro-Canada gas station where the attendant, Tate Passer, came out to see what was wrong. When he lifted the hood the V8 engine rattled alarmingly. "It's probably something in the cylinder, she's knocking on the first piston," said Passer. "But we can't do nothing here. We got nobody on." Better, he told Andrew, to drive on to the Husky station at Bradford which was some miles away.

Whether the car would make it was doubtful, for it looked as if the engine might seize up at any minute. He advised Andrew to get a tow truck. "No," said Andrew, "I'm only going to Barrie and I can get it fixed there. It's my sister's car, I've just borrowed it." Passer and another attendant, Jeffery Plouffe, noticed that Andrew was wearing girls' clothing. "After he left we laughed about the way he was dressed: women's track pants, white with a purple stripe down the side, and the license on the car, TYGER. We thought he was a fruitcake, gay."

So Andrew drove on, slowly but desperately, the twenty or so miles to the Husky station at Bradford, near highways 88 and 400. There, at a quarter to eleven, the car almost ground to a halt, oil leaking from the engine. Andrew switched on the flashers and walked to the station to get help. Would the garage be able to help him fix the car, even temporarily? Surely if a rag could be stuffed in the hole in the motor, more oil could be poured in which would enable him to continue on his journey to nowhere.

Dan Reynolds, the attendant on duty and not much of a mechanic, grunted; his shift was just about to end and he wanted to get back to the warmth of his home. He saw that little could be done at that time of night and told Andrew so. "You'll have to get a ride someplace else because that car ain't going nowhere tonight."

It looked as if a tow truck was the only answer. Dan's pal, Kirk Griffith, offered to phone for a truck. It would cost only twenty-five dollars. Andrew's answer struck them as odd. He didn't have twenty-five dollars, only fifty. The long day was obviously beginning to take its toll. Kirk thought it strange that, after Andrew said that the car was his sister's, he asked Kirk if he knew her. But they were used to having some pretty weird customers late at night and shrugged their shoulders, thinking nothing of it.

They were much more concerned about Nancy's car. It was right in the middle of the ramp where it would obstruct other vehicles entering the gas station. Since plainly it could not be repaired that night, it would have to be towed. Andrew repeated that he didn't have enough money and asked Kirk if he would help him push the car. "Are you crazy?" replied Kirk. "Move it yourself. And you better get it out of here real fast or I'll call the police and have it towed away. It's blocking our entrance."

Desperate, Andrew went out to the laneway, hoping that he might be able to push the car himself, and it was at the moment he got back to the car that an officer from the Ontario Provincial Police drove up.

As soon as the Metropolitan Toronto Police found that Nancy's car had disappeared, they sent out a red alert to apprehend the car and its driver. Among others, Constable John Madden received a telex message from Homicide telling him to be on the lookout for a 1979 white Buick Skyhawk, bearing the license plate TYGER. At five minutes after eleven he received a further message, requesting him to go to the Husky Restaurant and Gas Bar where a motorist who had been involved in an accident on Highway 400 would be waiting for him in the coffee shop. It was on his way to deal with this that Madden drove to the service station, noticing as he drove down Highway 88 that there was a stationary car in the middle of the ramp. The young man who was standing by it flagged him down. At first Madden thought that this was probably a person connected with the accident, but the youth asked him if the police cruiser could push him as far as the gas pumps in the parking lot so that he might get help. It was only then, looking through the windshield of his car, that Madden saw in the light of his headlights the significant word TYGER. "Sure," he replied. "Go and sit in the car, and I'll get behind and give you a push."

Andrew got back in the driver's seat to steer. Madden, uncertain as to whether Andrew was armed or not, took advantage of the brief interval to alert police headquarters in Barrie and to ask for reinforcements. Then he moved his own car forward as if he was about to push Andrew's car but, before he made actual contact, he turned off his engine, drew his revolver out of its holster and told Andrew to get out, warning him that he was under arrest. "Put your hands on the roof of the car," he ordered, "and spread your legs." He gave him a quick search, was relieved to find that there was no gun, put on the handcuffs and made him sit in the back of the police car. It was a big moment in P.C. Madden's career, for he had never had to arrest a suspect on a murder charge before. So when two other police officers, Kenneth Dolan and Taylor Hunt, arrived on the scene, he was relieved and felt he could safely put his revolver back in its holster.

They took Andrew to the Bradford police station where they subjected him to a more thorough search. All they found was a small pocket knife and a wallet containing various identification cards, a Grey Coach bus receipt, fifty dollars and, in the side pocket, a folded two-dollar bill containing a white powder.

And there was one more thing — a bronze medallion card from the Royal Life Saving Society.

At 1:58 A.M. Andrew was taken from the detention cell to the interrogation room where two officers from the Homicide Squad, Staff Sergeant Ed Stewart and Sergeant Joe Cziraky, were waiting for him. He was subjected to a long investigation lasting nearly four hours. They managed to elicit from him his chilling account of the events of the early morning.

> It was getting bright when I woke up. I went into her room. She was sleeping. I stabbed her with a knife I got from the kitchen. It was a big knife, about nine inches. It had a sharp blade for trimming fat. After I stabbed her I took off my pants and had sex with her. I ejaculated into her. She was dead when I raped her.

When they asked him about Nancy's car, he replied, "I stole it early this morning and I was on my way to Blue Mountain when it broke down." Why was he making for Blue Mountain? "Because I was not stupid. There's a cliff at the top of Blue Mountain and I planned to drive the car over it and kill myself because I felt bad for what I did and I wanted to die."

Throughout the interrogation he remained remarkably calm and self-possessed, rarely showing any emotion. But what was the turmoil of the past years and even more of the past hours, which passed then through his mind?

At length the interrogation came to a close, drawing together the thread of events but failing to explain why they had happened. Its conclusion was inevitable. "I am arresting you for murder," Stewart told Andrew. "It is my duty to inform you that you have the right to retain and instruct counsel without delay. Do you understand?" Andrew nodded, and at nine minutes past six, on a bleak Tuesday morning, he was taken away by the Metro Police to the Don Jail in Toronto.

It was less than twenty-four hours since he had been sleeping safely and soundly on the couch in Nancy's living room.

11

NANCY

Love, sweetness, goodness, in her person shined.

JOHN MILTON

NANCY EATON WAS BORN INTO THE Canadian Establishment, a world of old money and pedigree, a private, even secret, club whose members attend charity balls and polo matches and live comfortable and secluded lives in graceful mansions with manicured lawns and elegant drawing rooms — a life of privilege and influence insulated from the outside world.

Her forebears on both her mother's and her father's side were charter members of the rich WASP establishment in Ontario. Her father was an Eaton. For every Canadian, Eaton is a household name. What the Wanamakers and Marshall Field have been to New York, the Whiteleys,

Harrods and Selfridges to London, the Eatons were, and still are, to Canada. They are the merchant aristocracy of Canada. Eaton's is the largest privately owned department store chain in North America, operating some three hundred branches, and its activities have proliferated into many other areas of commerce and capital. What the Medici family were to Florence, the Eatons have been to Canada — rich, with an extravagant lifestyle, philanthropists and builders, if somewhat less conspicuous than the Medicis in their patronage of culture. They are on a first-name basis with premiers and prime ministers. They get what they want when they want it and their power and influence pervades Canadian life, even though they have always sought to preserve their privacy. As a general rule, the Eaton name appears in the press only when an Eaton wants it to. When an armed robber murdered a finance-company manager on Yonge Street, fleeing through Eaton's store in an attempt to get lost in the crowds, the dramatic chase was reported in the press as "being through a downtown department store and south across Queen Street."[1]

Timothy Eaton, the founder of the Eaton empire, was Nancy's great-great-grandfather. He came originally from a Scottish family which had settled in northern Ireland, and he was born in 1834 on his father's small holding at Clogher, near Ballymena, in County Antrim. Twenty miles away was the growing commercial town of Belfast, and Ballymena was not far from Slemish where St. Patrick, the apostle of Ireland, once tended sheep. When Timothy was eleven years old, Ireland was afflicted by a terrible potato famine which so ravaged the population and ruined the economy that emigrants made for a new world where they hoped to find a better life. Ships sailed from Liverpool crammed with emigrants huddled in great discomfort and drenched by sea spray as they sought their fortunes overseas.

Timothy's father had died before he was born, so that his mother had not merely to look after the farm, no easy job in itself, but also to bring up her children. He went to the local school at Clogher, and managed to get an apprenticeship to a draper in nearby Ponteglenne, a small market town on the banks of the river Banne. But it was a one-eyed job in a one-horse town, and so year by year Timothy put his savings aside until he had enough to purchase a passage to Canada.

On his arrival he set up a general store, at the little town of Kirkton in Huron County. But he soon found out that life there was primitive and even harsh. There were no railways and Timothy had to transport all his stock by himself in his own ox wagon. But he prospered sufficiently to make a move, from Kirkton to St. Mary's, near Stratford. He hankered after something bigger and more challenging. So he moved yet again, to Toronto, a thriving town that was growing fast and attracting commerce and industry.

He set up his store on 8 December 1869 at 178 Yonge Street, transferring, in 1883, to 190 Yonge Street. A fanatically hard-working and teetotaling Methodist, Timothy's motto was "Early to bed, early to rise, never get tight and advertise." His concern for improving the lot of mankind dovetailed neatly with his passion for making money. He worked relentlessly, supervising every aspect of the business personally. The store soon expanded, spreading with great rapidity, to towns outside Toronto.

The secret of Timothy's success lay in his shrewd appreciation of what the public wanted. He was the first store owner in Canada to introduce cash dealing, "one price for all and spot cash," and to enact a policy of "goods satisfactory or money refunded." In 1884 he launched a sales catalogue which gave Canadians in remote rural areas the opportunity to buy a great variety of goods. Its arrival in distant homesteads was eagerly awaited, and it was sometimes the only book in the household other than the Bible. It was possible to order almost anything by catalogue — from Eaton's mail-order toupees, to patent medicines such as Greaves' worm syrup, and the Sahlin bust distender for ladies which "guaranteed to give the wearer that full bust and small waist so much desired." At one time it even offered a seven-room house, delivered by train with instructions on how to erect it, which sold for $999.77. "On Saturday nights," someone from a small township in Saskatchewan remembered, "everyone would get dressed up and go into town to see what everyone else was wearing. When they got home they'd look up the items in the catalogue and see what they cost."

Timothy was a patriarchal figure, high minded, enterprising and stern. He refused to sell playing cards or tobacco in his store, was a pillar of the Avenue Road Methodist Church and a generous benefactor of charities. The great department store which he had masterminded was further extended by his son, John Craig. Sir John Eaton, knighted for his patriotic services in the First World War, amassed a great fortune. He had two Rolls Royces (he owned the first motorcar in Canada and was the original owner of license plate No. 1 in Ontario) and a 173-foot ocean-going yacht, *Florence*, which he placed at the government's disposal in the war; it was used to patrol the Labrador coast until it was sunk. In 1901 he married Florence McCrea, a carpenter's daughter from Omeemee. They lived at Ardwold, a Toronto mansion with fifty rooms, fourteen bathrooms and a private hospital. Lady Eaton, who was to long survive her husband, later built a Norman-style castle with seventy rooms on a 700-acre estate at King, north of Toronto, and traveled the country in a private railway car. After a visit to Italy in 1927 she expressed her appreciation of Mussolini's reforms, regretting only that the dictator "is not really in good health and his only relief is in distracting his thoughts by playing the violin."[2]

Sir John Craig had four sons and two daughters, but by his will he provided that trustees must select the most suitable son and buy out the others. His eldest son, Timothy, who was passed over, lived in England where he devoted his life to building and operating model railways. So the succession passed eventually to John David Eaton, who was president of Eaton's from 1942 to 1969. He lived in a large house in Forest Hill but had a country seat in the Caledon Hills, a villa in Antigua and another on Georgian Bay. He owned a diesel yacht, the *Hildur*, and regularly commuted to work in a helicopter which he had learned to fly himself. He died in 1973 shortly before the completion of his pet project, the 250-million-dollar Eaton Centre, which was to become the prototype of the great shopping malls of North America. He was succeeded by his sons John, Frederick and George. Today the company shows some signs of decline but the Eaton family remains at the heart of Canadian commercial, political and social life.

Nancy Eaton was descended from Timothy Eaton's granddaughter, Alice, who had married Edward Browse. When the marriage ended in disaster, Alice reverted to her family name which was kept by her son Edward, Nancy's father, who was to marry Nancy Leigh Gossage at the Timothy Eaton Memorial Church on St. Clair Avenue, which Timothy's widow and son had erected to his memory.

On her mother's side Nancy was descended from the McCarthys, Campbells and Gossages, who, though not as affluent as the Eatons, had contributed much to Canadian life in the fields of law, politics and commerce. All these families had their roots in the British Isles. Nancy's maternal great-grandfather, Archibald Campbell, treasured a distant lineage which took his family back through the mists of Scottish history to bold and turbulent nobles, the Campbells of Breadalbane and even, though dubiously, to King Robert the Bruce himself. The Campbells arrived in Canada in the 1840s, settling first at Montreal, a town which had only recently replaced Kingston as the capital of the united province of Upper and Lower Canada.

Archibald obtained a job with the Commercial Bank, later the Bank of Montreal. In 1865 he started a flourishing timber business at Ashburnham near Peterborough, and profited greatly from the economic boom which the building of new railways had stimulated. As the demand for timber grew, so Campbell managed to exploit the riches of two million acres known as the Queen's Bush in the vicinity of Lake Huron and Georgian Bay, founding the Muskoka Mill and Lumber Company in 1875. His business interests proliferated; he presided for many years over the British Canadian Loan and Investment Company as well as the Toronto Electric Company. Like Timothy Eaton, Archibald Campbell managed to combine capitalistic ethics with high principles. It was characteristic of him that when he set up the Toronto Coffee Association in 1881 he defined its objectives as to "keep the working man from strong drink and to pay a comfortable dividend to the shareholders." He was deeply involved in the foundation of Wycliffe College, Toronto, in 1882 and the well-known girls' school, Havergal College, in 1894; his house, Carbrook, became the west wing of the Royal Ontario Museum. His ninth child, Muriel, married Leighton Goldie McCarthy in 1900.

Leighton McCarthy, Nancy Eaton's other maternal great-grandfather, traced his ancestry back to a distant line of Irish chieftains, the McCarthys of Munster and, on the female side, to Anne Burgh, a daughter of the Lord Chief Baron of the Exchequer in Ireland, whose forebears included Robert de Burgh, supposedly half-brother to William the Conqueror. Through his great-grandmother, Martha, Leighton looked back to another distinguished if somewhat tarnished ancestry, for Martha's father, Colonel Bucknell, so it was said, was an illegitimate son of Frederick, Prince of Wales, son of King George II. Leighton's more immediate ancestor, D'Alton McCarthy, was a Dublin lawyer whose practice at Blackrock near Dublin had been ruined by his partner's financial fecklessness. In June 1847 he settled at Kempenfeldt Hill, by Shanty Bay, near Barrie, on the western shore of Lake Simcoe. Here he and his elder son followed their former profession of the law; a formidable independent Tory, he was for ten years the member of Parliament for North Simcoe.

Leighton McCarthy was also the name of his nephew and he succeeded him as a member of Parliament. He expanded his family law firm with such success that it became one of the biggest corporation law practices in Canada. The Oslers, the family from which Andrew Leyshon-Hughes was to be descended, were for a time his partners. McCarthy had such a flair for attracting much-needed American capital for investment in Canadian industry that it was once said of him that the list of the companies with which he was associated read like a *Who's Who* of the Canadian business world. He reemerged into the mainstream of political life when Mackenzie King invited him to become Canadian minister (upgraded in 1943 to the rank of ambassador) in Washington during the important war years. His appointment was greeted warmly by President Franklin Roosevelt. The two had been friendly since McCarthy had sent his son to be treated for paralysis at Warm Springs in Georgia, which Roosevelt himself patronized. Leighton retired at the age of seventy-five and was succeeded by Lester Pearson. His daughter, Frances Leigh, married Brookes Gossage at St. James' Cathedral, Toronto.

The Campbells were descended from Highland lairds, the McCarthys from Irish chieftains, but the Gossages traced their ancestry to a Northamptonshire squirearchical family. On one side of the family tree they managed to trace a connection with the Elizabethan family of Ferrar, one member of which, John, had become a deputy governor of the Virginia Company. His brother Nicholas was better known as the founder of a high-church community in the Northamptonshire village of Little Gidding, one of the settings for T.S. Eliot's classical poem *The Four Quartets*.

Brookes Wright Gossage arrived in Canada in the early 1850s. The Northamptonshire family from which he came had been afflicted by declining fortunes. His grandfather, Thomas, had started a lace-making business but after initial prosperity it fell on hard times. His father, who acted as a land agent to a Cambridge college which had estates in the area, lost his wife when she was thirty-two and he himself died at forty-five, leaving an orphaned family of seven children. Brookes, who was the youngest, decided to seek his fortune abroad. He was a sturdy, ill-tempered boy, but strongly ambitious. It was his original intention to sail to Australia but when he arrived at the port of Liverpool he found that there was a berth on a ship sailing to Canada, so he changed his mind.

Brookes Gossage was not blessed with the success or distinction which had been showered on Archibald Campbell and Leighton McCarthy. On his arrival in Canada he became apprenticed to a Colonel Stoughton Harris as a land surveyor and civil engineer. In the 1860s he started a brewing business, Aldwells, on Simcoe Street in Toronto, but it failed. So he went back to land surveying, the boom in railway building serving him so well that he became chief engineer of the Canadian Southern Railway. He was evidently as cantankerous in old age as he had been as a boy. "You know," his daughter, Mrs. James Gill, told his grandson in 1935, "I was only sixteen when he retired from all activities, and when I look back he was always at the house at Creaton Lodge [Creaton was the name of the Northamptonshire village from which the Gossages came] and decidedly unpleasant he made it for us all."

Brookes' son, Charles, became a banker. He died in 1930. By his marriage to Georgiana Davidson, he had a son, Brookes Ferrar Gossage, who served with distinction in the First World War, winning the Military Cross. He became a successful businessman and married Frances Leigh McCarthy, the daughter of Leighton McCarthy. It was their daughter, Nancy Leigh Gossage, affectionately called "Snubby," who was to promote what might be called a dynastic marriage when she became the wife of Edward Eaton on Saturday, 17 September 1960.

Although he had been married before, Edward Eaton, Nancy's father, was not by nature designed for married life. Blessed with a large family inheritance, he drifted comfortably through life but contributed comparatively little to it. He took no interest in the family firm and after his mother Alice died he was ostracized by the Eaton family. But he continued to live the life of an Eaton in his large Forest Hill mansion and at his condominium in Palm Beach, where he roamed the bars like a night owl. He liked to drink and to talk but rarely to listen, so that he lost friends more easily than he gained them.

> Edward [observed Mrs. Eaton] was dreadful. He had no friends.
> I felt sorry for him...was going to completely change him...
> was going to make everything better.
>   I didn't marry Edward until I was thirty-four but I met him
> when I was twenty-six, I think. His first wife left him and he
> chased me for eight years. If I went to Ireland to visit my friends
> to get away from him, who would show up? Edward. If I was in a

hotel he'd bang on my door all night. If I went to London, same thing. If I went home, he came home. I just couldn't get away from him. Finally, finally, I married him. And it's a very bad reason for marrying anybody but I just got tired. Anyway, somewhere along the line Edward decided that he wanted to assert his manhood and have a child before he was forty. The result of that was Nancy Alice Edward Eaton. His mother's name was Alice, his name was Edward and mine is Nancy so I named Tiger, Nancy Alice Edward Eaton. Edward nicknamed her Tiger.

When Tiger was born she did something to my back and I had to stay in bed in hospital for three months. She was born on the twenty-eighth of May as opposed to the thirteenth or fifteenth of June so I was on one floor of the hospital and she was in an incubator. So I didn't see her until she was about three weeks old.

She was ill a lot of the time and "Harry," her nursemaid, came to stay with us when she got out of the hospital. Tiger constantly screamed as a baby. She was miserable, she was ill, she screamed. She seemed to scream twenty-four hours a day.

At other times she appeared serenely unaware of her surroundings, as if immersed in a sea of silence. Mrs. Eaton began to sense that something was wrong.

I took her to the Institute of Child Studies, which was my grandfather's house which he had given to the university. They phoned me and said that they had some terrible news for me. They said my child was deaf.

She was profoundly deaf in both ears, about 98 or 99 decibel loss. One ear was better than the other. [Hearing aids, though unable to correct her hearing, amplified sounds and made her life much easier.] She hated the hearing aids but I made her wear them and she eventually got to the point, about age five, where she didn't even know she had them in. She'd go to sleep with them in. She'd wash her hair in the shower and all of a sudden I'd hear a scream, "Mother, I got my hearing aids wet!" So I'd go and pull them out. But then she became ill and she found that her ears would perspire and they became very irritating. She never really got used to them again.

Life with Edward became more and more unbearable.

> We weren't allowed to talk on the telephone, I couldn't have
> any servants, and we couldn't have any friends in because
> Edward was paranoid of people. He was an awful father. He
> never held her, never so much as touched her. Not even once.
> He'd go out when it got dark and come home about seven in the
> morning. Smashed. I'd have to get him, drunk, up the front
> stairs while I brought Tiger down the other stairs or else I'd
> have to whack him in the car, drive the car into the garage and
> pull the garage door down. He'd sleep all day so if there was any
> noise Edward would get up and give us hell. We had to keep
> quiet. So the two of us were forced to become a very close
> twosome.

By 1972 Edward had become so difficult that his wife walked out and
divorced him.

> When I finally left him I was sitting there like a bride with
> flowers coming in from all my friends saying, "Congratulations!
> You finally sharpened up."

The break-up of the marriage naturally created a crisis for both his
wife and daughter. For while the Eaton name ensured their social
position, they lacked the Eaton wealth and their lifestyle had to change
drastically.

> I kept the Eaton name because it wouldn't have been fair to
> Tiger to change it. But I have a real hang-up about it. I've had
> planes held up for me because they didn't know which Eaton I
> was.
>   I don't know and I never want to know whether some people
> were nice to Tiger because her name was Eaton. It would never
> have entered her head, and she would have been terribly hurt.
>   She used to say to me, "Can you imagine what I would have
> been like if you had stayed with dad and there had been all that
> money around? I could have turned out to be one helluva
> bitchy snob!"
>   She knew what real money was. But we didn't have it. With
> all my twenty-one times at court fighting Edward, he never

supported Tiger or myself. She got angry when she saw her father eat a hundred-and-fifty bucks worth of caviar at dinner. The big deal in our house was beef stew. She saw how my mother lived as well so she knew both sides of the coin. We just didn't happen to live that way. But it didn't bother Tiger. It bothered her for me.

So in the ensuing decade Mrs. Eaton lived with her daughter in semi-seclusion in a quiet flat on a quiet Rosedale street, contemplating her failed marriage, disappointed by the fact that her financial resources imposed severe limitations on her social life and activities.

I sometimes wouldn't see Snubby for a year and a half [recalled a close friend]. I'd put a Christmas present on the doorstep and leave. There were long periods when she simply never saw anyone. But I don't think, like her mother, it was a form of agoraphobia. It was just that she had some real problems. I think Snubby had a real feeling that these were her battles and that she had to fight them by herself.

She's probably the single most courageous person I've ever known. You can see that flame burning inside her — and you can almost see it literally these days, she's so thin, poor lamb.

Throughout, Mrs. Eaton showed the dogged courage which was a principal ingredient in her character, devoting herself to her daughter and trying, with the financial aid of her mother, to keep things on an even keel. "Without my mother," Mrs. Eaton said, "we'd have been out on the streets."

Snubby's mother, Leighton McCarthy's daughter, Frances, who had married Brookes Gossage, was a formidable personality; even her father christened her in later years "Mrs Bossage." Her own marriage had ended in separation. From the early 1960s she had an intimate relationship with the Canadian statesman, Vincent Massey.[3] When he was working on his autobiography, he recalled from an early diary that in the summer of 1912, after graduating at Oxford, he had spent a particularly happy time at a cottage on Georgian Bay built by Archibald Campbell, where he met four charming young girls, the daughters of Leighton McCarthy. He decided, after half a century had passed, to renew his acquaintance with the eldest, then ten and now sixty, Mrs. Leigh Gossage. "I can," she told him after their meeting, "vividly remember each incident, especially you and Herman Boulton demonstrating the fireman's lift, the knitting lesson with you... you must come and revisit the old place. After so many years it was delightful seeing you again."

Until Vincent Massey's death in London in 1967, Leigh Gossage was his constant companion, often visiting him at his home, Batterwood. She was once introduced as Massey's mistress. "I wouldn't," she responded sharply, "be anyone's mistress for a million dollars." "And wouldn't you," her questioner said, "just love to have the million!" "I have two," Mrs. Gossage replied frostily, "on deposit. In the National Trust."

Mrs. Gossage was sixty-three, Massey seventy-five; but they became fond of each other and, had it been easier to cut through the legal entanglements of their respective marriages, they might well have married.

> I was particularly happy [Hilda Neatby told Massey in 1966] to meet Mrs. Gossage and to be able to share with you your hopes of continued happiness together in the future. She is indeed, as you told me, a gifted and charming person, with such good sense, and a sense of humor, and great kindness. I shall be happy to learn that all has gone as you both hope. And what makes me very happy is that I believe with her encouragement you may feel able to do even more of the work for our country that you do well.[4]

They did not marry, but they were constantly in each other's company, spending social evenings at Massey College and at the Stratford Festival, and exploring the country around Grafton in eastern Ontario where the Masseys had first settled. He gave her an Italian enameled bowl as a birthday present. She showed an enthusiastic interest in his plans for the future of Massey College, and when he was taken mortally ill on a visit to London, she flew over and was by his side when he died on 30 December 1967.

But somehow she never seems to have developed a very close or deep relationship with her daughter. Although she was a rich woman, Mrs. Gossage kept a tight control over the purse strings and, for a time at least, Snubby did not find it very easy to make both ends meet.

Bearing her own experience in mind, Mrs. Eaton was determined that Nancy's childhood would be happier than her own had been.

Snubby said something to me that I think was very revealing [an
intimate friend commented]. She was talking about her mother
and she said, "I guess the one good thing that came out of my
relationship with my mother was my marvelous relationship with
Tiger, because there was no way any child [of mine] was going
to be treated the way I was."

I had a lousy bringing-up [said Mrs. Eaton]. My mother and
father did not get along. We were brought up in the back of the
house by the servants. Cook or Betty, the nanny, basically
brought us up. There are really no happy memories. They're
mainly sad-little-girl-crying-in-the-corner memories.

I remember coming home one day all excited because I'd
found a little kitten. My mother immediately took it up to the
Humane Society and had it destroyed. So when Tiger started
picking up stray cats and dogs I'd keep them. At one point we
had seven kittens in the house.

I wanted my mother's love and did everything I could to get it
and I didn't get it. There were no hugs and no love and no
warmth at home. So I did the complete reverse with Tiger by
giving her as much love and warmth and hugs as I could. This is
why Tiger and I were so close.

When Nancy was eight years old and in grade three at Branksome
Hall School she wrote in the school magazine, *The Branksome Slogan:*
"My mum has a funny color of hair. It is gray, brown and white. She has
a hard time keeping the cat and dog from running away. Once she made
a cake and it came out flat. My mum is a funny mummy. She likes me
and I like her." But in spite of her closeness to her mother, Nancy, in
some respects, was an unhappy child. She felt rejected by her father and
her handicap dogged her throughout her checkered school career.

I can't tell you how many schools Tiger had been to. I think
we added up eighteen. She refused to stay at the school for the
deaf. She loathed it, she hated all the sign language. So I sent
her to Forest Hill Public School which lasted about a month,
then she went to Rosedale Public School and then she went to
Branksome where she stayed for three years. After that, any

little private school that opened up in the city, that's where she would go, until they went belly-up. She had the lousiest education that anybody could ever have.

Kids at school teased her. Because she was so hard of hearing they thought she was slow and because her name was Eaton they said she was stuck-up. In the playground her classmates would gather in little groups, chatting and giggling. But Nancy felt alone and isolated. She did her best to appear normal and tried to participate, listening and concentrating to the point of exhaustion, trying desperately to lip read. Sometimes it worked out but more often than not she'd embarrass herself and the other girls would laugh and make fun of her.

Life became so stressful that instead of trying to make friends, as she desperately wanted to do, she withdrew into herself, becoming more and more dependent on her mother. Her strained relationship with her father made things even worse.

He'd sit outside their house all day with binoculars [recalled a neighbor]. Then he'd come by at three or four in the morning and ring the doorbell. Ring, ring, ring. And then he'd start phoning at all hours in the morning.

He'd take her out [Mrs. Eaton said], get drunk and humiliate her. He would tell her things like her mother was very ill and was going to be sent away and that he was going to look after her.

These situations began to overwhelm Nancy, leaving her so depressed that by the time she was eleven she suffered an emotional breakdown which lasted for three years.

Luckily she didn't have to be sent away. She was on very strong therapeutic medication and I had a lot of help in the house.

Eventually she recovered only to go through the normal trials and tribulations of the teenage years. She was no goody-two-shoes. She started roller-skating at the Mutual Street Arena and hanging out at the Scarborough Bluffs with a group of kids whom I suppose you would call rough. One of them, Todd, was a roofer and she spent a summer roofing. But these rough guys

took care of her. They always made sure she got home. And
when she got home, sometimes at three in the morning, she'd
come into my bedroom and sit on my bed and tell me all about
the evening.

When she turned seventeen, in spite of the traumatic nature of the
break, Nancy moved out of her mother's Rosedale residence and took
an apartment on Farnham Avenue.

We were living in very close quarters. So that I could live a life
and so that Tiger could live a life, instead of us both being so
entwined in each other's lives, it was decided that Tiger would
get a place of her own. Dad died and he left some dough so
there were funds to provide Tiger with an apartment and a bit
of pocket money. It was definitely the right decision but, my
God, at the time it was so upsetting for both of us.

A few days before she was supposed to move out she was lying
in her bed moaning. "What's the matter?" I said. "I've got such
a pain in my side," she said. "I'm sure it's psychosomatic
because I don't want to move out." But it wasn't. I took her to
the Toronto General and sure enough it was appendicitis.
Before she was operated on I went into her room and she was
crying. I leaned down, hugged her and said that the operation
would be over soon and that everything would be all right. But
she kept on crying. She looked up at me and said, "I've never
been cut before."

The four-storey block of apartments on Farnham Avenue is situated half
way up the Yonge Street hill, just north of Toronto's busiest liquor store
at Summerhill. It is situated in a kind of no-man's land between the
more fashionable areas south at Rosedale and north at Forest Hill. The
buildings are nondescript, even dingy, and few people, if any, would
give them a second look.

Her first apartment at Farnham Avenue [Mrs. Eaton recalled]
was very tiny. It was absolutely awful before she got her hands
on it. "This place stinks," I said. "How can you stand it?" It was
filthy but she turned it into something very cute. All she could
fit in the bedroom was a bed, and if you put one foot out of bed

you'd have been in the bathtub and if you put the other one out
you'd have been on the john. There was no door in the
bedroom or the bathroom so when she moved into the next
apartment, which had a door in the bathroom, all her friends
said, "Thank God!"

Her second apartment was much bigger. It was on the top
floor and it had a fake fireplace and a little entrance hall. To
the left was her bedroom which had a bathroom off it with a
good-sized window. To the right was the living room which had
two windows facing east and then a little dining area and a
kitchen with a back door leading outside. She completely did it
over. The living room was very attractive. It was big enough for
one three-seater and a two-seater sofa and two wicker chairs
and her stereo. She had her television in her bedroom. All her
kitchen stuff was yellow. She also had a roof deck and she'd go
up there with her Sony Walkman and her tea or her diet Coke,
which she was addicted to, and sit in the sun. She loved that
apartment. It was full of greenery. Lots of plants and lots of
flowers and lots of candles. Chip off the old block. She loved
music and she loved her space and she really enjoyed being
there by herself. But she also loved having people around. She
used to cook a lot. It was sort of a drop-in center. Of course,
there she was at seventeen with her own apartment. And she
had a car, Edward bought it. But he had to choose the make
and color and he was the first to drive it.

She was the person people called in the middle of the night
when they were in trouble or had a problem. Or they would
show up at her apartment at three in the morning. She'd say,
"All right. On the sofa." And there they would be in the
morning. She had a lot of male friendships which were
non-sexual. But she also had people she liked to snuggle with.
She was a very warm person, she liked hugging. As for the
other part, she really didn't see what all the fuss was about.

The move to Farnham Avenue, however, did not mean that there was
a change in the close relationship with her mother. They were in
constant touch with each other and if anything they became even
closer.

They phoned each other eight, maybe ten times a day [remembered one friend]. And they'd talk for hours. Like girlfriends, not like mother and daughter. Mrs. Eaton's life revolved totally, one hundred percent, around Nancy. She was always at the apartment doing a laundry or something for her and I thought to myself, "God, doesn't this woman have a life of her own?"

But in spite of having her own apartment, her own car and lots of friends Nancy was in some respects at a loose end. She was anxious to grow up and do something with her life but she was insecure and always tended to underestimate her capacity. She was, after all, only seventeen. She tried a number of odd jobs: cashier, waitress, babysitter. None of them lasted very long and in any case she found them tedious and unsatisfying. She was overweight and still suffered from occasional bouts of depression.

She was extremely emotional [a close friend recalled]. She could be terribly hurt by people. But she'd always forgive and forget. If you said the wrong thing to her she would burst into tears. My kid brother once made a stupid comment about her weight and she cried for hours. She used to cry a lot. She was something of a hypochondriac in those days. She always had a migraine or she was sick or she was at the doctor's or else she was always getting pills from the pharmacist. She was unhappy a lot and would sometimes sit in her apartment by herself, turn off the lights and feel plain miserable.

Those first two years on her own Nancy seemed to float through life like a particle in a solution. And then suddenly, when she was nineteen, she began to blossom. Life, she decided, was not going to pass her by.

Nancy completely turned her life around [her best friend Kristi Morrison commented]. She took a real-estate course and passed and got a job at Bill Joyce. Things really began to happen for her after that. It wasn't so much the job as it was going out and doing something she really felt proud of.

At first, though [Mrs. Eaton reflected], Tiger's emotions had a hard time dealing with the up-and-down nature of the business. She couldn't keep her upsets inside — they would come out all over the place and she'd end up in tears. "Of all the stupid, damn jobs for me to get," she would say. "Me, who's up and down like a yo-yo. Here I am in real estate. But I know it's going to work some day. I know it will." And it was. It was just starting to turn the corner for her. She had just sold her first house.

"Having a stimulating and challenging job," said Kristi, "gave Nancy a real feeling of self-worth, which she never had before. For the first time in her life she had responsibility and she began to feel worthwhile and intelligent."

Socially, too, she began to bloom. In social situations she took the initiative and, instead of hiding her hearing problem, she admitted it freely. She became an expert lip-reader and, along with her limited hearing and the guessing techniques which she had developed in order to survive, she was usually able to manage with minimal difficulty, even in group conversation. Still, things weren't always easy. There was the constant need to apologize and life sometimes became a steady repetition of, "I'm sorry, what did you say? What was that? What? What? What?" But she was learning to view her handicap with a sense of humor. Her deafness, she would say, had its advantages. Whenever it suited her she could pretend not to hear things people said, and she wasn't harassed in the middle of the night by the noise of wailing sirens on Yonge Street nor by the ecstatic groans of the over-sexed couple across the hall.

People couldn't get over how good Nancy now looked.

Everything about her was transformed [remarked Kristi]. She cut out all the junk food — she used to have potato chips and candy beside her bed — and she became very involved in athletics, especially windsurfing and tennis. She joined Super Fitness and began exercising nearly every day. And then the weight started to come off. Even the first twenty pounds made a difference. She was on such a high about the twenty pounds that twenty soon turned into thirty and so on until she eventually got down to a hundred and eighteen pounds. She looked absolutely fantastic! She changed her hairstyle, her nails were always perfectly manicured, she was always suntanned. She had a healthy, scrubbed, wholesome look about her and she was always beautifully dressed. She used to wear a string of pearls that her mother gave her. But she was never conservative, Nancy always had flair. Her favorite color was pink — everything was pale pink, white and pale blue. In her last three years Nancy was incredible looking and she was very proud of the way she looked.

She once gave me a picture [her friend Patti Sifton recalled] which showed her about forty pounds too heavy, and after she lost weight whenever she visited my apartment she tried to find the photograph so that she could destroy it.

The old Nancy and the new Nancy were completely different [another friend commented]. Suddenly everyone began to notice her. She used to complain that she had "no boobs and no legs" but in a crowd she always attracted stares — even in her sweatpants, Porsche sunglasses and tennis shoes, which she used to wear a lot. All of a sudden her phone never stopped ringing and she became very very popular. And these were good catches — guys who go after prime stuff.

Her whole attitude changed [said Kristi]. Instead of bursting into tears she learned to confront people when something was bothering her. She wouldn't take any guff from anyone. I'll never forget the first time she told me off. It was something to do with real estate. Anyway, she screamed at me, she really gave me hell. I was shocked, it was so unlike her. She had every right to yell at me but in the past she never would have done so. It was a good sign.

She even learned how to handle her father. Whenever he was difficult she used to laugh it off. Or she'd tell him to "go stuff it" if she felt like it. And he'd laugh. He loved it when she told him off. It was great. They began to enjoy each other.

She grew an awful lot in those three years. The real tragedy is that, after all the struggles she had to go through to get there, she really only had three good years.

Nancy made other people's well-being the central purpose of her life. Her need to be needed was the fundamental ingredient in her character and formed the basis of nearly all her relations with other people. "She was always running around doing something for somebody," a friend remembered. "She was a sucker for anybody who needed help." Above all, she wanted a permanent attachment, someone she could love and be loved by in return, but she inevitably seemed to become involved with unloving, emotionally unavailable partners instead. There had been some close relationships but they had not, in the long run, come to anything. One disastrous affair followed another, perhaps an expression of her own unhappy relationship with her father. As a young girl, every time she hugged her father or tried to show him affection he failed to respond. "It got to the stage," Mrs. Eaton said, "where she would say to him, 'Dad, why don't you tell me you love me?' "

As she grew older she often became involved with similar men in an attempt to win the old struggle to be loved by her father. But she tried too hard and she loved them too much.

> None of Nancy's boyfriends were long-term [a close friend revealed]. She smothered them with love. She was far too nice and generous with them, and always went way out of her way, hoping that if she bent over backwards they would love her as much as she loved them.

Nancy was warmhearted. It was hard for her to evaluate people or situations objectively and her overwhelming need to be needed drew her especially to those who were down on their luck or in some sort of trouble, and even, occasionally, to people who were dangerous or unwholesome. Her first boyfriend at one time carried a revolver in the glove compartment of his car and is currently before the Supreme Court accused of cutting the wires of the CHUM transmission tower, causing it to fall dangerously onto Yonge Street. He wrote to Mrs. Eaton in January 1985:

> I once shot a man, and felt remorse only for the place in which I had done it. Nancy . . . was determined to capture and mold me. And so with her soft stern unmoved voice, resolving eyes, and captivating wink, she did just that.

Another *liaison dangereuse* concerned Zach (not his real name), a

Yorkville drug dealer of unsavory reputation with whom Nancy had become involved while his girlfriend, Michelle (not her real name), was vacationing in Europe.

> She met [Zach] playing baseball [a friend recalled]. There used to be a mixed league that played in the park across from the liquor store in Summerhill. Most of the people who played were part of the really fast set in Toronto, the so-called 'beautiful' Yorkville crowd — models, actors and rich playboys, who'd pull up in their Mercedes, looking to go out with a model. [Zach] was one of these.
>
> The first thing I said when I found out that she was seeing him was, "What are you doing with a scumbag like that? The guy's a creep." But Nancy rushed to his defense and said, "He's a nice guy, he's not a bad person. He does what he does because he doesn't know any other way of life." She always overlooked people's faults. She couldn't distinguish between bad and good, that's for sure.
>
> Anyway, [Zach's] girlfriend, [Michelle], came back from Milan in September '84, after which she immediately phoned Nancy and screamed, "Keep away from my boyfriend!" So for fun, Nancy and I told her that we were going to squeal to the RCMP and get [Zach] busted, which was a lie. We never intended any such thing but we thought we'd have a bit of fun and get her back. Before you know it we got a threatening phone call saying, "You're messing with the wrong people. If you two don't shut up there's going to be big trouble."
>
> Nancy and I were completely freaked. We thought, "Oh God, they're going to murder us!" We must have stayed up until five in the morning talking about it. Nancy said to me, "If you get murdered, I'll know who did it and I'll tell the police, and if I get murdered you'll know who did it and you can tell."

In January 1985 Nancy Eaton had never been happier or busier or more beautiful in her life. She didn't have to strain for sincerity or high spirits. She was naturally bubbly and her luminous face was continually lit up with a smile. She was not so unlike most girls her age, more sensitive perhaps, more trusting and kind. She believed what people said and assumed that everyone's motives were as pure as her own. She saw good qualities in even the most dubious of characters. She looked at the world with hope and love and truly believed that down deep everyone was basically good at heart. She was wrong.

III

——*ANDREW: BEGINNINGS*——

Were you born of some queer magic?
Is there something strange and tragic,
Deep deep down?

NOEL COWARD

Thou cam'st on earth to make the earth my hell.
A grievous burden was thy birth to me.

SHAKESPEARE, *RICHARD III*

But children, you should never let
  Such angry passions rise;
Your little hands were never made
  to tear each other's eyes.

ISAAC WATTS

ALTHOUGH THEY CAME FROM SIMILAR social backgrounds, Nancy and Andrew were to grow up very different people. And yet, there was a tragic common ground on which they often met, a ground compounded of Nancy's caring self and Andrew's deep, even traumatic, need for care.

Andrew was born on 14 July 1967 at the Royal Victoria Hospital, Montreal. His mother Sarah, on the instructions of her physician, Dr. Primrose, had been admitted to a private ward shortly before noon on the previous day. She was a healthy young woman, twenty years old, with no serious medical history; the only comments made were that she was allergic to penicillin and smoked fifteen cigarettes a day.

The pains began in the early evening and eleven hours or so later she gave birth, at 6:25 A.M. to a boy, seven pounds, two ounces in weight. Ten minutes later, as was normal, the placenta was expelled. The hospital report noted that the placenta was "infarcted," that is obstructed, and there was a measure of calcification, suggesting that this might have been the case for some time. The baby was delivered vaginally, the umbilical cord (so it was said, though there is no reference to this in the reports) wrapped round the baby's neck.

Neither this nor some other minor features were thought to be dangerous. The medical reports showed that the baby had been "slow to breathe." "After first minute he responded to oxygen." First breath, two-and-a-half minutes. First cry, four minutes. The fetal result showed some shortness of breath ("moderate asphyxia") and low blood sugar ("hypoglycaemia," thirty-two milligrams). But these symptoms raised no undue comment at the time. Mother and baby were doing well and were soon discharged. Such was the way in which Andrew Leyshon-Hughes first saw the light of day.

The bad fairy must have been present at his birth. Yet at the time the omens were not ominous. His father Ernest, who was a Scot by birth had come with his parents to Canada and had been educated at an exclusive boys' school, Trinity College School, Port Hope; Ernest's parents later moved to Mexico where he, Sarah and Andrew regularly visited them. A childish drawing in Andrew's hand depicts an airplane labeled "Toronto to Mexico." Sarah was an adopted child, her adopted parents members of a well-known, wealthy family, the Oslers. Her elder brother, Stephen, and his family lived in New Brunswick; her younger sister Amy and her family resided in Toronto.

The Oslers, like the Eatons, had a British ancestry. The patriarch of the Canadian Oslers was the Reverend Featherstone Osler, a Cornishman and officer in the Royal Navy who had been ordained as an Anglican minister. In 1837, he and his wife Ellen, who lived to celebrate her hundredth birthday in 1906, emigrated to Canada to minister to the people of the townships of Tecumseh and West Gwillimbury at Bond Head, forty miles north of Toronto. It was an arduous job, looking after his sometimes difficult flock and raising a family of eight children. So, in March 1857, in poor health, he moved to Dundas near Hamilton. Featherstone, a strong evangelical, did not always see eye to eye with his high-church bishops and had to wait until he was seventy-six before he received an honorary canonry for his long service to the Church.

Four of his children achieved distinction in the fields of law, politics, business and medicine. The eldest, Featherston — he dropped the *e* — became a judge in the Ontario Court of Appeals, but in 1888 refused a seat on the Supreme Court because he had an inadequate knowledge of French. Britton Bath Osler, "B.B.," dominated the Canadian legal scene in the late nineteenth century and was much involved in the prosecution of murder cases.

Britton's brother, Edmund Boyd, "E.B.," was to win fame and fortune as a financier and broker. He started life as a teller at the Bank of Upper Canada and had to face the angry crowds who lost their money when the bank crashed in 1866. Later he became the president of the Dominion Bank as well as president of the Ontario and Quebec Railway which was absorbed in 1884 into the reconstituted Canadian Pacific Railway, of which he was a director for many decades. E.B. Osler was a founder of the Toronto Ferry Company and of St. Simon's Church which was later to be the scene of Nancy Eaton's funeral. He sat in the Canadian House of Commons, representing West Ontario, for seventeen years, was invited to take cabinet office and to become Canadian high commissioner in London. He was knighted in 1912.

William Osler, after a fractious childhood which involved his being expelled from two schools, entered the medical school at McGill where he taught for ten years. (His ashes rest in the memorial library there.) He was appointed first to a chair of medicine at the University of Pennsylvania and then at the newly established Johns Hopkins University in Baltimore. From 1904 to 1919 he was regius professor of medicine at Oxford University, and is still commemorated there by a medical center, Osler House. Sir William was a highly esteemed teacher, a research worker and a man of wide human sympathies, the first practitioner to organize a clinical unit in any Anglo-Saxon country.

Their descendants, spread geographically through Toronto to Montreal and Winnipeg, continued to play a prominent part in Canadian life as politicians, lawyers and businessmen. Featherston retired from the bench to become president of the Toronto General Trusts Company, dying in 1924. His grandson, John G. Osler, a distinguished lawyer, was Andrew's grandfather.

Yet, fine as his future prospects were in theory, there were soon shadows over Andrew's early life, not because of health but because of what may be broadly described as his environment. When he was born, Ernest and Sarah were still students, Ernest twenty-two, Sarah twenty. They had first met on the boat coming back from Europe when Sarah was thirteen and Ernest fifteen. At McGill romance blossomed. Sarah became pregnant. They discussed the possibility of abortion but decided against it. They were married on 19 November 1966.

Andrew was, his mother insisted, very much a wanted child, but in a sense he was unplanned, a mistake. Dr. Carr wrote to Dr. Norman Saunders, the family pediatrician: "Both parents suffer from a lack of good parenting themselves and Andrew was the cause of their marriage. Both parents feel they never should have had children and feel themselves miscast in the role of parents."

"They didn't want any more children," Joy Freeman, a social worker, recalled Sarah telling her. "They both wished to pursue careers and consequently they did not wish to compromise their desired life styles."

Circumstances made it difficult for Sarah to be a mother. She was still a second-year student. Both Ernest and she were career-oriented and in due course, in a worldly sense, they were to make good, Sarah as an estate-planning counselor with Canada Trust and Ernest as a chartered accountant with a bankruptcy firm in Toronto, where they moved in 1970 when Andrew was three.

But what of the child? Although his parents lived near the campus, his mother had to attend classes at the university, leaving Andrew in the care of babysitters who came and went. Au-pair girls followed the babysitters, and at two he was placed in a nursery. From the nursery he was moved to a daycare center where he was to stay until he started school. However much his parents tried to demonstrate their love, Andrew, from the start of his life, seemed insulated from their affections.

Later when the psychiatrists began to probe into Andrew's early history, they were puzzled to find it littered by tantrums. When he was only two years of age, he struck a child with a baseball bat and he cut another small friend's head with a metal toy car. More worrying, because in some sense unnatural, was his hostility to some of the housekeepers, and his seeming lack of affection for his parents. Sarah and Ernest were concerned about his childish outbursts, Sarah more than Ernest, for he believed that Andrew would grow out of them in time. He seemed moody, sullen and ill-tempered. But he showed a more cheerful side at his first school, Sunnybrook, a small private school on Merton Street. It was a carefree environment. The classes were small, so that the teachers could give their pupils personal attention. The atmosphere was friendly and the discipline liberal. The school's principal, Mrs. Irmingard Hoff, and Andrew's teachers, Mrs. Cameron and Ms. Burn, were pleased with Andrew's progress. It was said of his performance in grade one in December 1973:

> [In oral expression] Andrew has a substantial vocabulary and is always interested in the meanings of words new to him... He loves to read and his increasing knowledge of phonics allows him to sound out many new words... Andrew is already beginning to write his own stories.

At mathematics he "enjoys this subject immensely. He is enthusiastic about all subjects and always tries his best." The report at the end of the summer of 1974 was similar in tone. "Andrew loves to read both aloud and to himself. He reads with comprehension. He is capable of writing interesting and well-expressed stories as his command of the English language is good." Math remained his favorite subject. "He works accurately and quickly. He has an excellent understanding of number concepts and relationships." The report ended on another positive note: "Andrew enters into all activities with enthusiasm. He is always ready to discuss his own opinions as well as to listen to those of others."

He was promoted to grade two. And the report at Christmas 1974 showed that Christine Burn was still very satisfied: "expresses himself articulately"; "reads with expression and comprehension"; at arithmetic, "works with care and accuracy and greatly enjoys working with numbers." The report for 1975 summarized his achievement. "Andrew has taken real pleasure in the projects this year." Only in English was there a hint that he needed prodding if he was to give his best.

> Andrew [Margaret Ronning-Philip wrote on her Christmas card] has always been a favorite of mine. He is doing extremely well. He's happier and more confident of his own abilities and more at ease with himself in relations to his peers. He is charming and a little monkey and I am so happy to have him in my class.

No one could have wanted more glowing reports. There was just a suggestion that there were times when all was not well in his relations with the other children. But here at least there were no signs of the mental aberration nor the deep psychological problems which, it was to be said later, had been inaugurated at birth. He seemed a sunny, hard-working, interested and intelligent little boy. What were the circumstances which so steadily and inexorably changed his personality and reversed the hopes and expectations which reports such as these surely must have raised?

His school reports, not from Sunnybrook but from his new school, Blythwood Public School, were soon to show a downward turn. He was eight when he left Sunnybrook. By 1976, when he was only nine, his teachers were beginning to find him an enigma. While he had a good auditory and visual memory, his recall was often poor and confused. He was beginning to read badly, leaving out words and omitting whole sentences.

Worse than that, he was ceasing to communicate, even with his teachers, often with his peers, and more and more with his parents. Andrew seemed to live much of his time in a fantasy world and grudged being brought down to earth. Sunnybrook had been the highlight of his life. But he hated Blythwood. As the time drew near for him to leave for school, he would linger, sometimes bursting into tears. He began to sulk whenever he failed to get his way. "Go and finish your homework," his mother said sharply to him on one occasion. He snatched his papers from the table and ran out of the room. The front door slammed behind him. Simmering with rage which his mother's rebuke had evoked, he stalked the streets until his temper cooled. At midnight he came home. He was very young when this happened, but the seeds of future rebellion had been planted.

He reacted in a similar way at school. He had a "short fuse." His fits of ill-temper were the more disconcerting because it seemed impossible to predict when a minor explosion would detonate. "A pretty aggressive little boy," was how a school fellow remembered him — a boy who bullied smaller kids, easily got into fights and pelted dogs with stones. His parents were puzzled and troubled. The words which the Duchess of York used of her son in Shakespeare's *Richard III* were beginning to seem only too appropriate:

Tetchy and wayward was thy infancy
Thy schooldays frightful, desp'rate, wild and furious.

Andrew was getting further and further behind in his work. "He is very slow to complete assignments," it was said of his reading in grade three in March 1976. His written expression is "below grade level... produces little and very slowly. Content lacks detail and interesting ideas." Even at math, where he showed the capacity to understand new concepts, "his enthusiasm for enrichment activities varies greatly." Inattentive, it was only on the sports field that he let himself go. In seven out of nine subjects his work was deemed unsatisfactory. A solitary, puzzled, introverted boy in a large class of thirty, he stared out at nothing. His teachers were too busy to give him much personal attention. His parents were often away. He looked inward and found a vacuum. His egocentrism rendered him vulnerable to impulsive wishes to satisfy his needs.

Perhaps unjustifiably but inevitably, Andrew was beginning to develop a grudge against society, more especially against his parents. Worried by this, they sent him when he was nine, dragging his feet to Mary Hackney, a highly reputed child psychologist.

> Andrew [Mary Hackney reported] is certainly withdrawing from his present problems and dreaming of being much older, when he imagines that his problems will probably be solved. There is no doubt that he is engaged in a "power" struggle over attending the kind of school he is in now. His parents are not inclined to "give in" in the power struggle and wish him to adapt to the public school.

In Dr. Hackney's kindly presence, he thawed and she seemed to win his confidence. She found him, as everyone else was to do subsequently, well above average in intelligence. "There is no doubt at all," she reported, "that he is a very bright child." She was disinclined to think that his learning disability which she described as "very mild" was irreparable.

But she came back to his environment, concerned about his general attitude to his parents and school. To Andrew the best line of defense was attack. He thought that he was being "set on." Sensibly, Dr. Hackney wondered whether he might be more likely to respond to persuasion rather than to force. A show of strength might well be counterproductive. "This boy," she said, "will certainly not adapt to force." She doubted whether he was going to settle at Blythwood and suggested "some individual tutoring from a skillful remedial tutor. He obviously prefers a one-to-one situation."

But it was back to Blythwood and to the difficulties of home life that

Andrew was to go in 1976. Then, in August of that year he was sent to another psychiatrist, Dr. Norman Saunders, partly to cope with problems arising from inadequate toilet training, for he was a bed-wetter and suffered from constipation and soiling well into adolescence.

That summer the clouds temporarily lifted. He left the family home on Alcorn Avenue and spent a month at Camp Kandalore. It was a serene and happy time which showed Dr. Hackney's good sense in suggesting that Andrew was capable of responding to friendly and happy surroundings. Camp Kandalore in the Haliburton Highlands was not far away from the Muskokas where his grandfather, John Osler, had his summer cottage. The Muskokas had an air of enchantment for Andrew. His friend, Stephen Niblett, described how elated they had both felt when, rowing on the lake one night, they had watched the orange moon dappling the still waters. Here there seemed a harmony which passed him by at home and at school. So Camp Kandalore turned out to be a success. "Andrew," wrote his camp counselor Bob Hatchwell, "proved a most enjoyable person to have around and he mixed well with the other campers." He threw himself into the camp's activities, winning awards at archery and climbing; and on a three-day canoe trip showed that he possessed some powers of leadership.

At school, however, his behavior pattern showed a curious oscillation between good and bad, acting sometimes as if he was in control, and at other stages seeming to allow the bad fairy, another Andrew, to direct his footsteps. "It seems," he told Dr. Solursh some time later, "as though I was watching television through my eyes and it seems as though I was not commanding my muscles to do what I had done." He said he hated his teachers but then pronounced that he was likely to have a good teacher next year, a Mr. Philips. He neglected his homework and things went downhill, but then things improved. When he was in grade four his teachers reported that he "had an excellent attitude to school and his schoolwork." Then there was talk of his expulsion. He looked forward to going to a private school, Crescent, but failed the entrance exam. He quarreled with his school fellows. He kicked Kenny Hudson down the hill because he had been "bugging" him, just as he later told Dr. Solursh of another boy, Robert, who had given "me a lot of trouble" so that "sometimes I feel like chucking a rock through his ugly face. I just want consistency from one minute to the next," he complained, but consistency of mood there was not.

Things seemed to be deteriorating at home as well, though here too his conduct oscillated. He wanted to do well at school, he said, mainly because then his parents would cease to "bug him." One week he would be even-tempered. "He has been really calm," Sarah said on 8 November 1976. "He's trying to be cheerful; he has volunteered to write to Granny; he's more home centered." Christmas that year was a success.

Then all hell broke loose. He stole five dollars from the food larder. When it was discovered, he was told that he could not go to the movies, but he had already spent the money. Then he took ten dollars from the housekeeper, Mandy, and was spanked. "I knew I would get caught," he said. Perhaps he wanted to be caught, to draw attention to himself. He resented the punishment, but he had done what he wanted to do. He was "like an angel afterwards," Sarah said.

Andrew believed that he was not getting the love and affection he needed; his ego needed to be boosted. He wanted, he told Dr. Norman Saunders, "to please Dad and Mum. . . . would like it better if they showed their love, not disapproval and concern. . . . I want and deserve, at least sometimes, some praise. . . . I'm frightened of my dad getting mad at me."

"My father's very quick to anger, uncontrollable. He hits out at mother," so he complained to Dr. Carr a year later. "When my parents fight," he told Dr. Saunders, "I went up to cry in my room. When my dad hit Jennifer [the dog], I went up to cry."

But though he was afraid of his father he wanted to be on good terms with him. He even began to learn chess in secret so that he could play with his father. He grudged Sarah's absence. He felt she should be looking after the house, not the housekeeper, Mandy, whom he rattled. "When I'm not here," Sarah said, "Mandy has a bad time." Andrew once pointed a knife at her. "She yells at me, ignores me," he complained. She left, partly because of Andrew. If he would act in a more mature fashion, his mother said, there need be no housekeeper. But Andrew was only ten.

His parents undoubtedly meant well and did all they could to show Andrew their love, but he seemed unable to respond. They hardly seemed to be on the same lifeline as their young son. "I can't put things in a gentle way," Andrew confessed. And Sarah began to be at her wit's end. "I love my husband," she exclaimed on 6 August 1976, "I love my son. I love my work but I hate my life."

After the spring of 1977, there was another calm. Andrew's behavior, Dr. Saunders noted on 22 August 1977, had been excellent. Camp had gone well too. Andrew had shown, his counselor Richard Schroeder reported, "a particular interest in archery" for which he had won an award. He had also enjoyed shooting, swimming, at which he excelled, sailing, two canoe trips, one an overnight trip of twelve miles, and another in a thirty-six-foot canoe up the Trent Canal for three days. "Very helpful to me in both trips. He got along and fitted in well with his cabin group."

But calm with Andrew preceded a storm. He was still so fractious that his parents, afflicted by their own problems, decided once again to look for help. Their new counselor was Dr. Robert Carr. He found that Andrew had "developed a rather sterile and obstinate personality and spent most of his emotional energy in controlling with little spontaneity or enjoyment." There were to be weekly sessions, interrupted only by a vacation to Mexico and by camp, between December 1977 and July 1979, sessions which Dr. Carr sometimes found frustrating.

At his meetings with Dr. Carr, Andrew showed many disturbing signs. The traumas of childhood, which he should have outgrown by now, seemed somehow to have become more conspicuous. Dr. Carr, like Dr. Saunders, had to cope with Andrew's toilet training, with his constipation and occasional fecal incontinence. But, apart from playing floor hockey with him, he also tried to draw Andrew out, so that his life might take on a happier hue. Their conversations often seemed to turn on two dominating themes: conflict and, less directly, sex.

Andrew seems to have been obsessed by war games and conflict, though this is a pastime which attracts many boys of his age. The brief notes in Dr. Carr's hand are graphically descriptive. 2 February 1978: "war, soldiers"; 9 February: "army-game broke down when no rules"; 2 March: "war card game"; 13 April: "more powerful new gun — the ultimate weapon — allowed me to use his first but had to overthrow its power supply"; 21 April: "war game — total mutual destruction"; "war again" equals "chaos, feelings of separation," Dr. Carr noted in November 1978. "War games — repeatedly demolishing me, the center of his explosions," on 30 January 1979. 13 February: "War again — end all killed. He's not happy because no more wars. No you're left. Shot me." 17 April: "space war — my station demolished." 30 April: "Army battle — destroyed me."

Andrew always wanted to win and seemed to see Dr. Carr as the enemy who had to be destroyed. 23 February 1978: "Army men — always wants to push first, go first." 16 March: "Army to start — again need to have all best defense — atom bombs his also." 5 March: "Began dragging out boxes for war games. I was fed up, so decided my side had found the 'elixir of life' which could reconstitute everything, even if destroyed. He wound down to silent sulk." "You and I have been fighting a war for over a year." Dr. Carr observed. "My father," Andrew said, "would never buy me a gun."

There were also sexual undercurrents, a preoccupation with what Dr. Carr described as "anal-erotic" themes. The allusions were often indirect but nonetheless there. "Fears and shame," the doctor noted on 16 January 1979, over "masochistic, sexual impulses." "Much sexual tension throughout; often zipping, exposing rear and back." A week later, 23 January, Andrew was "embarrassed about sexy thoughts." 8 May 1979: "Soccer — rolling on floor to seduce/entice contact with him." "Let's play horsey," Andrew suggested. "No," the doctor responded, believing it alluded to masturbation. "What are you getting at doctor?" Andrew angrily replied. He talked about "his fears that he might be a fag." On 5 June 1979: "Continual sexual themes. I confronted 'blow job'. Andrew showed signs of being upset but showed a positive response." "Do you know what a flasher is?" he asked.

The crude drawings that Andrew made during these sessions were concerned with similar themes. A missile, very phallic in shape, bears the words "power," "nitrogliceron [*sic*] war-head." Others demonstrated his feelings of personal desolation: a boy looking at nothing. In one an airplane or rocket to which a figure is attached flies towards the sun, with a caption inserted, "Dear Jim I've gone to Hawaii, Andrew," while in a sort of cot or bed a smaller figure exclaims, "Why did he leave me alone? I'll kill him." Two other drawings seem to express his annoyance at not being allowed to smoke. "Well, you smoke...," a young boy says to a pipe-smoking figure, obviously his father. "Dad," he wrote on another, "you smoke to [*sic*] much." "What's wrong with that?" Perhaps his feelings on the human situation were summed up in the one word, *shit*. Andrew showed signs of anger, Dr. Carr noted, when he "turned round" his drawings.

During the two previous summers, 1976 and 1977, Muskoka had afforded a release of tension and a happy environment. Andrew was much looking forward to going to camp and to staying at the Windermere cottage in 1978, the "best place" where he could be alone. But then news reached him of the death of his grandfather John Osler. For Andrew, John had become an idealized father-figure. He felt the news intensely. In Andrew's memory, his grandfather stood for solidarity, security and serenity. When he spoke of him, tears came into his eyes. He told Dr. Veeder later that he frequently wept when he was by himself as he thought of his grandfather. Apart from an incident at camp when he lost a knife and tempers flared, there was no complaint about his behavior but, in comparison with the two previous years, he was depressed, lethargic and apathetic.

Next year's camp, Camp Hurontario at MacTier on Georgian Bay, was worse. Andrew, the acting director, Donald Marston admitted, was an intelligent and active boy who participated well in the camp's general activities; but in the groups of six into which the camp was divided he did not hit it off well with his companions, proving so disruptive an influence that they had no alternative except to send him home. "Andrew," Joshua McHugh reported, "was very temperamental and aggressive towards the other campers and the staff... constantly bickering and fighting with the boys in the camp."

By midsummer 1979, Dr. Carr was wondering himself whether they were really getting anywhere. At times Andrew was grateful, at others uncooperative and resentful. Would the doctor, he asked, see patients in his own free time? Was he doing it simply for the money? Andrew complained, on 11 May 1978, that the doctor was too intrusive and liked bossing him around. When the doctor talked about him to one of his teachers, Mrs. Johnston, Andrew was angry. Yet, in some respects, Andrew had become dependent upon him as one of the few people to whom he could confess his fears, the difficulties he had in making friends at school, in keeping up with his studies, and his problematical relationship with his parents.

Even Dr. Carr had not always found conversation with them very easy. When he saw them at the beginning of 1978 he found the interview very "uncomfortable." Ernest puzzled him. "A very secret person... A very fearful man," but of what? He said he thought there was nothing fundamentally wrong with his son. Sarah seemed "very guilty at not wanting to be a mother and feeling she was able to hide this for years but Andrew has let out the secret." "We both work," Ernest said. "He's missing something there. We're very demanding parents." "When mother comes home," Andrew complained, "she starts to get at me." "You have," the doctor remarked to Andrew, "two parents." "Not really," he replied sadly. In any case Sarah and perhaps even more so Ernest, began to wonder whether the lengthy and expen-

Andrew's drawings for Dr. Carr in 1978 and 1979

sive sessions were really accomplishing anything and, in the autumn of 1979, by mutual agreement, they decided to call it a day. Although Andrew complained bitterly about going to the sessions, he was upset by their conclusion and Dr. Carr was a little worried that Andrew would think that he was "throwing him out because I couldn't be patient with him."

Andrew left Blythwood. His final year there had shown that when he did apply himself he could do reasonably well. Evidently his failure to get into Crescent School had rankled, so he put on a spurt and the results were reflected in his school reports which made relatively encouraging reading. "I'm very proud, so are my parents," he commented when he heard that he had been accepted at Crescent which he entered (at grade seven) when he was just over twelve.

Robert Carr had hoped that in a new environment Andrew might regain his self-esteem and be less aggressive. There were some signs in 1979 that this might be the case. "This is called adjusting," his French teacher observed in October 1979. "Come on, Andrew, you know what is expected." There was no hint of trouble and in manner he was said to be polite. At the end of the year he needed to make a more concentrated effort, but the results were not bad. "Keep your goals high," his French teacher observed, reporting better work. "Hard work is the answer," was the comment at half-term 1980, and in October the school was able to report that "Andrew's competence in his classes improved due to his diligence and determination to succeed. Bravo. . . . Keep this up and by Christmas the report will be one to be proud of." He showed a marked improvement in most subjects — grade A in math and French. Nor were there any complaints about his conduct, though it was noted that he lacked "assurance with his peers at times."

But the improvement was short-lived. Andrew was easily discouraged. "I hope," his headmaster wrote grimly at the end of the school year, "Andrew is not pleased with his results." He had "got off to a slow start and refused to maintain a level of effort which is necessary for academic success." Books continued to have little interest for him. His prose was infantile, his spelling dyslexic. Even his French teacher, with Gallic rhetoric, was less complimentary than usual: "Don't choose your moment of glory, Andrew. Give EVERYTHING. ALL YOU'VE GOT. . . ."

The comments on his reports may have screened what was really happening. He lacked any real sense of purpose. He often skipped classes, drifting towards his rootless contemporaries. More and more he felt unwanted.

> He talks a great deal about feelings of depression [Mary Hackney was soon to comment] and these feelings are related mainly to his feeling that nobody loves him. He has a great tendency to blame all his problems on his parents and wants them to take responsibility for "getting him off the hook" of any problem. He feels that the reason he is unhappy is that they have neglected him. He tends to make unreasonable complaints about his parents, and there is little reality to his resentment of them.

Home had become by 1980 something of a misnomer, not perhaps due to anyone's direct fault but because of the mutual incompatibility of the personalities involved. Andrew's father, who was suffering from a peptic ulcer, was often away. When he left the office he frequently went to play squash and would only return half an hour or so before Andrew went to bed. He thought his son's problems were the teething pains of adolescence. "It's normal for boys to get into fights. I got into fights when I was his age."

His mother was apprehensive, disappointed and often angry with herself. The gap between mother and son seemed to be widening. Andrew, Sarah said, was so "slovenly and sneaky" that she could "not really stand his company for more than a limited period." She, too, stayed purposely late at the office. There were fierce quarrels in which mother and son both lost their tempers and hit out at each other. Once when Andrew shouted that he was damn well not going to school, his mother struck him. He got hold of her arms and pinned them at her side. She turned and bit him on the arm. Home had become a house to which they all dreaded to return. The only happy member of the household seems to have been the dog Jennifer.

IV

ANDREW: ── THE DOWNWARD PATH ──

I and the public know
What all school children learn,
Those to whom evil is done
Do evil in return

W.H. AUDEN

Children begin by loving their parents.
After a time they judge them.
Rarely, if ever, do they forgive them.

OSCAR WILDE

WHAT HAD THE FUTURE IN STORE? There was as yet no Sibylline Oracle to provide an answer; but there were portents of ill-omen. Andrew's school reports showed a falling off, drawing a warning from the headmaster: "The writing is on the wall Andrew, get down to it."

More alarming than his lack of progress at school was Andrew himself. He was moving away from the settled environment of school and home, however uncongenial, mixing with high-school dropouts, drawn to alcohol and drugs to exalt an artificial self-esteem. Even with his peers he felt less and less comfortable. "He is both desirous of human contacts and mystified of how to mobilize and use them," a

44

psychiatrist, Kenneth Keeling, later reported. "He can sit for hours with friends, and yet not feel part of the group. Though with others, he senses a separation, aloneness."

He was self-centered and had a wanton incapacity to exert any moral discipline. When things went wrong, he blamed other people. "I'm easy going," he once said, "until somebody crosses me. Then I've got quite a temper and an aggression towards them." Anger blew like gusts in a storm when he was thwarted. When his school fellows teased him, the teasing acted like a detonator. When it was all over, once passion had been spent, he rarely showed any signs of remorse but rather embarrassment, depression, shame.

> Afterwards [Dr. Neil Morris wrote in a perceptive analysis of his problems] he will be emotionally exhausted but not confused. Often he will experience shame for the event although the outburst of anger will relieve the tension that has been building up for a period of several days. These visceral and emotional experiences... occur in the context of anger [and] frustrating thoughts. ...

His acts of aggression so far had been neither dangerous nor very serious: fights with boys, conflict with his parents, petty theft. Then came the first of the frightening explosions, on Monday, 21 September 1981. There was a row with his parents. He stomped out of the house, took the car keys and drove away in his father's Volvo. He would show his parents. He drove fast, making almost automatically for his grandmother, Ursula's country house near Pickering. (After her husband's death in 1978, Mrs. Osler had married another lawyer, an Englishman, Alistair Patterson.) When Andrew arrived he turned off the engine and asked the gamekeeper, Mal Albright, for the key to the gate of the estate, which Mal gave him. He made his way to the house but, as he had no key, he took a shovel and broke the kitchen window. When he got inside, he swept up the broken glass, pushing it into a vent in the floor. He ran from room to room, overturning the mattresses, seizing some blankets and taking two bottles of liquor, one of Kamchatka vodka and another of Chemineaud brandy. Then he drove to his grandparents' cottage, West Winds, where he intended to stay the night.

Ernest and Sarah were outraged. His father reported the loss of his car to the police. Andrew's uncle, Bill Jephcott, drove up to the cottage to see what was missing. A family conference followed, which included Nancy Eaton's uncle, David Gossage, their insurance agent. In fact little actual damage had been done. No good would come from advertising the incident to the world. Better to close the ranks. Better to hope that this was a solitary episode, not a prelude to further acts, and that the threat of police action would bring Andrew to his senses.

The police proved amenable. It was, after all, a first offense; his parents were highly respected members of the community. Andrew was brought face to face with his parents at the Youth Bureau at Ajax on 29 September 1981. The police were rather taken with Andrew, finding him a likeable boy. They suspected, with some measure of truth, that there was a lack of communication with his father. Sergeant Sturgeon put it to Ernest that it might not be a bad idea if he tried to spend rather more time with his erring son. Andrew, his anger spent, was hangdog, "sad and depressed."

His parents, lacking confidence to deal with their son, turned once more to Mary Hackney. She had given sensible advice in January 1976. Now, five years later, in the autumn of 1981, Andrew was in her office again. He was late in arriving, glum and characteristically blamed his mother for a mistake in timing which he had made himself. He looked ill and tired, for he had recently recovered from a bout of pneumonia.

Andrew played along with Hackney. Most of the psychiatrists mentioned his courtesy and readiness to talk. Perhaps he was gratified by the attention he was receiving. There was an element of self-congratulation in being diagnosed as an unusual case. Perhaps Andrew was genuinely curious as to whether he was suffering from some sort of mental derangement. The more numerous the consultations, the more confident he was that he was in the grip of forces outside his control.

Once more the tests showed that, according to the Wechsler intelligence scale for children, Andrew was well above the average. He solved the mathematical puzzles put to him without difficulty. Once more, however, Mary Hackney came to the conclusion that it was less a question of learning disability than of a personality problem. He lacked self-assurance, self-esteem, self-confidence. The bullying in which he engaged at school was a defense mechanism. He refused to admit that he was an intelligent boy with potential.

Even more distressing, "he doesn't care sufficiently about other people." Andrew still had no conception of how to establish a trusting and loving relationship. He wanted desperately to be loved, resented what he felt to be his parents' seeming inability to give him love; but love was something of which he too seemed incapable.

In her report, Mary Hackney again showed her good sense. "My examination suggests that he has improved somewhat in the past five years, but, partly because he is now a teenager [Andrew was fourteen and three months], his opportunities to do really delinquent acts are increased." The next few years were to show how incisive and relevant this statement was, as the range of temptations put before him expanded, and the opportunities for giving vent to what he called his "bad vibes" multiplied. After suggesting that Andrew would benefit from being schooled in a "highly structured and disciplined setting," such as a good boarding school with small classes, she concluded, "I think it unlikely that he will last much longer at Crescent School."

Her prediction was fulfilled sooner than she might have anticipated. On Tuesday, 3 November, C.B. Gordon, the headmaster of Crescent School, requested Andrew's parents to withdraw him from the school. His work record continued to be very poor; he had to repeat grade seven and was not making any progress in grade eight. But it was a breach of school rules which led to his expulsion. He had made a fierce attack on a classmate which caused his teachers to worry that perhaps "next time Andrew hits someone he will have a rock in his hand." "And, yesterday afternoon," the headmaster wrote, "at the southbound bus stop on Bayview Avenue, across from the school, Andrew was smoking." In fact he had been smoking for at least two years, getting through three-quarters of a pack a day.

> Andrew either does not understand or does not wish to acknowledge school rules; the school rule in particular — smoking, which says that a student is not permitted to smoke in, on, or around school property. However, the smoking itself is a minor problem. The fact that Andrew took a cigarette and purposely burnt a hole in a schoolboy's jacket is an example of his irresponsible behavior. I consider Andrew to be a threat to his fellow students.

So once again Andrew was on the move, this time to Deer Park Public School on Ferndale Avenue, where he was to get C grades in most of his subjects.

Of course it was less what was happening at school that was significant than what was happening to Andrew. He was always easily provoked and ill-temper erupted into an explosion. Asked later how he felt before these explosions, he replied, "hot inside," the hot flush which passionate feelings inevitably bring. Then he had to release the tension, the "energy," which bubbled up inside him. There was a rush of adrenalin to the head, a feeling of tightness in the chest, of palpitation and tremulousness. Yet experience suggested that such feelings were only activated when something or someone aggravated him. Then the dam would break and the water would gush out. He said that sometimes he'd scream and actually bruise and cut himself, until the mood passed.

His parents' faith in psychiatrists had wilted. The family, as one of them said later, was "going in circles... spinning its wheels," voicing their frustration with the many helpers they had sought. Through Andrew's uncle by marriage, they made contact with his sister, Ann Taylor, a psychometrist at the Toronto Western Hospital, and she arranged for Andrew to see Dr. Lionel Solursh, an associate professor of psychiatry at the University of Toronto. He saw the boy first in February 1982 and continued to see him regularly until he fell out with Andrew's parents. His last interview with Andrew was in August 1983.

Andrew remained depressed. He felt he had not been forgiven for taking his father's car and breaking into his grandmother's farmhouse. He felt lost, isolated, without roots, in need of attention, wanting the world to take notice. In early March 1982 he went up to the bathroom, took a bottle of 222s and swallowed a handful of them, three at a time with a glass of water. He threw himself on his bed and collapsed into a comatose sleep. It is unlikely that he really intended to do away with himself, but whatever he did was unconsciously a desperate cry for help, which went unanswered.

He awoke the next morning, feeling so dizzy and groggy that he groaned, turned over and went to sleep again. Downstairs Sarah could not understand why he was not up. "It's time to get up," she shouted, "if you're going to make school." His head split, his body ached. He dressed hurriedly, splashed cold water on his face and dashed downstairs and out of the house. Still dazed, he went to catch the subway, but when it reached the station for his school, he remained seated and stayed on the train until it turned round and took him home again.

He got out and slouched home, full of resentment at the lack of sympathy which the world seemed to show him — resentment against his parents, resentment against himself. His parents were ignorant of what had occurred, but Andrew's mind, still partly under the influence of drugs, saw them as "the enemy." It was "they" who stood for all the things which prevented him from being an achiever.

The house was silent, empty. Sarah and Ernest had left for their offices downtown. So Andrew was there by himself. He trashed the house, in his own words "destroyed," vandalized it, scattering the family papers, "messing up" his parents' bedroom, engaging in a positive orgy of senseless destruction.

He seized what money he could find, pushed it in his pocket, again took the key to his father's car and drove it away, making as before for the cottage at Muskoka, the illusory haven of peace and security. He drove fast with eyes glazed. He wanted to get away from home and show his resentment by taking his father's car.

His eyes were not on the icy road and, driving carelessly, he crashed the car into a bank of snow. The accident brought him back to earth. He got the staff at a nearby service station to pull him out, used his father's Shell credit card to fill up with gas and then, on impulse, changed direction. He decided to go to his grandmother's farmhouse near Pickering. Within a mile of his destination, the car skidded again on the ice and plunged into a snowbank. Andrew left it where it was and trudged through the snow to the house, forcing an entry as he had done a year before. He stayed the night.

When he awoke the next morning, he found he was out of cigarettes. At half past eight, on a gold-colored snowmobile, which he had taken from the garage of his grandmother's house, he made his way to Balsam General Store. The storekeeper Grant Jones, who lived next door, was opening up when Andrew arrived. Clad in his red-plaid lumber jacket and holding a hunting knife, Andrew went up to the counter and ordered Jones to give him a carton of du Maurier cigarettes and to hand over all the money in his till. Reluctantly, he gave him all the ten-dollar bills. Andrew saw that there was still a five-dollar bill and told him to hand that over too. Then, with thirty-five dollars and his cigarettes, Andrew ran from the store. He had really acted big. Who said he couldn't do things when he wanted? He had driven his father's car away; he had forced the storekeeper to hand over his cash. In his exhilaration he took the snowmobile for a joy ride and careered about on it. Its engine was still warm when the police eventually caught up with him at the farmhouse shortly after eleven that morning.

As P.C. Smith approached the house, he noticed that the lights were on, the back door open and a rifle lay on the counter inside. A figure ran swiftly through a room, and came through the kitchen to the room which the police constable had entered. Andrew made no attempt to resist. "Yes," he said, "I robbed the store." He showed the policeman where the knife was and handed over the money and cigarettes. "Why," Smith asked him, "did you pull the knife?" "I don't know," Andrew said. "I knew I'd get caught." In a bigger way, on a larger scale, history was repeating itself. One day there was to be a larger stage still. The message which he was trying to give to his family and the world was to grow louder and louder.

He spent the night in the local jail and next day appeared in juvenile court and was charged. His parents, incensed by what he had done, came up to the Durham Youth Bureau. Andrew was taken back to Toronto where he was placed in a detention center before being brought before the court. Away from home his temper seemed to subside. Since he had given no trouble at the center and because of his family's support, he was placed on probation for a year and allowed to return home.

But home for Andrew was in some respects another detention center, and he, like his parents, was relieved when in July he went off to summer school at Lake Rosseau. Physical activity provided a release from tension and an opportunity for achievement; it did something to bolster his lagging self-esteem. He made excellent progress in swimming and earned his white level in Red Cross. At games he "exhibited sportsmanship and a good degree of athletic ability." He loved sailing. Academically, his record, as usual, was less impressive, but his house-master commented that Andrew was a "pleasant addition to the Clarkson House family." Later, however, there were some reports of his getting into fights with other students. So, with the detention center and the school at Lake Rosseau, summer had passed and Andrew was at home on Alcorn Avenue again.

After the traumatic happenings in March, he seemed more than ever set against his family. His father, he complained bitterly to the psychologist, Dr. Grant Harris, was "an alcoholic," a "bit of a prick" when sober, and "quiet while drinking." Rows between father and mother continued. Andrew was disturbed because he supposed that he was often the cause of their disagreements. "Ernest," he was to write a few years later, "I feel extremely guilty about your drinking and fighting

Nancy, age three

Andrew, age eight

Age ten

Age eleven

Andrew, age twelve (Ronald Miller)

Age thirteen

Rockledge

West Winds (inset: Canada Wide Feature Services Limited)

with mom. I feel I was the whole cause of it." With his mother, of whom he saw so much more, he was engaged in verbal squabbles. Indeed by April 1983 the situation was becoming impossible. It was as depressing for him as it was for them.

> By mid-May [his mother recalled] the situation had deteriorated. He wasn't living by the rules. My nerves were totally shattered and we would have row after row. I would shake him and I would hit him because I was so cross with him and he would hit me back and he hit me back hard and I don't know why. One night we had a big fight [Ernest threw a screwdriver at Andrew] and he ran out of the house and I ran out after him and I said, "Don't roam the streets. Go up to my sister's." And I phoned them and said, "I just can't cope anymore and Ernest can't cope anymore," and I said, "Would you keep him for a while because I can't let him live at home."

Andrew had always liked and got on well with his mother's sister, Amy, and her husband Bill Jephcott. So he moved from the family home at 109 Alcorn Avenue to the Jephcott residence at 278 Glengrove Drive, where he was to stay to the end of the year. At first this seemed to work. "He got on very well with my children," Amy said. "He seemed happy with my home life. His only problem, a perennial one, seemed to be his inability to get up in the mornings." With Andrew living away from home and without much frustration, Dr. Solursh remarked, "explosive outbursts were not noted." The Jephcotts were sympathetic and understanding. Bill's sister, Ann Taylor, who was experienced in dealing with psychiatric problems, was available to help with advice. Yet with Andrew there seemed a sort of cycle in his existence of which crisis was an inevitable feature. Perhaps the Jephcott residence had come too much to resemble home. At any rate, a crisis was to occur in December 1982 which was to be nerve-racking for the Jephcotts.

It came on without warning, a small cloud ballooning into storm, minor friction giving rise to a frightening scenario. Andrew had just come back from school. Perhaps something had left him angry there. He went down to the basement where the Jephcotts' children, aged six to ten, were playing with their friends, bouncing up and down on some mattresses. Amy was upstairs having tea with her mother-in-law.

What happened exactly we do not know. Perhaps Andrew was already in a state. Perhaps the children teased him. But Amy's son came running up to his mother, complaining that Andrew "was bothering them." Amy heard the children screaming and ran down to remonstrate with Andrew but when he heard her coming he ran into the bathroom. "I was really mad at him," she recalled. But when he finally emerged from the bathroom, she was utterly horrified when she saw the look on his face. It was as if Dr. Jekyll had become Mr. Hyde. "It was like the devil looking at me."

His aunt came to the conclusion that Andrew was over-reacting to her disapproval, and decided that it would be better to leave him alone for a while. So she told her children's friends to go, and took her own children upstairs.

Angry with his aunt, angry with himself, Andrew ran up to his bedroom where he smashed everything of his own, including his stereo, but carefully left untouched anything that belonged to the Jephcotts. Amy went up to his room and sat on the bed, trying to calm him down, but he refused to speak, simply continuing to break up everything that belonged to him. It seemed in a sense as if he were admitting his own guilt, but he was too uptight to apologize or heal the wounds. Andrew went downstairs, pacing backwards and forwards "like an animal in the zoo." Amy retreated to the top of the stairs and watched him. "I felt," she said later, "that he was losing control and I was afraid for the children." When the children said they were hungry, Amy left her vantage point and took them into the kitchen.

Andrew came downstairs. "I am going to go and do it now," he declared. His aunt thought that he was about to go off to the pool where it had been arranged for him to take a swimming test that afternoon and replied simply, "Good luck." But in fact, Andrew, knowing that his uncle kept his gun locked in a cupboard in his daughter's bedroom, took the key, unlocked the cupboard and loaded the revolver, putting the extra shells into his pocket. Then he marched to the garage. Amy heard the garage door open. Fearful of what Andrew might be going to do, she followed him.

Andrew was sitting on his uncle's motorbike, the helmet on his head and the gun in his hand. "I got really mad," Amy said. She pushed him off the bike and said, "Don't you dare take that." But he got on the bike again, and again she pushed him off. Andrew responded by cocking the revolver and shouting threateningly, "Get out of the way or I'll kill you." "Don't shoot," she screamed as she crouched behind the car, then ran for safety.

If Andrew had driven the motorbike away where would he have gone? Northward, to the Muskokas? Would he have been actually capable of shooting his aunt? It's not outside the realm of possibility. When Andrew's will was crossed, as he confessed, he had quite a temper.

But the storm had in fact reached its peak. Even before Amy started to run for the house, Andrew had begun to cry. "It was real sobbing. It was heart wrenching. He was in agony." He followed Amy, telling her to "go and get the gun. It's outside. The kids..." The macho man turned out to be made of *papier maché*. He was flat, drained of emotion, yet distressed. Just as he had surrendered the goods he had taken from the Balsam store without putting up a fight, so now he crumbled. Even Andrew seemed to have perceived that he had hurt, perhaps irreparably, two people whom he had grown to trust and who had trusted him, but the people whom he had wanted to love were always the people he also wanted to hurt. "He kept bouncing off the walls, crying, 'Oh I've blown it. I've ruined my life.'"

When Bill came home, he found Andrew "in a high state of anxiety and he wouldn't look at me." His aunt and uncle felt that Andrew's outburst may have been a sudden irrational tantrum rather than the manifestation of a long standing grudge.

So they decided to go ahead with plans which had been made already for Andrew to take his examination in lifesaving. His anger faded, he was in high spirits as he went to the swimming pool, and the test went well. "I got my bronze badge, I can now be a life saver," he boasted proudly. It was an ironical comment in the light of future events, but a proud moment for a boy who sensed so strongly that he was a failure.

The Jephcotts could hardly get what had happened out of their minds, though Andrew himself put it aside, showing no evident sign of remorse or regret. Bill Jephcott did, however, decide that it would be wise to take him along to see his sister at the Toronto Western Hospital. Her examination was fairly perfunctory but she was sufficiently apprehensive about her findings to wonder whether Andrew might be suff..ing from a brain dysfunction. The Jephcotts had had Andrew for eight months but they could not risk a repetition of the recent outbreak. He would have to return home.

This was not something which Sarah or Ernest wanted. Somehow or other home had become a focal point for his outbursts. His mother said she was really scared to have Andrew alone in the house with her.

Ernest was often late home after playing tennis or squash. Andrew was low-spirited and uncommunicative, though to Dr. Solursh he admitted, "I sometimes think that my body's falling apart, my mind's falling apart." He seemed strapped to a wheel of fortune which left him calm and depressed one day or high and excited the next. He was making occasional use of drugs. "Reasons for me staying out late at night," he told his father, in July 1984, "getting high, being with 'fair-weather' friends were that I felt like dirt, that I was a failure." He wore clothes that suited his mood, one day clean, neat, brightly colored clothes and then, as his mother said, "he starts wearing black and lets his hair grow long and things end up in disaster."

His parents were determined to try to prevent any repetition of the events of the past few months. The list of psychiatrists, public and private, whom they were to consult, and in whom they seemed for one reason or another to have had ultimately little confidence, grew even longer. On Dr. Solursh's advice they decided they would try Dr. Raymond Veeder at the prestigious and expensive Institute for Living in Hartford, Connecticut. And it was to Hartford that the unhappy family were to go for a few days at the end of February 1983.

Dr. Veeder had long interviews with Andrew and his parents. Andrew appeared casually dressed, looking younger than his fifteen-and-a-half years but mature in manner. He impressed Dr. Veeder favorably. Nervous at first, he then loosened up, seemed ready to talk, and occasionally a smile lit up his otherwise somber face. He was, the doctor commented, "a very engaging young man." What was more, he appeared to take a real interest in the many psychological and physiological tests to which he was to be subjected in the course of the next few days. He expressed surprise that he had actually been talking to Dr. Veeder for two hours. He had certainly gained confidence in that first session.

Next morning, 23 February, when Andrew accompanied his parents, the story was a different one. Sarah was evidently ill at ease. At one moment she appeared depressed, at another angry. Ernest seemed rather detached. There was an undercurrent of disagreement and the atmosphere was uneasy. They found it difficult to agree over specific incidents which had occurred and even over when they had happened. "Whenever she attempted to give particular examples her husband would contradict her and she would look at him and appear to be very angry although she would say nothing." Andrew's father seemed, on the other hand, to be underplaying the seriousness of the situation.

When, the same afternoon, Andrew was alone with Dr. Veeder, he was again much more relaxed. He expressed relief that some attempt was being made to resolve his problems, seemingly convinced by now that they were outside his control. "He was worried," Dr. Veeder recalled, "where he was going." When he had been told that he was going to Hartford he had been "real scared," but he felt that the talks were doing him good, and he was now prepared to talk freely about some of the episodes which had recently given rise to so much alarm: his attempt at armed robbery, the episode with his aunt. His impulses, he said, made him afraid. More than once he repeated that, "he did not feel that he could control them even though they bothered him." He wondered many times, apart from the night that he had swallowed the 222s, whether he shouldn't try to kill himself and end it all. He was not averse to dramatizing the situation, and here at Hartford he was the center of the stage. Dr. Veeder thought the talks had been useful and that something might yet be done to help Andrew.

But the next morning, when he saw Andrew again in the company of his parents, he was less optimistic. Alone with Andrew the atmosphere had been relaxed, but with Sarah and Ernest present it was again tense. Andrew shut up like a clam, fidgeting and staring at his shoes. "Why don't you say something?" Dr. Veeder asked him. "I get a kind of lump in my throat," he said, "in these sorts of situations and I don't want to say something that may hurt my parents."

His parents were as ill at ease as their son, and were again reluctant to go into detail about specific events in which Andrew had been involved.

> Mr. and Mrs. Leyshon-Hughes [Dr. Veeder reported on 25 February 1984] tended to attempt to intellectualize about the whole situation.... Mrs. Leyshon-Hughes stated that she was really afraid of Andrew and was afraid that one day he might hurt her.... At times, Mrs. Leyshon-Hughes looked as though she was about to cry but much of the time she appeared hopeless and angry. She stated that they were not a family, that she did not want to come home at the end of her day, and that she felt Andrew did not want to come home either.... She accused

her husband of having become pompous and tending to pontifi-
cate. Ernest commented that people might think they have
failed as parents and that possibly they had but my impression
was that he did not really believe what he was saying.

It was a real relief when the session came to an end after what seemed
an overly long two hours. Andrew remained behind. He was utterly
depressed and began to weep. Where was all this leading to? It seemed a
journey without end. A waste of time. No one could really help him.
He would never change. At least, with his parents away, he talked more
freely.

Throughout his stay Andrew had submitted to a series of tests. The
results were by and large encouraging insofar as they were for the most
part negative. On the Bender-Gestalt Test, which was based on the
capacity to recognize a series of different designs, he made accurate
copies of the designs and was able to recall seven of them, which was an
above average performance. The psychiatrists did comment that as his
designs were always smaller than the originals, this might suggest an
underlying feeling of inferiority.

His performance in the Trail Making Test was satisfactory, the results
accurate and rapid. Nor did the Rorschach Test indicate that there were
any significant signs of a mental disorder, even though Dr. Shearn
noted "some strangeness in his perceptions." His results seemed to show
that he was highly imaginative. The encephalogram revealed nothing
important, the results in the main negative and inconclusive. There was
an abundance of 6 and 14_z spiking, which might, but not necessarily,
indicate that there was just the slightest possibility of epilepsy; but no
abnormal responses or other types of seizure or dysrythmic activity could
be deduced from the test.

What did all this reveal? That Andrew was, what could be inferred
already, a self-centered, narcissistic youth who was often hostile to his
environment, who felt rejected by his parents and the world, and who
had more or less come to the conclusion that his problems lay outside
his control, a solution which was later to be offered and accepted in the
courts. What the report brought out even more strongly than previous
reports was his inbred sense of inferiority, his lack of self-esteem.
Outwardly aggressive, he was inwardly dependent, with strong feelings
of weakness, personal inferiority and lack of achievement. He saw
himself as "an actually or potentially worthless person who is likely to

end up losing everything." His life was governed by outbreaks of passion which he thought he was unable to restrain. "He is," Dr. Shearn said in a telling, prophetic remark, "likely to demand and even to take by force what he wants, without appropriate restraints on his behavior."

In their final recommendations the experts were, as often happened, divided in their prognosis. "The likelihood of achieving basic changes in these patterns via psychotherapy," Dr. Shearn noted, "or via psychology seems remote." Dr. Veeder was somewhat more optimistic: "With intensive therapy, he could have a reasonable prognosis." But the problem was, which therapy? There was no definite evidence of any focal organic disease of the central or peripheral nervous system. The neurologist had considered whether Andrew's past history, together with the EEG findings, might not suggest that his rages could be "organically engendered," a suggestion already hinted at by Ann Taylor. It was possible that certain anticonvulsant drugs might relieve the symptoms. In a letter to Dr. Solursh in Toronto, Dr. Veeder suggested tentatively that the use of anticonvulsant drugs which had been found "very useful in this kind of dyscontrol syndrome" might well be advisable.

Aware of the uncomfortable, emotion-laden atmosphere of his own home, Dr. Veeder believed there was some case for suggesting that Andrew might receive treatment away from his family, in a hospital or similar surroundings. If he were away from home he would feel personally less threatened. If he were somewhere where his impulsive behavior could be examined without prejudice, he would be himself less afraid of the consequences of his paroxysms. But experience was to show that he rarely had fits of rage in these circumstances. If he were to be hospitalized, it was important to reassure Andrew that he was not being locked up but helped. Dr. Veeder ended his letter on a gloomily prophetic note: "I am most concerned about the possibility that his behavior might escalate in such a way that he does serious harm either to himself or to others."

The findings of the Institute for Living were more penetrating and thorough than any that had yet been done on Andrew, but the recommendations fell on stony ground. The Institute's fees were high — amounting to some 10,000 dollars a month — and the Leyshon-Hughes were not very happy with the conclusions. They wondered whether the diagnosis which Dr. Veeder had sent, not to them directly but to Dr. Solursh, was worth the money. They discussed with Dr.

Solursh whether Andrew should be given anticonvulsant drugs and decided against the treatment.

In any case, their relations with Dr. Solursh were soon, in his words, to become "stressful." Equally, they were convinced that something should be done for Andrew. The family had been told that Andrew might be labeled a psychopath needing ten years of residential treatment, as Dr. King was to tell Dr. Vinegar on 14 July 1984. Fearful of this outcome, in desperation his parents sought an alternative explanation for their son's bizarre conduct. So, as first advised by Dr. Solursh, the seemingly endless trek to some psychiatric El Dorado was embarked on yet again.

In the next three months Andrew went to three different centers for examination and treatment and at each the diagnosis was inconclusive. In general they came to the conclusion, perhaps not wholly unreasonable, that there was nothing very fundamentally wrong with Andrew.

Dr. Vera Bril, the neurologist at the Toronto General Hospital which he attended on 8 March 1983, described him as a "healthy young man in no acute distress."

> He denies blackouts or seizures. Vision, hearing, speech and swallowing are normal. He does not have any weakness, numbness or tingling anywhere. His reading and writing are normal. He is able to understand everything which is said to him. . . . He was alert, cooperative and very quiet.

Nor did Dr. Bril's test reveal any abnormality; the EEG was perfectly normal. There were no signs whatsoever of any epileptic tendency. Andrew himself had hoped that the results might have been more positive and that epilepsy, as had been half suggested at the Institute, might provide an explanation for his behavior. It looked, however, as if on that score he was in the clear.

From Dr. Bril he trudged three weeks later to the Toronto Western Hospital where Dr. Kenny submitted him to a formidable array of tests over two days: the WAIS-R, the Standard Raven Matrices, the Peabody Picture Vocabulary Test, the Wechsler Memory Scale, the Ray Auditory Learning Test, the Hooper Visual Organization Test, a dichotic listening task (dichotic digits), tests of speech, sound, discrimination and auditory rhythm perception, finger tapping, grooved pegboard and hand dynameter tests of bimanual coordination and strength, Trail-

Making Tests A and B, the Wide Range Achievement Test, a test of verbal fluency and the Wisconsin Card Sorting Test. He was also submitted to a short series of reading tests. "Andrew," Dr. Kenny commented, "was exceptionally polite and cooperative and he displayed a keen interest in his results. He spoke freely, fluently and intelligently." It's hardly surprising, given the battery of tests to which he had been subjected, that he seemed rather restless and at times inattentive. But the tests revealed no major disorder, only feelings of frustration and impulsiveness, and "an inattention deficit disorder," thought to be the sequel to and a minor aspect of hyperactivity or diminishing hyperactivity. The bland results must have been reassuring.

This was not, however, the end. In early April, Dr. Solursh referred him to Dr. Angus Hood at the C.M. Hincks Centre for Children and Adolescents. Andrew attended unwillingly on and off during May and June, for he must by now have become sick and tired of the seemingly endless round. When the Centre made its assessment, its findings were very similar to those which Dr. Solursh had reached earlier: that Andrew's problems were rooted in his relationship with his family and with his environment. Although Andrew had had abnormal sleep scans, Dr. Broder and Eric King, of the Hincks Centre, wrote on 9 July 1984:

> Several normal EEGs have left inconclusive the possibility of an organic basis to his highly impulsive angry outbursts.... At a meeting with Dr. Solursh, the family members heard Andrew labeled a psychopath who would need ten years of residential treatment. The treatment recommended in 1983 was a time-limited trial of family therapy as a last chance for this family to mobilize its resources before proceeding to residential treatment, particularly given the inconclusive medical answers and the fact of the family's long-standing 'spinning its wheels' in search for a concrete medical label.

Andrew welcomed the Centre's suggested treatment but his parents dithered. "It was left that the parents would contact us for a decision about following through with our recommendations," Broder and King reported. "We did not hear from them again."

Andrew was not far short of his sixteenth birthday. In outward appearance he seemed like most boys of his age: five foot nine, shoulder-length brown hair, dressed usually in blue jeans and sneakers. He was a slim but sturdy boy and his normally sullen face was occasionally lit up by a winsome smile. Although he was no reader of books, he was bright and managed to pick up a good deal of general information. "Intelligent, well informed and thoughtful" were the adjectives used by Dr. Grant Harris who was impressed by his knowledge of and interest in literature and related topics.

Andrew enjoyed most sports. He was a keen swimmer and water-skier, and in winter went downhill and cross-country skiing. He liked to play pool, to engage in target shooting, both with guns and arrows, and to take part in tennis and squash, baseball and football. Nothing gave him greater pleasure than tinkering with old cars. He built model cars, and loved riding motorcycles at high speed.

Although he did not find it easy to make real friends, and was uneasy in company, he had a growing number of acquaintances, some as unstable and uprooted as himself, and they found him congenial company. Andrew was physically fit, healthy and intelligent. In the medical reports there was only a minor cautionary note — that he was allergic to bee stings. If bee stings had been his only nightmare he could have looked ahead with reasonable hope to a normal, rewarding future.

But in fact a deep problem remained. He was still haunted by outbursts of black anger which seemed to transform him into a different personality. In these outbursts of temper he seemed to become so depersonalized that he was detached from the other Andrew.

He was aware that there was a deep-seated canker in his personality. How indeed could it be otherwise, given the ever-lengthening list of psychiatrists that he was to consult, and the hospitals to which he had been referred since he was eight years old? There were times when he despaired utterly of ever finding a solution to the disorders which seemed so inexorably to afflict him. Either he lacked the will or the capacity to exert the controls needed to circumvent a show of ill temper.

His relations with his parents had become strained to the breaking point. As they saw it, they had done all they reasonably could on his behalf; arranged his change of schools — and another one was on the way — and paid high fees for medical and psychological treatment but to no avail. His mother was frightened, not only of what he would do to others but of what he might do at home. His father, it seemed to Andrew, was both aloof and hostile. "It got to the point," his mother recalled, "where there was no life. It was a hotel. It was who could check out first in the morning, my husband or I, and get to work and hope that nothing went wrong."

His aunt Amy, whom he had come to regard as a surrogate mother, could not banish from her mind the horrifying experience when he had run amok; neither she nor her husband, Bill, who had more faith in psychiatrists than Andrew's parents, could ever be as close to him as they had once been.

Andrew remained desperately lonely. There was no one among his acquaintances in whom he could confide or who would understand his problems. There was no one to give him the affection which he so badly needed but which he found almost impossible to evoke or reciprocate. For all his aggressiveness, he was an insecure and apprehensive young man, haunted by the conviction that he was a failure. Nor, significantly, was he any longer really a boy. A few months earlier Mary Hackney had remarked that as a teenager he had to face different and dangerous allurements which the very process of growing up brought into being. As the boy became a young man, the problem of finding an appropriate niche in society and of discovering a genuine identity became more rather than less difficult. He had, Dr. Solursh noted, "no clear sense of self." He needed a close friend, and in the summer of 1983 he was to find one in Nancy Eaton.

V

BIG SISTER
——AND LITTLE BRO'——

He who believes in nothing still needs a girl to believe in him.''

ROSENSTOCK HUESSY

Beauty thought the Beast was very considerate and that, perhaps, there was nothing to fear from him, after all.

BEAUTY AND THE BEAST

THE SUMMER OF 1983 FORMED A HIGH plateau in Andrew's life, for it was full of sunlit vistas which fleetingly dispersed the dark clouds, its setting the popular summer resort of Muskoka. The Muskokas are situated ninety miles north of Toronto at the lower reaches of the Canadian Shield where, at the end of the last ice age, retreating glaciers left hundreds of clear-water lakes. The original white settlers found the acidic soil of Muskoka unprofitable and moved further west, leaving the land to be bought up cheaply by city dwellers attracted by the natural beauty of the area, rich in fish, game and wildlife. So the Muskokas became the summer playground of the Canadian rich, the Eatons,

Seagrams, Southams, Bassetts, Blacks, Labatts and Rogers. They constructed palatial summer homes along the water shore and cruised the lakes in their sailboats and sumptuously outfitted yachts.

The Oslers had a summer cottage, West Winds, at Windermere on Lake Rosseau where Andrew had spent happy vacations as a boy in the company of his grandfather, John Osler, who had died in 1978 and whose memory he cherished so strongly. Something in the placid atmosphere of Windermere softened or quietened Andrew's tensions, for Alcorn Avenue was not merely out of sight but also out of mind. There was plenty for him to do, sailing, swimming and water-skiing.

The Oslers' neighbors were the Eatons. When Windermere was first beginning to take shape as a resort, old Timothy Eaton with the shrewdness which had made him such a successful businessman, bought some eighteen acres of land for a mere 125 dollars; and on it he built a noble house, Rockledge, which became his favorite home. He loved nothing better than to cruise on the lake in his steam yacht *Wanda*. Edward Eaton inherited the house and, in June 1983, Nancy Eaton was staying there. It was natural that the Eatons and the Oslers should have known each other. Indeed Nancy and Andrew had been acquaintances since they were children but six years difference in their ages had operated against a close relationship. Now that Nancy was twenty-two and Andrew sixteen, the age gap no longer counted for so much. In some ways Nancy was younger than her years, Andrew older. It was in the summer air of Windermere that acquaintance ripened into friendship and burgeoned into affection.

Andrew had come to West Winds with his father. Away from home their strained relationship mellowed in the companionship which sport and sailing provided. In later years he spoke affectionately of their winter skiing together. In the normal routine of existence neither was able to break through to the other, but in the relaxed atmosphere of Windermere they were able, if briefly, to let down their guards.

Andrew attended Lake Rosseau Summer School:

> When I went to Rossoe [*sic*] Lake Summer School and did really well [he wrote to his father] and you said 'WELL DONE' and man I really felt great after you said that. It meant a lot thank you. I really wish we had more times when we [went] downhill skiing at Blue Mountain. I was really proud of you, my dad — out there with me, and I really enjoyed it.

In his heart Andrew wanted to love his father just as his father wished to love his son, but for the most part the channels of communication were blocked.

It was at Windermere that Andrew discovered Nancy. He had first taken a fancy to her, he confessed later, when he was thirteen. "I have had a crush on her since I was thirteen, ever since she gave me shit for having a beer with her father." Andrew normally resented it when people gave him "shit" but there was something about Nancy which immediately attracted him. Right from the start Andrew felt easy in Nancy's company. She laughed a lot which made him feel that he was amusing and fun to be with. She made him feel good about himself. They would sit on the Eaton dock for hours at a time telling each other more and more about themselves. They found that they had many things in common. Both of them came from wealthy families and did not get on well with their fathers. Both were subject to depression. Nancy always sat close to him and listened carefully to everything Andrew said, making him feel that he was the only person in the world who mattered. They formed a perfect foil for each other. Nancy was a cheerful, kind extrovert who took the introverted Andrew into her confidence and he, grateful for her sympathy, responded by a readiness to talk, unusual in his normally inhospitable character. Taken out of himself he had less time to ruminate over his own wrongs and for a lugubrious contemplation of his future.

So a close relationship developed during those sunny days, Andrew's unhappy state and her eagerness to help him forming the basis for their mutual attraction. "It wasn't really a friendship as such," Nancy's mother commented later, "Tiger was more like a mother to him." Nancy tended to think of him as a brother. "This," she would say as she put her arms around his neck and hugged him, "is my little bro'." Nancy was an only child, and a brother-sister relationship was new and intriguing. It made her feel needed, important. "She treated me cute," Andrew said.

But whenever he was in her presence he felt stirrings of a deeper kind. When the bartender, Christopher, at the Inn on the Bay at Muskoka, came over to talk to Nancy, Andrew showed his resentment. He was up early in the morning and went to Rockledge to make tea for Nancy and bring it to her in bed. But he was too shy, perhaps too inarticulate, to express his feelings more strongly. "I did it by actions. I brought her tea...and things like that." Stimulated by common conversation and companionship they became in different ways fond of each other. There was at least now someone to whom Andrew could go and describe the woes of his world.

But as the idyllic summer gave way to autumn, and the leaves of the trees turned to burnished gold, so the bewildering cycle in Andrew's life began to reassert itself. He had now left Deer Park School and had joined a mixed private school, the Annex Village Campus, which at first seemed to suit him well, for its atmosphere was adult and liberal. He felt less constrained and made more friends there than at any other school to which he had gone. His academic record did not, however, improve. He was backward with his assignments which required greater effort and more attention to detail, and the outlook for his grades was poor. "A sad showing," his English teacher said. "Andrew is very talented, but rarely cares to let it be shown."

He was no longer living at home but, supported financially by his parents, was experimenting dismally in community living. He was subject to the temptations of his age and easily fell to them. He could obliterate the realities of everyday life by getting high on marijuana, hash, acid, cocaine and occasionally engaged in drug dealing. The movies gave him entry into another unreal world. Inevitably life at school deteriorated. Given his unstable temperament it could only be a matter of time before, what had seemed at Windermere a spent volcano, erupted again. Toronto was not Windermere.

What happened was not, however, wholly predictable. He had managed to hold down a part-time job from October to March at the Bathurst Street Theatre where he acted first as usher during, among other plays, *Talley's Folly* and later was promoted to assistant general house manager in charge of the concession stand. "I was very happy there," he recalled. Unfortunately financial difficulties caused the theater to close in March 1984. But he worked as a contract worker at the Colling Tire Shop, clearing the yard of scrap and doing some auto repairs which seemed to give him some satisfaction. To keep a job was for Andrew in itself a remarkable achievement, and served to boost his self-esteem.

When things seemed to be going modestly well, he met, dated and became enamored of one of the girls at his school. All went well for a time until another boy showed an interest in her. Andrew, angered by his advances, grabbed hold of the boy and shouted, "I'll kill you for this!" Later that day at a nearby tavern, Andrew got into conversation with a 260-pound ex-motorcycle thug, with whom he had become acquainted. The biker advised Andrew that the best way to kill his rival would be to catch him off guard when he least expected it. Andrew, however, contented himself with smashing the boy's head into a fountain as he bent down to take a drink. As soon as Andrew's teachers realized what had happened, they became alarmed and warned the girl's parents that it would be better if the relationship came to an end. The rupture of this incipient romance was a humiliating blow to Andrew's pride. His world collapsed, not surprisingly initiating a chain reaction of a violent kind, in its components strangely similar to earlier incidents in his checkered career.

In February 1984 Andrew was once more living at home on condition that he attend school regularly and obey its rules. After his girlfriend rejected him, he dropped out, much to his parents' chagrin. At the beginning of April they went away. Andrew used the opportunity to drive their car which they had forbidden him to do, and to hold a noisy party which led the neighbors to complain. He continued to stay away from school and, when arrangements were made for him to be interviewed for possible jobs, he failed to keep the appointments. His parents told him that he must not bring his friends home. "Why," said his father, "don't you go out and do something for society?" "You always do things to piss me off," Andrew responded sharply.

Towards the end of May his parents went away again, for a night. They told Andrew that because of what he had done in the past he must find other accommodation. He said that he had, but in fact he had failed to do so, and that night climbed up to the third floor and broke into the house where again he invited friends in for an all-night party. He also took the car keys as well as money from his mother's purse. When his parents returned, they were horrified to find that Andrew had once more vented his anger against them by making the house, in his mother's words, "a pigsty." They had had enough. They had the locks on all the doors changed and told Andrew that he had two days in which to find alternative accommodation, adding that they would help him pay for it, but for the time being he was not to darken the family home.

Where could he go? To whom should he turn? Solitary and resentful, he spent the first night after his parents had turfed him out in Nancy's car. Later, in her apartment, he found a temporary sanctuary where he could sleep on the living-room sofa. He poured out his troubles and found a sympathetic hearing. While Nancy recognized that Andrew had problems, she believed that they were evoked by his difficult relations with his parents, and had faith that in time he would be able to overcome them. So she gave him a key to her apartment, though she told him firmly that he couldn't drink or do drugs there, and she forbade him to bring his friends to the apartment without first telling her.

Nancy's neighbor, Sue Milne, remembered:

> There were periods when Andrew was there all the time. His bicycle was always outside and his construction boots outside her door in the hallway. Once when I was passing Nancy's apartment he was banging at her door as hard as he could with both fists. And then he began kicking with those boots and yelling for her to open the door. Finally I screamed at him, "Look, you idiot, she's obviously not at home." But he didn't pay any attention to me and just kept on banging. He gave up about ten minutes later. The next morning I told Nancy what had happened. But Nancy was always very protective of him. She just shrugged her shoulders and said, "I know he can be kind of violent sometimes but he'd never do anything to hurt me."

Nancy didn't know Andrew's parents very well. But she remembered one irate conversation between Mrs. Leyshon-Hughes and her son while Andrew was staying with her that spring. Andrew yelled into the phone, swearing at his mother, for nearly half an hour — a big change from the quiet and considerate sixteen-year-old who brought her tea in the morning. Finally, in a rage he slammed down the phone. "My fucking parents," he cried, "they hate me." Nancy felt so sorry for him. It was heartbreaking. No wonder, she thought to herself, he acted strange once in a while.

After a time he tried once again to live on his own and to get a job, but there was soon a fresh crisis, which like the others conformed to a pattern that was symptomatic of Andrew's life. One morning, about half past seven, Andrew went to his uncle's house on Glengrove Avenue and, knowing where the car keys were kept, took them, unlocked the driver's door of his uncle's 1983 Volkswagen and drove away at high speed. He only had a temporary license. Bill Jephcott saw the car being driven away and, aware of Andrew's predilections, told the police that he suspected that his nephew was the culprit.

Andrew did not get very far. By Casa Loma, at the junction of Spadina Road and Austin Terrace, he lost control, hit a hydro pole and smashed the front of the car, causing some 5,000-dollars-worth of damage. Andrew was unhurt. If he was, as his uncle thought likely, making once again for the family cottage at Windermere, his object had been forestalled early. Just about a quarter past nine the police caught up with him at the parkette behind his home. He sprinted across the railway tracks, running away as he was continuously to do from the realities of existence. But not for long. When he was apprehended, he collapsed like a pricked balloon, and admitted what he had done. A day or so after the episode with his uncle's car, he stole ten dollars from his mother and, in a furious argument, smashed the tiles on two walls in the basement.

Andrew was obsessed with taking away and driving cars at high speed. He did not take cars from strangers but from people whom he loved or who had tried to love him: his father, his uncle, even Nancy. Was what he did an unconscious demonstration of resentment, either at their failure to give him the love he sought or at his dependence on them? His parents, as he saw it, had failed in their duty towards him. He said explicitly, "My parents never showed their love for me, so I struck out against them by getting myself in shit." He had sought dependence on his uncle and aunt, but that too had proved disastrous, ending in a threat of violence. He was becoming increasingly dependent on Nancy, but dependence was a sign of weakness which he resented. He was showing contempt for a society which constrained him. The thrill of driving away at high speed was itself a masturbatory rapture. In driving north towards Muskoka he was not merely experiencing an enviable and exciting sensation but he was escaping from home, casting his troubles into oblivion and fleeing from reality into the never-never land of illusion. And that he should drive towards the place where he had experienced some happiness signified his search for the Shangri-la which was ever to elude him.

Two weeks later there was another scene at Alcorn Avenue. His parents told Andrew that he could not be in the house unless they were there. He reacted violently. He stole his father's wallet and left home. Once more it was to the ever-faithful Nancy that he went. He asked her if he might borrow her car. As she had arranged to visit friends in

Brockville the next day — 7 June — she said she was sorry but she wanted it herself. The next morning while Nancy was asleep, he crept from the apartment where she had given him refuge, took twenty-five dollars in cash, her car keys and somewhat inexplicably her passport and, starting the engine of her Buick Skyhawk, planned to drive north. His capacity for striking at those who tried to help him and to show him affection had no limits.

As soon as Nancy realized what had happened, she deduced that it could only have been Andrew and reported the matter to the police. Once again the family cottage at Windermere was his destination and here, for the next few days, he indulged in a spate of robbery and violence, shooting up one of the neighboring cottages belonging to John Hamilton, with a .22-caliber rifle. Andrew was acting out the role of the superhero of his childhood dreams. Then, passion spent, he relapsed into flat normality and gave himself up to the Bracebridge police. He was charged with breaking and entering and the theft of an automobile, and was remanded in Parry Sound Jail.

From Parry Sound he was sent on a remand warrant to the mental hospital at Penetanguishene where he was to stay at least until the outcome of the trial at Bracebridge. His mother and step-grandfather brought him to Penetang on 15 June. Penetang, which was to become so familiar to him, has the unenviable reputation of being what a former inmate described as "a bug-house Alcatraz." It was built in 1933 on the southern shore of Georgian Bay — three kilometers from downtown Penetang and five from Midland — to accommodate the criminally insane. Although it was to evolve from a prison into a mental hospital, nothing could soften its forbidding exterior, a bleak two-storied fortress built on a ridge, surrounded by dense forest and a high wire fence, its gates, doors and windows bolted and barred. Its reputation, like its appearance, is daunting. "If you're not a good boy," parents warned their children, "you'll be sent to Penetang."

In 1984, Keith Norton, Ontario's minister of health, appointed a committee under the chairmanship of Dr. Stephen Hucker, a psychiatrist at the Clarke Institute, to investigate conditions at Penetang. It was none too soon. "Overall," the Hucker Report (*Oak Ridge: A Review and an Alternative*) commented, "the place is most unattractive," too cold in winter, too hot in summer. Its physical layout makes it difficult for the inmates to enjoy any degree of real privacy and the rooms themselves with their heavy metal doors, tray ports and concrete-slab beds look like prison cells. The toilets, in full view of everyone, and the only source of running water in some cells, are nicknamed The Fountains of Youth.

The most criticized aspect of the regime was the social therapy program, pioneered by Drs. Boyd and Elliott Barker in the 1960s and '70s but since then largely abandoned. This was based on the belief that faulty communication was the chief cause of mental illness and that remedial treatment could be effected by breaking down the "barriers of communication." Central to this was the experience of what was called the "total encounter capsule." Inmates confronted each other in a specially constructed room isolated from the rest of the building. It had no windows, was constantly lighted and barely furnished, but there were concealed microphones, closed-circuit television and a panel of one-way glass in the ceiling.

The patients sat stark naked on the theory that clothes were themselves a distraction and that an unclothed body helped to reveal the uncovered parts of the mind. There were no set mealtimes, but patients sucked hot and cold drinks from straws through holes drilled at an angle through the door. Patients were obliged to submit to experimental drug treatment, including LSD, scopolamine, amphetamines and alcohol, to help break down the barriers of communication. The patients lived together in this way for as much as two or three weeks. "We've been eating, sleeping and defecating in each other's presence without any judgment," complained one patient.

> Sooner or later someone breaks down [a psychologist explained] . The most entrenched guy, the most pathological guy, the strongest psychopath — in the fourteen days got to some kind of limited point within himself, surfaced it, either cried out, was angry with it, or did a sick thing with it. And then the group has a chance to tend to him or care for him and it's resolved...I saw guys who never cried in the ward — not even in drug treatments — suddenly cry out their crimes with their trusting group. They resolve their feelings about themselves and their crimes, or their victims and their crimes.

Such was not the experience of former inmate Roger Caron who wrote about conditions at Penetang in his autobiography *Go-Boy*.

[For the] first two weeks I was made to swallow twelve pills a day. . . The result was massive muscle spasms every thirty seconds, from the top of my head on down to the tip of my toes. . . All that while I was kept in that ice-box sleeping on the floor and eating off paper plates with a wooden spoon. My toilet was a hole in the floor and I had no drinking water.

Penetang's inmates include those who have been charged with criminal offenses and have been sent on remand for assessment; those who, because of mental disorder, have been found unfit to stand trial; those who are on warrants from the lieutenant-governor who have been found not guilty by reason of insanity; and those who have not been charged with criminal offenses but who have been sent to Penetang by other Ontario psychiatric hospitals because they are too violent or unmanageable.

One patient who said that he heard voices blamed them on his parents and so hit them over the head with a hammer. Another had a girlfriend who kept reminding him that Friday the thirteenth was an unlucky day, so on that day he "picked up a fucking knife and fucking stabbed her in the fucking face." "I wanted," a third commented, "to commit suicide but I couldn't, so I thought that if I killed a guard they'd kill me."

Another patient, Paul Conway, a black man who was found not guilty by reason of insanity to a charge of sexual assault in Windsor, Ontario, in 1983 insisted that he was not mad. "I am not crazy," he declared, "I'm here by mistake. . . but the torture I face could end up making me crazy." He refused to cooperate, would not take medication or take part in rehabilitation schemes. As a result he found himself in solitary confinement and the victim of punitive action.

My daughter [his mother, Frances Conway, said of a visit which she had paid] got up and began hugging him as he sat down because he was so upset. I got up to comfort him and all of a sudden six guards barged in and pounced on him. . . one choked him, two grabbed his arms and two grabbed his legs. . . his face began to puff up. He hadn't done anything. . . [but] they dragged him down the hall like they were dragging an animal. I was afraid he was going to die.

"It's a disgusting institution," Carla McKague, the head of litigation for Toronto's Advocacy Centre for the handicapped, declared. "It provides poor therapy by unqualified staff. There are reports all the time of physical and verbal abuse of patients by staff." "In its current state [Penetang is] hopeless," commented Howard Richardson, the executive director of the Ontario division of the Canadian Mental Health Association, who had himself been a member of the Hucker committee. "It's not geared towards the rehabilitation of human beings, no matter how sick they are."

During his first month in Penetang Andrew proved to be well behaved and socially adept. There was a slight hint of what one report called a "smart-alecky" impression but no outburst of rage. In general the authorities found him pleasant and cooperative. He spent much of his time in the music room, watching TV, playing ball games, reading and swimming. He socialized with the other patients, apparently without difficulty, playing cards with them. At the end of July a report from the Occupational Therapy Centre described him as "a bright, personable and mature individual. He is quite industrious and always busy. At times his work skills are not at the level that he would have one believe and he indicates a low level of frustration tolerance."

The authorities, persuaded by his previous mental history, realized that Andrew was no ordinary delinquent, and before sentence it was thought expedient that he should have a thorough psychological assessment. Once more he had to submit to a formidable series of tests, the high-sounding names of which screened some relatively straightforward examinations: the Hartford-Shipley Scale, Intake Survey, Sack's Sentence Completion Test, the Self-Rating Depression Scale, the Beck-Depression Inventory, the Minnesota Multiphasic Personality Inventory, 16 Personality Factors Questionnaire, Bender Gestalt Test, Benton Visual Retention Test, Reitan Neurophysiological Battery, Wisconsin Grooves and Maze Tests, Stroop Color-Word Naming Test and the Wechsler Memory Scale. Andrew recognized that he had been put through some of these before but cooperated without criticism. Previous assessments were also available, but strangely enough Dr. Vinegar never received the valuable and revealing report which had been drawn up in February 1983 by the Hartford Institute for Living. In the first instance the Institute had replied that it had no record, and the Mental Health Centre seems to have been satisfied that there was no necessity to pursue the matter further.

From all these little that was new emerged. There was some evidence of impulsive, unconventional behavior, which would have been obvious to anyone who had the least knowledge of Andrew, and of a "mild mood disturbance" which was thought to be "quite likely situational and transient." More seriously, temporal lobe epilepsy was suspected but was never to be proved. There was really nothing to suggest any real grounds for organic dysfunction or impairment.

What was plain from all the reports was the unhappy state of Andrew's relations with his parents, against whom he nourished a strong resentment. Whether or not his complaints were groundless, he made his parents, and his father in particular, the scapegoat for his behavior. His father, he told Dr. Grant Harris, wanted him to act as if he was a man of twenty-five rather than as a boy of sixteen. Andrew reported, the doctor added, "that when his father was drinking or when they had been arguing, he would often retire to his room and take drugs."

Andrew blamed his recent escapade on his parents' neglect. Eric King, of the Hincks Centre, thought that Andrew's "poor affective expression has risen in part from a family which is well defended against emotions," adding, somewhat obliquely, that Andrew's egocentrism had been fostered "by models in two previous generations."

> Overall [King concluded] Andrew presented a sense of hope-lessness and despair particularly with his situation at home. He acknowledged that he is closed up with his family and it's very clear that matters are terrible at home.

Andrew spoke, however, very warmly of Nancy Eaton and her supportive role in his life; she was like a "real sister to him."

When he was asked what he would like most to be when he grew up, Andrew replied promptly, "a cop." Given his sticky relations with the law, his choice might seem astonishing. But the visual image of the high-booted, leather-jacketed policeman riding on his powerful motorbike, with an implied threat of violence, fitted in with Andrew's own macho aspirations. Gloria Curtin, however, of the Ontario Department of Social Work was optimistic about Andrew's future, judging him to be a "warm, sensitive, intelligent teenager, who, given the opportunity, could live a productive life." "He is very sincere," she added, "about wanting to change."

At the time this may well have been the case. It was the judgment reached by Dr. David Vinegar, the psychiatrist under whose supervision he was to be placed for the next three months. His report covered the same ground and came to very similar conclusions. He was convinced that Andrew did not suffer from an incapacitating mental illness which would have led to his being certified under the Mental Health Act. He was absolutely fit to stand trial and perfectly aware of the legal consequences of what he had done. Andrew, he supposed, was an emotionally immature young man who had recourse to drugs to escape his problems. He had responded well to group therapy and the doctor felt sufficiently confident about the future to recommend to Judge Bice that psychotherapy would prove a more effective remedy than a prison sentence. "His present actions can be seen in the light of a 'cry for help.'"

The functional assessment, made shortly after his arrival, was not without interest. Andrew admitted that he had been experimenting with drugs and drank moderately, a "moderate to heavy marijuana smoker." He could cook for himself and do his own laundry. He did not trust himself with large amounts of money, not that he had ever had any. He was "more of a listener than a talker," and felt that he was moody. With most people, his parents excepted, he could communicate easily enough. Separation from home family life, he said bluntly, "does me good. My parents," he said on his first day at Penetang, "didn't get along. They'd fight. I'd go to my room and cry. There was no ballgames. We did nothing together." When he came back from the court on 18 July, he confessed that he could talk much more easily to other people than to his parents.

His parents were to visit him on his seventeenth birthday, 14 July. He became increasingly nervous as the day drew near. His arm and leg began to shake when he heard that his father had phoned to find out how he was getting on.

> This Saturday [Andrew wrote] is my birthday and my parents are coming to visit me. I feel that they will expect a great change in me and I want them to see that because there is a change. I want to make things work as [far as] a family goes and I feel that is [a] possible reality. I know also that it is going to be hard on my dad and mum, just the feelings that I'm going to reveal to them. I'm not going to let them do the talking any more. I will speak for myself once in my life, and am going to confront them

on as many feelings as possible and try and deal with them at the same time. I realize that this may not work but I feel that this is a very important step to my mental health [even] if it does create BAD VIBES. I'm not sure if I'll be able to continue trying AND I'M AFRAID OF THAT. I hope to open my father's and mother's eyes about my TRUE feelings towards them and to be able to receive a 'True' Response.

But when his parents came to Penetang's gray fastness he was as tongue-tied as ever. He sat gloomily smoking, feet on a chair, head bent forward, refusing to look his parents in the eyes and saying very little, obviously ill-at-ease. To relieve the tension he went out to greet the dog, Jennifer, which they had brought with them.

Three days later he was due to appear in court. On the morning of the trial he was so nervous that he got up at six and was allowed to smoke a cigarette and listen to music before the police arrived to take him there. He was found guilty of breaking and entering his uncle's house on the Joseph River and of seven other offenses. But Judge Smith put him on probation for three years on condition that he receive treatment at Penetang, and during that time perform three-hundred hours of community service. Andrew was delighted with the verdict and full of good resolutions.

Six days after sentence on 23 July, he wrote a letter home which was unusual in length but also genuinely touching. Yes, he did really want to talk openly to his parents. He didn't think that such an aim was mere fantasy. "Ernest," he told his father, "I realize now how much you care about me; someone who did not care wouldn't be phoning often and asking how I was doing and how long I was going to be here." Of course Andrew could not say how long he was going to be at Penetang but he hoped that when he left he would be really "mentely [sic] fit."

I could understand why you, Ernest could not show how much you care by physical emotions, if grandpa did not, and you felt that it wasn't manly to do so, but damn it really hurts to see other famillys [sic], father[s] showing love to their children, and not being part of something like that I guess made me really jelous [sic] and hurt. And to see other famillys [sic] going to 'THE BALL PARK' and you not taking me made me feel unwanted...I felt...I was a failure. After hearing stories you've told me about T.C.S. [Trinity College School], how you played soccor [sic] and did 300 sit-ups to prove yourself really got to me. I wanted to please you, so that you would be proud of me, but when I did try you would critsize [sic] me and I would feel that I had failed again. Saying things like "you could be really good if you apply'd [sic] yourself" really got to me. I did apply myself. I need the positive renforcement [sic].

Now, however, there was a chance to make good, to show his parents that he could apply himself and that he could communicate with them. "After other people's experience I realize how *fucking lucky* I am and that I've still got that one chance left.... I think we can work things out; AND THIS TIME NO BANDAID TREATMENT." He reported proudly that he had been given full privileges, so that when his father came to visit him he wouldn't feel embarrassed by having to talk to him in the ward, but they could go for a walk together, "and we could talk 'Son and FATHER' — 'FATHER and Son.' I'm going to give you 100% and I also NEED your 100% of TRUE feelings I LOVE YOU."

What he had to say to his mother was less effusive. He apologized to her "for not talking good," but he was so afraid of hurting her feelings that he found it difficult to communicate. "I would like to have both of you into group [therapy] because I think it would help me."

"Long letter, eh" — and so it was. His father was moved by so unusual and unexpected a display of emotion. After visiting his son in early August he sat down and wrote a four-page reply in which he tried to be reassuring:

> We all make mistakes but if we help each other we can put them right. I hope you listened carefully to the judge in Bracebridge and understood how fortunate you were. He felt you were worth another opportunity and both your mother and I agree.

How desperately they wanted Andrew to be really happy. "You may not believe me, Andrew," he wrote, "but I do understand your frustration.... You wonder who you are. Why? What is the purpose? It is a stage through which we all go."

To ram home his point Ernest related an apposite but somewhat banal story:

There was a good Buddhist monk who took the young student into the forest and asked him to describe what he saw. The student replied "I see trees, branches, leaves, flowers and grass." The monk told him to remain and live in the forest. Ten years later (the Orientals are not too concerned with time) the monk returned and asked the same question. The student replied that he did not know what he saw. Again the monk left the student in the forest returning ten years later and repeated this question. The student answered, "I see trees, branches, leaves, flowers, and grass." The monk sighed and said, "Now you see for the first time." What the monk meant was that the student saw because he understood.

"What I am trying to say," Ernest continued, "is that growing up takes time, you will find problems to overwhelm you. . . . Andrew," he confessed, "I am sorry I am unable to communicate the way you think I should."

Neither Andrew nor his father were letter writers. Andrew rarely wrote if he could avoid it, preferring to use the phone. His father said that it was the longest letter that he had composed since he had written to his own father telling him that he needed money. The rapprochement was affecting; if only it could endure. "If you would like to reply," Ernest said in a postscript, "I will love to receive it." A few days later Andrew replied enthusiastically:

Dad that was the most feeling I ever got from you and it was terrific. . . . Your letter really lifted me up Dad. It felt true, honest and sincere. So what's this Bullshit that you can't communicate, you came across as if you were here. It was great to feel YOU. Like your Zamboudhist [sic] monk I can see you, now I am starting to understand you.

Andrew was momentarily determined to try to make a success of his treatment at Penetang. After all, it was the first time that he had been hospitalized and that a hope had been held up to him not merely of a reprieve but of a cure. While he was waiting for the trial he had bridled at the idea of going to the Mental Health Centre, thinking that it was perhaps more sensible to go to prison and get it over with.

Last Saturday [he told his father] I was thinking about when
the judge asked me if I was going to obey the conditions of the
probation. I thought, "Gee, it would have been much easyer
[sic] just to have gone to jail, do the hard time and be done
with it. That way there would be no "temptation" for me to
screw up on. After thinking about it for the week I realize, if I
did it that way I would not be doing it, the system would. So
now I'm looking at it as a way to prove to myself, that hell I can
do things, even when I have some restrictions.

The reports suggest that at first he was quiet and cooperative. He
mixed well with the other patients, playing cards and going on expeditions
down to the beach, playing some baseball and other games. "He chaired
a self-help forum today," it was reported on 31 July, "and did a good job.
Andy was able to get other patients to volunteer as buddies and also
help to spark some interest in the ward." He taught another patient,
Murray Parr, chess and played pool with him in the recreation ground.

So he started his course of treatment, resolved to do well and to make
the most of the three hundred hours community work which was part of
the course. At the subsequent murder trial Andrew's counsel, Clayton
Ruby, was to query the credentials of his medical supervisors at
Penetang, Dr. David Vinegar and Paul Henry. David Vinegar was
certainly not a trained psychiatrist. He was a medical doctor who had
done postgraduate research in drug therapy and pathology. Paul Henry
had a master's degree in psychology but he too had had no formal
training. Nonetheless Andrew had a good relationship with them both
and in the darkening days of mid-January 1985 it was to them that he
turned. If they did not have expert training, they had had ample
practical experience.

At first all went reasonably well. Catherine Anest, who was the
assistant of Dana Somers, the probation officer working with the
Ministry of Probation Services in Midland, was the coordinator of the
community service program in which Andrew was to participate. He
quite enjoyed supervising the work done either at the School for the
Physically Handicapped or with the Penetang Parks and Recreation
Department.

I have begun my community work [he wrote on 16 August] at a
place called Georgian View. It's part of Ark Industries in

Midland. This place is for Mentaly [*sic*] Retarded and physically Retarded adults. Here they do contract work for Companies such as Oxford (Bussiness [*sic*] Supplies). The people I work with are all girls, (witch [*sic*] is a nice change, pretty too)!! So as of tonight I have 276 more hours left, (slowly but surely).

Slowly but not surely, eventually not at all. He managed to clock up 62¾ hours of his allotted 300, then he came irregularly. As early as 14 August, it was reported that his participation was variable. As he became more at home, he was quick to anger if he did not get his own way or had a disagreement with another patient. He was argumentative and arrogant, speaking contemptuously of the "outside gang beneath me." He complained angrily after he had missed the bus for the community work at Midland because he had insisted on taking a shower, but shouted that it was the staff's responsibility to ensure that he rose in time. "They want you to be responsible," he grumbled to Murray Parr, "but they won't give you a chance." It was a trivial incident but only too characteristic of his growing failure to meet his obligations. On another occasion, 24 August, he created an uproar in the dining room. He failed to keep the curfew and disturbed the other patients by outbursts of temper if things didn't go his way. The other Andrew hovered in the background, threatening to take over.

On 27 August, Lisa Orsatti, a former patient, now an outpatient, who found Andrew attractive, drove to Penetang to meet him. "At the hospital," she said, much later, "we were really good friends. He was really nice." They left the grounds together that day and went down to the Red Dock Beach. Andrew did not return until after midnight. He said angrily that he was tired of having to stay in at night.

He was called before Dr. Vinegar the next afternoon. He told Andrew off for coming in late the previous night and informed him that as soon as he could find accommodation acceptable to his probation officer he would be discharged. Andrew was worried by this. He did not want to go home. That, he said, would destroy the improved relationship which he had been trying to build. Time was needed to regain his parents' trust.

But where was he to live? To live at home, as everyone recognized, would reactivate the trouble which had occurred at previous crises of his life. His parents agreed to help him financially if he found other accommodation. Dr. Vinegar and Paul Henry suggested that it would be better for him to live in a "structured setting" such as Sunnidale or Phoenix House in Barrie which provided cooperative housing for former patients from Penetang. At first he considered that this might be a viable solution, for he recognized that if he went back to Toronto he would soon return to the world of drugs and petty theft. But it was not really a solution that he wanted nor is it conceivable that it would have worked out well. He was given a pass to go to Toronto to look for a place to live and came back in "good spirits," reporting that he had found something that would do. So, on 18 September, Andrew was discharged from Penetang.

Given the extent to which he had ignored his obligations, his discharge seemed strange. His parents criticized his release, for it was plain that he had only responded partially to group therapy and had not kept the institution's rules. "I was shocked," his father said. "I just could not believe what I was hearing...I called to [Sarah], 'They are doing it again. What is happening?'" But since Andrew had given no indication of homicidal or suicidal tendencies, Penetang was free to dismiss him, more especially as his presence there was an actual disservice to some of the other patients. But in the light of later events the move seemed distinctly odd.

The psychologists at Penetang were, however, cautiously optimistic about Andrew's future. Dr. Vinegar, who believed that his parents were wrong to look for a physical cause for their son's ills, held that progress had been made.

> The psychological testing [Dr. Vinegar had written earlier] reveals absolutely no indication of perceptive deficit and the EEG is within normal limits. It also appears that Mr. and Mrs. Leyshon-Hughes have been looking for a physical answer to their son's illness when in reality it is a behavior problem made by all the family members including his mother.

Andrew had shown some insight into his difficulties. Although he still found it hard to communicate easily with his parents, he acted civilly towards them. Dr. Vinegar insisted that he had made some progress in group therapy. On the top of the letter which his father had written to him on 9 August, Andrew had written the cryptic words, the dating of which is uncertain: "I never thought that I would Last Long.

There are too Many things that bother me to even try any more." It was in effect an epitaph.

Unskilled and unstable, Andrew was again cast on the stormy waters of an uninviting world. When he was discharged he said that he would prefer to work for a few months before returning to school. Through Canada Manpower he enrolled in a steelworkers' course and managed to get a job with Nantucket Steel until an argument with a foreman led to his dismissal.

He drifted back to the bright lights of downtown Toronto where he could lose himself in the city's anonymity, wandering aimlessly from café to bar to disco. In the excitement and occasional stimulus afforded by alcohol and drugs, he had the odd furtive affair. At first he roomed in a squalid apartment at 181 Walmer Road, but then was offered accommodation by Csaba Szilagyi, who had met Andrew's family at the Toronto Tennis Club and later stayed with them. Szilagyi, who lived in an apartment on Gloucester Street, took Andrew in but, for undefined reasons, they quarreled and he turfed Andrew out.

Andrew enjoyed a modest social existence with salesclerks, waiters, and unemployed high-school dropouts. Once, while listening to Q107, a local rock station, he heard Scott Anger, who worked at an underground parking garage on Charles Promenade, say how bored he was spending his birthday on the night shift. Andrew went round to the garage at three in the morning; they talked for a while and smoked a couple of joints. They met up again on the morning of 8 January at Times Square Pool Hall. "He seemed," Anger recalled, "like a really nice guy.... He said he had a lot going for him with his trade and everything. He was a little shy.... He just spoke of things he liked to do, like going skiing and playing pool."

Beneath the quiet, even shy exterior rumbles continued. He had found a new friend in Lisa Orsatti, but it was still Nancy Eaton who remained his real confidante. She had forgiven him for absconding with her car, and was eager to do what she could to help him live a normal life. Wearing her heart on her sleeve, she had a puppy-like quality which made her want a world where everybody was kind, good and gentle. Nancy was convinced that many of the problems which dogged Andrew, more especially his bad relations with his parents, were not of his own making, and she hoped that by listening to him and sharing his company she could help him restore his self-esteem. Their friendship, as she saw it, was therapeutic. In spite of this she had been unable to penetrate the depths of his strange and aberrant personality, but she thought she knew Andrew well enough to entrust him with the key to her apartment. She still regarded him as her "little bro'" and he, so she supposed, thought simply of her as his "big sister."

VI

— PRELUDE TO TRAGEDY —

Things bad begun make strong themselves by ill.

SHAKESPEARE, *MACBETH*

I am malicious because I am miserable.

MARY SHELLEY, *FRANKENSTEIN*

Between the acting of a dreadful thing and the first motion,
All the interim is like a phantasma or a hideous dream.

SHAKESPEARE, *JULIUS CAESAR*

THE EATONS AND THE LEYSHON-HUGHES gathered at their homes to celebrate Christmas 1984. For the festival of peace, family dissensions were still, if only for the season. Edward Eaton joined his wife and Nancy for a traditional leg of lamb. Andrew was with his parents at the family farm at Claremont.

The January days which followed had the historic inexorability of a Greek tragedy in which events move fatefully towards a dire outcome. The colored lights of the Christmas trees no longer glittered in the frost. The New Year's celebrations had come to an end. Some fortunate

Canadians made for sunnier skies, Andrew's parents among them, going off on vacation to Mexico. Others made for the ski slopes.

Andrew was in a state of acute unsettlement; Nancy was readily sympathetic. She had everything to look forward to, a devoted mother, and the possibility in the future of a happy marriage, with, as her mother sadly said later, "some grandchildren for me. She once told me," Mrs. Eaton added, "that, in the profession she had chosen, it would be easy for her to have her children and then return to work." Nancy had managed to overcome her difficulties, and was living a full and enjoyable social existence.

For Andrew no bright lights seemed to shine. The jobs that he had done recently were of a temporary nature, requiring brawn rather than brain. He was too fickle, too argumentative, insufficiently conscientious, to hold down a job for any length of time. The unreliability and inattentiveness which had characterized his school days continued into the adult world. Curiously enough he was to look back on this time as a sort of halcyon period. After he was arrested for murder, he told Dr. Richard Meen at the Thistletown Regional Centre for Children and Adolescents that life had been really going well for him, working full time, earning a reasonable salary and spending it all having a good time. If there was some truth in the suggestion, it reflected a stretching of the imagination. Yet Andrew now numbered a good many acquaintances, had a close friend in Lisa Orsatti, and there was always Nancy. Fundamentally he was still a loner who was most at ease talking with Nancy and, on several occasions, spent the night on the sofa in her living room where temporarily he could shut out the glacial world which threatened to encompass him.

Andrew was now nearly eighteen. He could no longer be described as a disturbed child. He was a teenager with all the passions and temptations which form an inescapable part of growing up. Girls found him attractive but he was awkward in dealing with them, hesitant in making an approach. "He was very shy with women," a friend, Norman Nault, commented. "He found it hard to believe I could talk to women so easy because he was so shy." "Andrew was really shy," Lori McConnach, another acquaintance, said, "and I don't think he had a steady girlfriend." Real intimacy escaped him for, as ever, he found it difficult, if not impossible, to reciprocate the affection a girl might have given him.

While he was at the Annex Village Campus he became infatuated with Tami Mori, a pretty Japanese girl in the same grade. They played a game called Fire, the object of which was to "hit the hot spot." ". . . I was at his house," she said, "and we were playing this childish game. It's called Fire. And just like, you go up and you go up and you say 'Fire, Fire.' It's just basically getting closer and closer." But their relationship cooled somewhat (though Tami remained fond of Andrew and was to pay a moving visit to him when he was awaiting trial) and they drifted apart, so that he only saw her three or four times in as many months.

There was, however, Lisa Orsatti, whom Andrew had met at Penetang. As an outpatient recovering from depression, Lisa found a friend in Andrew. They had discovered, to their amusement, that they had the same birthday, 14 July, though Lisa was a year or so older than Andrew, and that they had some common interests. In the joyless surroundings of Penetang the friendship flourished and seemed to be growing into something stronger.

After Andrew left the center, he continued to see Lisa regularly. They went on expeditions together to the lakes and to the mountains, building sandcastles on the beach and skiing in the winter snow. Andrew would go up to Wasaga Beach where Lisa lived with her parents or, if her parents went to Toronto, Lisa would take the opportunity to come with them and see Andrew. Lisa's parents didn't take to Andrew. Her mother Ruth, in particular, felt that he couldn't be trusted. He rarely spoke and would never look her in the face. Just after Christmas she told Lisa that she mustn't bring Andrew home anymore. Unless she stopped seeing him she wouldn't lend her the car or give her any money.

But Lisa really liked Andrew and thought him an engaging young man for whom she had a growing affection; in her brother Tom's words, he was a "nice easy-going guy." They did not make love, she said "because of fear of pregnancy and I did not want to go to the drugstore for contraceptives because this is a small town." Their relationship was not, she said, "a heavy romance or anything like that," but she felt that it could evolve into something deeper. Andrew felt this too. She had helped to kindle a measure of self-confidence in him so that when, in mid-January 1985, he was to find himself again beset by problems, it was to Lisa that he would turn. Lisa was herself a somewhat temperamental and immature girl who had to cope with her own personal problems and was not in a position to resolve Andrew's. In early January they went skiing together at Blue Mountain but Lisa, who was then employed by a youth organization, Katimavik, which organized travel, soon after had to go for a week to British Columbia.

These first two weeks of January formed a crucial period in Andrew's short life. He had managed to secure a part-time job. Dr. Peter Samu, a radiologist at the Rosedale Medical Centre, who was a near neighbor of his parents on Alcorn Avenue, met him on the subway of the north-bound train between Rosedale and Summerhill on Wednesday, 9 January 1985. When Andrew told him he was between jobs, Samu suggested that he get in touch with his office manager as he knew that there were some files which had to be moved. "I did it partly to help him. I did have filing to be moved, but it wasn't that urgent." The job with Rosedale Radiologists at 600 Sherbourne Street involved shifting files and x-ray equipment and was not very demanding. In practice Andrew was not to do it for more than three days in all. Still, it helped to promote Andrew's *amour-propre* which was soon, however, to be sapped by another approaching storm.

The first real signs of its onset occurred on Friday, 11 January, the eve of his parents' intended visit to Mexico. Andrew, who was a little resent-ful that they had not asked him to accompany them, joined them for dinner that evening. His mother had been drinking rather too much and told him brusquely that he had better make sure that he behaved him-self while they were away. "Don't you dare screw up," she said. Given what had occurred when they had last left on vacation, the advice seemed understandable.

But thinking that he had been doing rather well recently, Andrew took offense. Time and time again he complained that even when he had achieved something, his parents failed to recognize what he had done. With a job in hand and no recent outbreak of ill temper, he felt bruised by carping criticism. A spasm of anger flitted across his flushed face. He withdrew into his private world, disappointed that his parents had so completely failed to perceive that, in spite of all his difficulties, he was actually doing "pretty well." Pretty well might seem to the outside world an indifferent level of achievement, but for Andrew, only a few months ago in danger of being sent to prison, his mother's remark was unjust. His parents, he felt, were "fucking him up again."

Sarah and Ernest flew off to Mexico. Depressed and distraught, Andrew felt "rising urges" of energy. He began to fear that his mind was again being propelled by irresistible impulses which might result in violence. He had been, he told Paul Henry later in the week, in "a lot of pain since Monday night." At half past twelve on Tuesday morning he tried to get through by phone to Mr. Henry, but his wife answered and told him that he wasn't in. Later that day Andrew had dinner with Peter Elcombe, a director of the John Howard Society, an association concerned with work in prisons and correctional services, as well as vice-president of Canada Trust where his mother worked. Earlier in the day he had told Peter that he was experiencing "surges of energy" which he didn't seem able to control, and which were interfering with his work to the extent that he did not know what he was doing. He imagined that there were two beings perched like angels on his shoulders whispering contradictory advice into his ears, "two of them, like good and bad angels, a sense of good and evil to them."

He did not know how best to deal with the situation. Dr. Vinegar had sugggested the value of physical exercise as an outlet to aggressive feelings, so Andrew played hockey; but hockey could not calm the restless turmoil of his mind.

Andrew was becoming increasingly irascible. He phoned Nancy on Wednesday afternoon in an agitated state and said that he needed to talk to her, knowing that she would listen to him and take his fears seriously. Just as she regarded him as a young brother, so he continued to think of her as an elder sister; but for Andrew their relationship was in fact slowly and subtly changing its nature. He had had a crush on Nancy since he was thirteen but he had never mentioned sex to her, he said. Their relationship, he asserted, was one of friendship without, so far as Nancy was concerned, any sexual overtones. Platonic was the word he used, which by a Freudian slip the future transcriber of the court's proceedings would write down as "plutonic."

Their talk that evening soon showed signs of turning into a heated argument. Andrew was having trouble with his roommate, Csaba Szilagyi, and wanted temporarily to move back into Nancy's apartment until he found somewhere else to live. Nancy put her foot down. She was seeing someone on a regular basis and he simply couldn't sleep on her sofa anymore. Tonight he could stay, but this would have to be the last time.

He told Nancy of the wild urges that were unsettling his mind. He felt "really alarmed," and asked her what he should do. She suggested that he go back to the Mental Health Centre to consult Dr. Vinegar and Paul Henry and to take part in more group therapy. Nancy, aware of the oscillations of his past history, knew that she had really done everything in her power to help him but there were depths which she could not penetrate. He needed professional help.

What he did next showed that he had real fears that matters might get outside his control. He handed Nancy a knife and told her to look after it for him, evidently afraid that he might use it on himself or attack someone else. Nancy was surprised when he told her to take her car keys and her purse with her when she went to bed.

When Nancy phoned her mother, she told her of Andrew's somewhat odd behavior, mentioning the purse and the car keys but not the knife. Mrs. Eaton was anxious but Nancy, used to the vagaries of Andrew's mind, laughed it off: "Don't be silly, Mother," she said. But Nancy was beginning to wonder how much longer she could cope with his black moods.

It was very late when they finished talking. Andrew slept on Nancy's sofa. He got up the next morning and left the apartment. Feeling that Nancy, too, had abandoned him, he grew increasingly ill-tempered and morose. His mounting anger gave him a perverse energy. He became pre-occupied with knives and those who saw him during the four days prior to the murder caught glimpses of his strange, aberrant behavior which, in the light of future events, might appear to form a pattern of intent.

In the next few days there were premonitions of the coming denouement. When Andrew met his friend Norman Nault he told him that he was so often depressed that he had thought of taking his own life. Norman (whose father had committed suicide) had no wish to talk about the subject and brushed Andrew's comment aside, putting down his depression to lack of money and accommodation. "Shut up. I don't want to hear about it, Andrew. Kill the subject. You're making me mad." Norman gave no further thought to their conversation and was not to see Andrew until the coming Saturday.

There was another disturbing incident that Thursday, 17 January. While Andrew put little trust in his parents, he continued to have some faith in his uncle and aunt, Bill and Amy Jephcott, with whom he had lived in the summer and autumn of 1983 until the incident with the gun made it impossible to stay with them longer. Nor had Andrew improved things by taking and smashing up Bill's car. But Andrew's anguish was such that he rang Bill and told him that he was "having surges and he couldn't sit still." Andrew couldn't concentrate. He said, "I feel like I am going to steal a car." Jephcott, who was at home with the flu, advised him to make contact with Penetang to ascertain whether they could see him.

Then Bill rang his sister, Ann Taylor, who arranged for Andrew to be examined at the Toronto General Hospital. Bill picked up Andrew at the squash club and took him there. After a quarter of an hour the doctor came out and said that it was "just a case of teenage hormones." Bill objected, but didn't get anywhere. Andrew still had his belongings at Csaba Szilagyi's so they went back to Gloucester Street where he started packing to go to Penetang. They ate some sandwiches, and drove to the bus station. Before they parted company, Bill gave Andrew ninety dollars.

That evening Andrew rang his friend, Lisa Orsatti, just as she was leaving for work, for she was now a waitress at the Golden Apple restaurant in Stayner, and arranged that they should both go to a group therapy session at Penetang on Friday morning. After her father had driven her home from work, at 2:00 A.M. on Friday morning, Andrew called her from the motel, the Panorama, at Penetang where he had checked in for the night, to confirm the arrangements. Next morning she borrowed her parents' car and at 10:00 A.M. arrived at the motel to pick him up.

Before they made their way to the Mental Health Centre, they had breakfast; Lisa had pancakes, Andrew a mushroom omelette. Lisa thought that Andrew was nervy, restless and "high-strung," but as they both liked Dr. Vinegar and Paul Henry she had some hope that the group-therapy session might help to put to rest their respective worries. When they got to the health center, Andrew immediately tried to seek out Paul Henry but, characteristically, he had made no attempt to make an appointment and, as Henry was a busy man, he could only spare him a quarter of an hour.

When they met, Andrew tried to explain what was going on or appeared to be going on in his mind. Uncontrollable urges, he said, were exerting such pressures on his will that he feared he might be tempted again to steal a car and drive it away at high speed. He spoke too of resolving the dilemma of his existence by taking his own life. While Henry did not doubt that he was "visibly distressed" and in a state of real agitation, he was relieved that Andrew had been so articulate about his problems.

Andrew told him that he had come to the health center because he wanted to talk things over, but he had no wish to become a resident again and believed that his difficulties could be resolved by attending group-therapy sessions as an outpatient. Henry was hopeful that talking about his anxieties had proved to be a release valve for Andrew's tensions, a sort of mental emetic. At the end of their brief talk, Andrew, he said, appeared to be "comfortable and relatively relaxed."

Andrew wandered off to the group-therapy session which was attended by a dozen or so people. At first he sat silently, taking no part in what was going on. Lisa Orsatti was tearful as she described, among other difficulties, her fear of being gang raped by groups of toughs around Wasaga Beach. To bring in Andrew, Dr. Vinegar asked him whether he thought that Lisa would be able to deal successfully with her problems. Andrew murmured something sympathetic, but he was too engrossed in his own anxieties to be concerned about Lisa's.

Once more he rehearsed his symptoms, of how he was being victimized by increased "energy levels" which might express themselves in violence. He recalled the disastrous dinner which he had had with his parents as a result of which he felt "fucked up." He repeated too how tempted he was to take a car and drive away. But he did really want to have a better understanding with his mother. When Dr. Vinegar asked him what he had been doing to surmount these difficulties, Andrew replied, "I've been playing a lot of hockey this week to try and work out the intense feelings I've been having." Dr. Vinegar expressed his satisfaction and told him to go on taking physical exercise. "I know," he was to say later, "that seems perhaps facile but it's what I did."

The psychologists were almost as confused by Andrew's symptoms as the boy was himself. They seemed simply to have put their faith in group-therapy sessions as a means by which his pent-up emotions could be released, unaware of the mental iceberg underneath. At some time on Friday Andrew had phoned his step-grandfather, the lawyer Alistair Patterson, to tell him of his worries and that he was going to Penetang. When later that evening Mr. Patterson got in touch with the Mental Health Centre, Paul Henry was reassuring.

> His grandfather was elated to hear that he'd been here seeking help. I indicated to him that Andrew had left in good spirits and I thought he needn't be too worried about him as I'd seen his coming here as a step in the right direction.

The session over, Andrew chatted briefly with the assistant probation officer, Catherine Anest. He asked her for copies of the document which recorded the hours of community service in which he had been engaged at the Health Centre. He did not strike her as being in any way under stress. Rather the reverse, he seemed polite and fairly happy. Lisa (who had told the restaurant she could not work that evening because she was sick) and he picked up a pizza from Pizza Delight and drove back to her house to eat and play gin rummy, which he was teaching her. Although Andrew seemed rather restless, he was less tense.

They drove in Lisa's parents' car to the Maple Motel in Wasaga Beach where he was to stay the night; Lisa gave him twenty-five dollars to pay for his room. They had to fill in the remainder of the day so they toured Georgian Bay in Lisa's car. They stopped for something to eat and Andrew said he wanted to smoke some dope. Lisa thought she knew of a place where they could get some, but they failed to find it.

Andrew, Lisa recalled, "was cheerful and was glad I was with him. I told him I believed he was falling in love with me and he said something like, 'You've got it right.' He told me he never was out with any girls he felt strong about since leaving Penetang." They came back to the motel about 10:00 P.M. but later went out again, following a snowmobile until it disappeared out of sight. It was nearly two in the morning before Lisa dropped Andrew off at the motel, promising to pick him up the next morning to take him to the bus station at Barrie where he could catch a bus back to Toronto.

Saturday, 19 January, did not, however, quite work out that way. When Lisa, who had got up at five that morning, arrived at the motel, she thought that it would be nice to have Andrew for at least part of Saturday, and she offered to drive him back to Toronto in her parents' car. Although she disliked driving in Toronto, she knew that Andrew would be ready to take over as soon as they reached the city's boundaries. It was perhaps a reflection of her own hope that the incipient romance was blossoming.

After breakfast they drove to Toronto, arriving about 11:00 A.M. Andrew had been immersed in his own thoughts and had little to say for himself, though he seemed pleased to have Lisa for company. On arrival in Toronto they needed gas, so she gave Andrew a check for twenty dollars but, as he couldn't get it cashed, she tried to borrow ten dollars from her brother Tom. She was crying and upset, worried that she had taken her parents' car without their permission, but she didn't tell Tom that Andrew was with her. He gave her the money and told her to go straight home. Meanwhile Andrew had gone to book a court at his parents' racquet club to play squash the next week.

What then? Lisa was still reluctant to leave Andrew and go home. She was very much hoping that he might drive her back to Barrie and return to Toronto by bus. But Andrew had other ideas. He was at a loose end. He thought he would go first to the apartment on Gloucester Street where he had roomed recently with Csaba Szilagyi. While Lisa sat in the car, Andrew, hoping that Szilagyi might let him live there again, investigated but without success. He came out shrugging his shoulders, suggesting they call on his friend Norman Nault. Norm was a twenty-year-old who had come to Toronto from Saskatoon eighteen months earlier, and who now worked as a busboy at Toby's in the Eaton Centre. Andrew was one of the first people he had met, and they became friends, going to the movies, playing hockey and backgammon.

When Andrew phoned Norman at his apartment at 115 Kendal Avenue to find out whether he was going to be free that afternoon, Norman was still in bed, but he invited them to come along and have coffee. Norm had his own problems, for his relationship with his girlfriend, Natalie, was tapering out, and the two of them were quarreling over money. By this time Lisa felt that things were not going quite as happily as she had hoped. Andrew was moody and rather silent. They had drifted from one place to another in an aimless sort of way. Now they were visiting a friend of Andrew's whom Lisa didn't really know. Her parents would be worried that she had taken their car to Toronto. Suddenly she felt that she wanted to go home.

Would Andrew drive her car back to Barrie and catch the bus back to Toronto? This would at least give them another hour together before they parted. Andrew said no. Instead, he suggested that Lisa drive Norman and himself up to Midland to see their friend Colin. Lisa became increasingly exasperated. Only a few hours ago Andrew intimated that he was in love with her but now he seemed more interested in going off with Norman. "I didn't want to hear any more. I didn't say anything to him at all." She picked up her things and with tears in her eyes flounced out of the room.

She went outside and got into her car. Andrew followed. By now he too was very angry, "really mad at me." He thumped the roof of the car hard with his hand. In her agitation she drove the wrong way up the one-way street. Andrew shouted after her. Alone, lonely and rejected, he stood in the cold with nothing on but his T-shirt watching her drive off.

Somehow the remainder of Saturday had to be filled in. A few minutes before Lisa's abrupt departure, Wayne Erwin and Lori McConnach arrived. They both worked for the same firm, Postal Promotions, Wayne as a machine operator and Lori as a payroll clerk. That Saturday they had been successful in acquiring an apartment at 37 Hallam Street. They all agreed to spend the evening at the Elaine Tavern in Scarborough. While Andrew and Norman spruced up, Wayne and Lori went out to buy a twelve-pack of Labatt's Blue and some Kentucky Fried Chicken. Norman had a shower and returned the shirt he had borrowed from Andrew. Andrew ironed it and put it on.

The two of them left with Wayne and Lori, making first for the Guild Inn in Scarborough where Wayne had been living with his father. While Wayne and Lori washed and changed, Norman and Andrew drank some beer. Then they all set out together for the Elaine Tavern on the Danforth which they reached about a quarter to ten.

The remainder of the evening passed in drinking, dancing and chatting together. As usual, Andrew had no money, so Norman lent him twenty dollars. The tavern was lively and noisy. While the others danced, Andrew sat alone, silent and withdrawn, sipping vodka and orange juice, perhaps still resenting Lisa's rejection of him that afternoon. "I sat and talked with him," Lori said, "and tried to get him to ask somebody to dance, but he wouldn't. He said he didn't like being rejected. We tried to get him to ask somebody to dance, and told him it wasn't that hard to do." Only once, prodded by Wayne, did he get up to ask a girl to dance, but someone else beat him to it, and so he retired to his seat. Wayne and Lori were dancing together. Norman spied a pretty girl, Fran, and went over to ask her to dance, a move which gave offense to her own boyfriend who suspected that Norman was making a pass.

When Norman went to the washroom, the girl's boyfriend followed him. Andrew and Wayne, wanting to protect their friend, got up and went after them, thinking that a fight might ensue. Whether there was an actual brawl seems doubtful, and the incident may have been another figment of Andrew's fertile imagination. Norman said that there was no fight, but this was not Andrew's story. Andrew told another friend, Frank Panos:

> One of the guys met a girl and this girl was with another guy and they got into a dispute and they went in the washroom and we beat him up and took all his money. He had some cocaine on him, and we took that too.

Whatever happened, they were bundled out of the tavern when it closed at 1:30 A.M. that Sunday morning, 21 January.

Andrew and Norman went in Wayne's car to Kennedy Station to catch a subway back to Toronto but, as they got to the bottom of the stairway, the train's doors closed. They banged on the windows but the last train went without them. Wayne had already left for home, so they were stranded. Fortunately a cab came along and they told the driver to take them to Yonge and Bloor streets. The fare came to nineteen dollars, and Andrew promised Norman that he would repay his share together with the other money that he had borrowed from him on Monday morning. They were in a boisterous mood, well oiled by the drink they had consumed, and decided to "check out the Connection," an after-hours club on Yonge Street, only to discover that there was a five-dollar cover charge which they were disinclined to pay. So they got into another cab which took them both to Norman's apartment. There they watched television and smoked a couple of joints until half past three when Norman gave Andrew a sleeping-bag and told him to sleep on the floor beside his bed. The day had been neither exhilarating nor exciting.

They rose sluggishly, a little hungover, on Sunday. Natalie, Norman's girlfriend, was up first, at eleven o'clock, making coffee. Norman rose soon afterwards and they argued over the rent for the apartment. He told Natalie that he didn't have the cash handy but she didn't give him the chance to explain that it was in the "Green Machine" and told him that he'd have to go. He phoned his brother who agreed to take him in. Norman said that this would actually save him some money. Meanwhile Andrew rose slowly and put on a white short-sleeved shirt with blue trim, black trousers and a grey suede jacket.

Norman was making arrangements for the day. He rang up the girl, Fran, with whom he had danced at the Elaine and arranged to meet her at 2:00 P.M. at the Spadina Station. He still had things to talk over with Natalie, so he told Andrew to clear off, lent him another ten dollars and told him to meet Fran and take her to the Castleview Tavern at the corner of Spadina and Dupont, intimating that he would join them there. But the plans went awry because Fran failed to turn up. While waiting for Norman to join him, Andrew called Natalie to tell her that Fran had not arrived. Norman eventually met up with Andrew at his brother's apartment at 503 Salem Avenue.

Norman phoned Fran and arranged another meeting, but he still had to remove his bits and pieces from the apartment on Kendal Avenue to his brother's flat. So he and Andrew went back to Kendal Avenue where they packed up his belongings, which Andrew carried to the cab while Norman said goodbye to Natalie. When they returned to Salem Avenue, they plunked it all down quickly, for Norman was late for his meeting with his new girlfriend. He and Andrew took the bus to Spadina Station to meet her, and there just before eight they parted company. Andrew would have liked to accompany Norman, but after twenty-four hours Norman had really had enough of Andrew and wanted to meet Fran alone. So reluctantly Andrew departed, telling Norm that he was going to call on his mother's friend, Peter Elcombe, to see if he could borrow some money to repay the loan, amounting now to some forty dollars, which Norman had made him.

It was not, however, to Peter's apartment but to Nancy's that Andrew was to make his way that Sunday evening. Seeking shelter for his body, mind and bruised spirit, he knew that Nancy in her kindness would not send him away into the city's darkness. He had nowhere else to go, no money to pay for a bed and no one else to turn to. The past week had been full of painful memories, and his mind still throbbed. All his efforts to obtain help had proved unavailing. His parents were on vacation in Mexico while he moldered on in Toronto. He had begun to doubt whether the group-therapy sessions accomplished anything. When he had consulted the doctors at Toronto General Hospital they had dismissed his case summarily. Norman Nault had failed to realize the power of the demon voices that seemed to be whispering into his ears. Even Lisa Orsatti had snapped her fingers at him. Only Nancy understood him — Nancy who was beginning to stand for something much more than mother, sister or friend.

But he resented that Nancy had so much that he lacked — a loving mother, a wide range of friends, the capacity to counter the difficulties which deafness and depression had brought her, the ability to hold down a job and to enjoy doing it, an adequate and assured income. It was Nancy's car which he had deliberately taken the previous summer, and it was through this and the major upheaval which followed the incident that he had been incarcerated in the harsh confines of the Mental Health Centre at Penetang. He did admire her, "adored her" were Mrs. Eaton's words. But if he cherished her, he was also jealous of her, of her possessions, of her boyfriends, and spiteful of his own growing dependence on her. What could restore his sense of achievement? Was there a case for striking at a person upon whom he was becoming dependent so showing the world of what he was capable? Ought he not to demonstrate that he could be the master of the situation? The ominous verses of William Blake, which were so inappropriate to Tiger, only too well describe Andrew's state of mind:

Tyger, tyger, burning bright
In the forests of the night,
What immortal hand or eye
Could frame thy fearful symmetry?
When thy heart began to beat
What dread hand and what dread feet?
What the hammer? What the chain?
In what furnace was thy brain?

What thoughts passed through Andrew's mind as he entered Nancy's apartment that Sunday evening it is impossible to say, for he cannot or will not talk about them. In all probability he was more immediately concerned with the outward superficialities of existence: a meal, television, a bed. Yet, the horrific events which were to take place in Nancy's apartment in the next twelve hours were already in gestation. The prelude was not unconnected with the act.

VII

—— MURDER ——

What shall be the maiden's fate?

SIR WALTER SCOTT

See how love and murder will out.

CONGREVE, THE DOUBLE DEALER

Murder most foul...
But this most foul, strange and unnatural.

SHAKESPEARE, HAMLET

IT WAS BITTERLY COLD AND SNOWING HEAVILY when Andrew arrived about nine o'clock on Sunday evening at Nancy's apartment; he was wearing the black clothes which he seems often to have worn when his mind was in turmoil. But if it was bleak weather outside, it was warm and cosy within. Nancy's flat was compact and comfortable. Tinkerbell, the cat, a silent and solitary observer of the events that followed, nestled comfortably by the warmth of the radiator. The curtains were drawn, the television was on and the partly decorated spruce tree in the corner of the living room was a reminder of Christmas joy and goodwill.

Nancy, who hadn't been feeling well, was already undressed and ready for bed when Andrew arrived. But she was as welcoming and sympathetic as ever. They sat in her bedroom chatting, smoking and drinking diet Coke, while they watched television. *Battlestar Galactica* followed the Super Bowl which was won by the 49ers 38 to 16, an outcome which greatly pleased Andrew since he had wagered and won forty dollars on the game, which covered what he owed to Norman Nault.

They talked about a lot of things that night, big sister and little bro'. About his bad relations with his parents. His lack of real friends. About having no money. No steady job. And nowhere to stay. But more importantly, Andrew told Nancy that he had taken her advice and had gone to Penetang to get help. This was good news, as Nancy felt increasingly unable to cope with Andrew's problems by herself, and was becoming uneasy about being his principal prop. So his willingness to go to the Mental Health Centre relieved her mind. It showed that Andrew might yet be able to take himself in hand and get on the right track, and she naturally displayed her enthusiasm. "That's fantastic, Andrew!" she exclaimed. "I'm really happy for you."

About ten o'clock the phone rang. Paul Fitzgibbon, a neighbor who lived on the ground floor and who had just returned from a winter vacation in the Caribbean, rang to tell her that he was back and to say hello. They talked for about ten minutes. Nancy mentioned that there was a program on migraine on television that she particularly wanted to watch as she herself suffered from this complaint. When Paul said that he too would like to watch it, she invited him to come around and watch it with her. Aware from the background sounds that Nancy had someone with her, he said he would watch it on his own TV. "Well fine," she said. "I'll phone you when it's over." She never made the return call.

Before the evening came to an end Nancy talked twice over the phone with her mother, for Mrs. Eaton usually called her daughter several times a day and always late at night, to discuss the day's events and to wish her a good night. When she rang, Nancy naturally told her that Andrew was with her. When Mrs. Eaton enquired how he was, Nancy replied, "Mom, I've got some terrific news for you. Andrew has been up to Penetang, is feeling much better and has a counselor and is going to see him on Monday." "Congratulations," Mrs. Eaton said to Andrew when Nancy brought him to the phone. "It's rough growing up. We all have trouble with our parents. But it'll all come out in the wash."

Nancy, taken in December 1984, a Christmas present for her mother (Peter Horvath)

4 Farnham Avenue (Metropolitan Toronto Police)

"He. . .found himself in the kitchen staring at a small piece of pottery. . . .From it Andrew took a long knife." (Metropolitan Toronto Police)

"He ransacked the apartment." (Metropolitan Toronto Police)

"He took the palm tree. . . and placed it as a symbol of victory on the blood-soaked bed." (Metropolitan Toronto Police)

The Royal Bank, Monday, 21 January 1985, 11:07 A.M.*, less than three hours after the murder* (Royal Bank photo)

Tuesday, 22 January 1985 (The Toronto Star)

So hang in there." "Yes, thank you," Andrew murmured in reply. But there was something in Andrew's tone of voice which made Mrs. Eaton feel slightly uneasy. Normally Andrew would ramble on, but that night he sounded subdued, a little down.

Nancy and Andrew watched the program on migraine but Nancy was so disappointed by it that she phoned her mother and asked her to find out from the head of the Migraine Foundation, Rosemary Dudley, what had gone wrong. Mrs. Eaton called Miss Dudley who said she would look into it and talk to her the next day. She decided to pass on the news to Nancy and phoned her back about 11:00 P.M. But when Nancy lifted the receiver, Mrs. Eaton was surprised to hear her say sharply to Andrew, "It's my mother, for heaven's sake! I'll speak to my mother any time I want." Inwardly Andrew resented any intrusion from the outside world into the private universe he was then sharing with Nancy. She had already spent more than enough time talking to her mother that evening, and he grudged Mrs. Eaton's seeming possessiveness, comparing the intimacy which existed between Nancy and her mother with his own remote relations with Sarah.

Mrs. Eaton asked Nancy if there was anything the matter, but she laughed and asked Andrew to come to the phone again. Had he learned anything from the program on migraine? Mrs. Eaton enquired. Nothing, he replied, that he had not known before. After this brief exchange, Nancy returned to the phone. "Now Tiger," her mother told her, "you've been feeling crummy all day, so for goodness sake, kick Andrew out early and get a good night's sleep." "Don't worry I will," Nancy replied. "Night, night Mom. I love you." "Night, night, Tiger. I love you too."

But Andrew was not to go.

It was getting late. Nancy did not feel that she could ask him to leave, for he had nowhere else to go, and it would not be the first time that he had slept on the sofa in the living room. When, towards midnight, Nancy's close friend, Kristi Morrison rang, she did not sense that there was anything unusual in the situation. Nor indeed was there. But there he was, sitting on her bed, with Nancy in her nightshirt. He was strongly attracted to her, and inwardly desire was mounting.

At 1:00 A.M. Nancy set the alarm on the TV, turned off the bedside lamp, took out her hearing-aids and went to sleep. Andrew, still in his clothes, stretched out on the yellow sofa in the living room.

A cold dawn was just beginning to break as Andrew stirred from sleep, awakened by the alarm on Nancy's television. He looked at the clock. Ten past eight.

Dressed in the clothes in which he had slept, he went into Nancy's bedroom. He stared at the sleeping girl.

He began to pace and found himself in the kitchen staring at a small piece of pottery fashioned like a canvas bag on which the words "Cooking is my Bag!" were inscribed. From it Andrew took a long knife with a black handle and sharp blade. A trimmer, a butcher's knife, used for trimming fat. Nine inches long. Grasping it in his right hand, he went back to Nancy's bedroom.

He stood, knife in hand, staring down at the sleeping girl. She was on her side, facing him, eyes shut. He tensed himself, arm coiled back. Then he sprang, plunging the knife into her head. Once. Twice. Three times. Four times.

She screamed. But there was no one, except Andrew, to hear. And Andrew was past hearing. The only sounds he heard were the demonic voices of his own unfettered desire. Time and time again he stabbed and ripped at her, at the life-force area, plunging the knife into her defenseless body in a series of phallic penetrations.

She fought back desperately. But the attack was so swift. So unexpected. She slumped to the floor. Helpless.

Blood was everywhere. Seeping from the gashes on her body across the carpet. Splattering the walls. The bedclothes. His face. His hands.

This excited Andrew to even greater frenzy. He was hard. He lifted her nightshirt, shredded and bloodsoaked. Pulled down his pants. Picked up the knife, bent out of shape. Slashed her panties into shreds.

Then he entered her, trembling with excitement as he reached orgasm.

He pulled out. Ecstasy turned to disgust. Panting like a rabid animal the killer stood, mesmerized, staring at his victim. Then he threw the bedclothes over her mutilated body, making sure that he buried her face.

It was all over now.

The frenzy in him, which had begun to wane, was back again. In a trance-like state of ecstasy he went into the kitchen, opened the refrigerator, took out two eggs and returned to the bedroom. In front of his victim he began tossing the eggs in the air, juggling them in a bizarre *danse macabre* of triumph and elation at what he had just achieved. One fell intact, rolling over the floor until it came to rest beside the body; the other smashed on the bathroom floor.

He felt powerful, totally in command. He ransacked the apartment, turning everything upside down, emptying drawers, not caring that some of the contents spilled over Nancy's body. He took the palm tree from the white plant pot near the body and placed it as a symbol of victory on the blood-soaked bed. "I myself," the psalmist wrote, "have seen the ungodly in great power: and flourishing like a green bay-tree."

At a quarter past nine he decided to phone Nancy's mother. "Good morning, it's a beautiful day today." "Who is speaking?" Mrs. Eaton said sharply. "It's a beautiful day today," Andrew repeated and hung up.

Finally, the ecstasy which had possessed the killer evaporated. The orgasmic powers had shrunk, leaving him a passive spectator of the scene in which he had been the prime mover. Andrew yawned. It had been a busy morning. He made himself a cup of coffee, added precisely one-and-a-half spoons full of sugar and, wondering what to do next, sat staring aimlessly into space.

Have a shower, he thought. Think it through.

He went into the bathroom, turned on the shower, and cast off his soiled clothes. He was covered with Nancy's blood. It had soaked through to the skin. Flecks of blood stippled the shower curtain and streaked the bath and sink, on the edge of which one of Nancy's black gloves mysteriously rested; her gold chain with a dolphin charm slipped partly down the drain.

Stepping naked into the bedroom he went to Nancy's closet and took out her denim jacket and down vest. As he dressed, the cat Tinkerbell scurried across the floor and hid under the bed.

What next? He was aware that Mrs. Eaton knew that he had been at Nancy's apartment the previous evening and that she would surely voice her suspicions as soon as the body was discovered. His fingerprints were all over the place. Andrew had nowhere to go and no cash. He was caught in a trap and for the moment had no plans for coping with the future.

C.. meet Norm, he thought. Pretend it had never happened. But first he needed cash. Rummaging around the bedroom he found Nancy's maroon purse. He emptied it on the floor beside her inert body, and took all the money, forty-five dollars. Her car keys were in her raccoon coat.

About ten o'clock he let himself out the back door in the kitchen, Nancy's private entrance, pulling it shut but taking care not to lock it. He knew that he would be returning later. From the garage behind the building he took her white Buick and drove south to Rosedale Radiologists on Sherbourne Street. Less than a block away, at One Ancroft Place, Mrs. Eaton was sitting in her study reading the morning paper, waiting, somewhat impatiently, for Tiger to call.

To the office manager, Mrs. Cowling, Andrew seemed perfectly normal, if a little pale. But she did notice that there were some fresh cuts on his hand and a spot of blood on his right cheek. "What happened to your hand, Andrew?' she asked him. "I was trying," he explained nonchalantly, "to pry two frozen hamburger patties apart." The cuts, he said, were merely scratches and did not require a bandage. "If you're going to be moving files all day," Mrs. Cowling replied, "I had better get you a Band-Aid anyway," and she went into the back room to get one. When she came back, Andrew, only too aware of the troubles looming ahead, said he thought it would be unwise to work at the office until the cuts healed. Could he be paid for the work he had done? "Well," Mrs. Cowling said, "you'll have to wait a few minutes. Why don't you have a coffee and I'll get it ready for you." While Andrew drank his coffee, Mrs. Cowling fetched his check which amounted to ninety-six dollars. "Well, come in," she said as he left, "when your hands are better." If Andrew had ever read Shakespeare, Macbeth's words would have seemed only too apposite:

> Will all great Neptune's ocean wash this blood
> Clean from my hand?

Whatever the inner turmoil, outwardly he remained composed and showed no obvious signs of panic. He was most concerned with collecting as much money as he could. From Sherbourne Street he drove to the Bloor and Bedford branch of the Royal Bank to cash his paycheck. The cashier, Colleen Miller, handed over the money without question. By this time it was 11:20 A.M., time to meet Norm at Toby's in the Eaton Centre.

A waiter, Gary Fox, recognized him as he entered the restaurant. "Hi Andrew, how are you doing?" "Fine, thanks," he replied affably, then ordered a draft and a Caesar salad and sat down to play the video game Gorf. With sufficient funds now at his disposal, he repaid Norm the forty dollars. Before he left he had two coffees, smoked a couple of cigarettes and then returned to Nancy's car which he had parked at the top of the Eaton Centre. Then he drove back to Farnham Avenue.

He entered the apartment. Nancy's cold body was stiffening on the bedroom floor. He switched on the answering machine to see if there had been any calls. To see if anybody had noticed her absence. A voice said, "I bet you didn't kick Andrew out and slept in. I've been expecting a call from you all morning. Where are you?" It was Mrs. Eaton. He checked his watch. Nearly twelve thirty. Time was running out. If there was to be any chance of making a getaway he had to leave the city as soon as possible.

But he needed cash. With cool precision he examined Nancy's bank statement to ascertain how much there was in her account. He then set about tracing her signature until he was satisfied that his own handwriting would pass for Nancy's. If Andrew's heart was void of warmth, his native intelligence and cunning were in perfect working order.

About one o'clock he took the check which he had forged to the St. Clair and Yonge Street branch of the National Trust. "I'd like to cash a check for my friend Nancy please," he told the cashier. "She can't come in herself because she's a real-estate agent and she's showing a house." But when the teller, Jean Pepperdene, examined the check, she noticed a minor discrepancy. The written part of the check said 190 dollars but the figures read 191 dollars — a small mistake which made the check invalid. "It should be for 190 dollars," Andrew told the cashier. "She owes me 180 dollars and she wants ten dollars for herself." Mrs. Pepperdene explained that by the bank rules she could not cash the check until the error had been rectified and countersigned by the drawer. "But since it's only a difference of a dollar and because I know Nancy so well," she told him, "I could phone her and have it okayed over the phone and have her initial it the next time she comes in." But Andrew knew that she was asking for the impossible.

Thinking quickly, he told Mrs. Pepperdene that it would be difficult to get hold of Nancy. "The house she's showing is up at Yonge and Steeles and doesn't have a phone." But Mrs. Pepperdene persisted. "I'll try anyway," she replied, "she may have come home for lunch." She dialed her number and of course only got Nancy's voice on the answering machine. So there was no alternative. "I'm sorry," she said, "I can't cash it." Andrew looked unworried. "That's no problem," adding that Nancy had asked him to find out what was the exact balance in her account. He was beginning to wonder if he had read her bank statement correctly. Mrs. Pepperdene replied that unfortunately bank rules made it impossible for her to divulge that information. Again Andrew replied, "No problem," which must surely have been the understatement of the day. Mrs. Pepperdene handed back the check and he left the bank. There was nothing unusual in his behavior and, had it not been for the scribal error, Nancy's check would certainly have been cashed.

All this was no more than a hiccup in Andrew's plans. Back once again to Farnham Avenue, with a snack to sustain him, another attempt to wash away the bloodstains, and a fresh set of clothes: Nancy's white track pants and her T-shirt with the words *Inn on the Bay, Muskoka*, printed on the front.

Although Mrs. Pepperdene had refused to tell Andrew exactly how much Nancy had in her account, she had inadvertently intimated that if she had cashed the check for 190 dollars it might have put Nancy's account into the red. Andrew ruminated on this piece of information and decided that it would be safer to draw a lesser amount, so he forged a check for 150 dollars.

It was now two thirty. Time to go.

But he didn't, not quite. Returning to the bedroom he took another look at what he had done, which for some reason pleased him.

At ten minutes to three he returned to the bank. Handing the check to Mrs. Pepperdene he said, "She made it out for a different amount this time because she wasn't sure she would have enough funds to cover the other check." This time, satisfied that everything was in good order, the cashier accepted the check and handed over the cash to Andrew.

Although he had given Norman the forty dollars he owed him, he still had more than two hundred dollars in his possession. On impulse he bought a gram of coke from a dealer on the street and then went to a record shop where he bought a couple of tapes by the Honeydrippers. Carrying his Music World bag he went back to Toby's where he played the pinball machine and ordered a coffee. Although he had reentered the real world and was to all intents and purposes behaving as a normal citizen, by this time Andrew realized that he was playing a charade which would sooner or later come to a bitter end.

What had the day brought? A few cups of coffee, some cigarettes, a couple of cassettes and a handful of dollars. But there was nowhere to go and no one to go to. Toby's was only a temporary refuge from the cold world outside, a world which seemed to be moving rapidly towards a

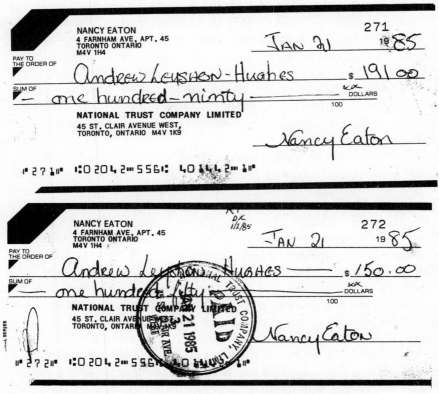

The checks forged by Andrew hours after the murder

tunnel of darkness. As the evening drew on, he would have to come to some sort of decision as to his next move. He could no longer return with safety to Nancy's apartment.

To postpone the fatal moment of decision, he called on some of his friends. He went first to 42 Glenallen Road to see Frank Panos, a sixteen-year-old whom he had known at the Annex Village Campus. To Frank, Andrew seemed perfectly normal and relaxed. Down in the rec room he discussed the events of the recent weekend and what had happened at the Elaine Tavern, especially the fight in the washroom involving the purloining of cash and cocaine. Frank himself began to get alarmed when Andrew took out some cocaine wrapped in a twenty-dollar bill. "Put it away," he said, "before someone comes down." Like

Mrs. Cowling, Frank noticed the cuts on Andrew's hands. They had been inflicted, Andrew said, "in the knife fight at the Elaine," a different story from the one which he had earlier given Mrs. Cowling. Frank reminded Andrew that he still owed him thirty-five dollars. Though he had the money Andrew postponed repayment, but said that he was quite interested in buying Frank's motorbike. When Andrew got up to leave just before eight, Frank asked, "Why don't you stay a while?" But Andrew said, "I'd like to leave before it starts snowing." But wherever he went Andrew would be unprotected from the winter of the spirit.

He decided that he would make one more visit before he fled the city. From Frank Panos', Andrew went to 981 Mount Pleasant where he found his former girlfriend, Tami Mori, with her friends Abbey and Rommell. Although his friendship with Tami, now a seventeen-year-old studying at Northern Secondary School, was a thing of the past, they regarded each other with some affection. Tami took him from the basement to the living room where, as with Frank, they talked about the previous weekend. He asked her if he could borrow a mirror, and, when she produced a piece of glass from under the Christmas tree, he again took out the cocaine wrapped in the twenty-dollar bill from his wallet. When Abbey saw it as he came upstairs, he told him to put it away. This time Andrew inserted the coke in a two-dollar bill. Once more he told the story of the fight at the Scarborough bar, and explained that the cuts on his hands were the result of it. After chatting for three-quarters of an hour, Andrew surprised Tami by suggesting that they might go for a drive together, pointing to the car parked at a gas station across the street. The request puzzled her, for she knew that Andrew had neither a car nor a license. Andrew explained that he had borrowed the car from a friend. Used as she was to Andrew's impulsive ways, Tami could not think why Andrew wanted to go for a drive on such a wintry night. "Where to?" she asked him. "Just driving around," he answered vaguely. But Tami was less than enthusiastic, knowing that it was in any case a school night, so she refused. As he was leaving, he held Tami tightly. "Don't let go now," he said as he hugged her, making one last appeal for affection before he departed into the night and crossed the Rubicon of his existence.

What should he do? Where should he go? He got into Nancy's car and drove north, away from the scene of his crime as he had driven away on so many other occasions from the crises of his life. But this time he was not to reach the never-never land of Muskoka. Ironically, his escape was to be frustrated by Nancy herself, his freedom of action brought to an abrupt end by the behavior of a car with the license plate bearing her nickname, TYGER.

VIII

REMAND

The vilest deeds like prison weeds
Bloom well in prison air
It is only what is good in man
That wastes and withers there...

OSCAR WILDE,
THE BALLAD OF READING GAOL

But the waiting time, my brothers,
Is the hardest time of all.

SARAH DOUDNEY,
THE PSALMS OF LIFE

AFTER THE MURDER, MRS. EATON'S house on Ancroft Place was filled with people. From early morning until late at night, countless relatives and friends, many of whom Mrs. Eaton hadn't seen for years, answered telephones, received visitors, handed out food and drink, listened for television and radio reports, collected press clippings, accepted endless deliveries of flowers, made all the funeral arrangements and provided for Mrs. Eaton's day-to-day living. In the midst of this confusion, Mrs. Eaton remained calm, even detached, part of her closed off, beyond grief.

The Anglican church of St. Simon the Apostle, just across the Rosedale ravine from her mother's home, was filled to capacity for Nancy

Eaton's funeral on Friday, 25 January, overflowing with people who had known and loved her. It was symbolic and appropriate that the last rites should take place in this church rather than at the Timothy Eaton Memorial Church with its mixed memories.

Naturally, Nancy's father, Edward, had taken the news of her murder badly, so overwhelmed by grief that he hired a private plane to take him from Florida to Toronto. Once he arrived in Toronto his behavior was characteristically unpredictable. He tried to insist that Nancy should be laid to rest in the Eaton mausoleum; but her mother, feeling that he had done little for the two of them in the last eighteen years, was determined that she should be buried in a separate plot at Mount Pleasant Cemetery. "I bore her, I brought her up. I'm going to finish the job." Edward was allowed to choose the coffin. He would likely select a good one, someone morbidly observed, because of his keen interest in boats.

At the funeral, as at the trial, a swarm of photographers and reporters descended upon Mrs. Eaton. Dressed all in yellow, wearing pearls, a large hat, dark glasses and a mink coat, she made no attempt to avoid the press. They seemed to admire her courage and strength and one by one they fell away.

After the short and simple service, the coffin, adorned by a mixed posy of carnations, tulips and daisies, was taken from the church, followed by Nancy's father and mother, who was supported by her brother, David Gossage, to its final resting place at Mount Pleasant Cemetery. As the snow fell, and the words of hope momentarily cast into the shadows the darkness and pain of the last few days, Mrs. Eaton threw a pink rose into her daughter's grave. "Goodbye Tiger," she whispered, "I love you."

The rest of 1985 was traumatic for Nancy's family and friends. Kristi Morrison was inconsolable. She and Nancy had known each other from the age of six and in the last decade they had become almost inseparable. Both worked for Bill Joyce Real Estate; he called them his "two princesses." They loved and confided in each other like sisters, and there was rarely a day in which they did not occupy each other's lives. Nancy's death left a hole in Kristi's heart which could never be filled.

Within months of his daughter's murder, Edward Eaton had a stroke while he was sitting on the toilet. He was discovered three days later, dead, lying face down on the bathroom floor, another indirect victim of Andrew's assault, for Nancy's death had been a shock from which he never recovered.

Mrs. Eaton was afraid to go to sleep. She dreamed the worst. Three or four times every night she discovered her daughter's mutilated body in a pool of blood, and would wake up in a cold sweat, the bedclothes in knots. Sleepless nights turned into weeks and then months. She walked for hours in the freezing cold because it was the only thing that would numb the pain. Everything reminded her of Tiger. She bought the white Mercedes sportscar her daughter always wanted her to have, and on the license plates she put "TIG'S MA." Christmas came and went. She did not buy a tree.

After the inquisition to which Andrew had been subjected on Monday night and early Tuesday morning, he left the Bradford police station shortly after 6:00 A.M. in the company of Staff Sergeant Ed Stewart and Sergeant Joe Cziraky of Toronto Homicide.

Staff Sergeant Stewart had been a policeman for more than two decades. In almost eight years as a member of the homicide squad he had never had an unsolved murder and never had a case successfully appealed. Stewart looked and acted like a typical old-fashioned detective-novel detective. Densely built and deliberate in his movements, he had a powerful face that easily identified his profession. His partner, Sergeant Joe Cziraky was born in 1943, the son of a Hungarian count who was forced to flee Europe at the end of the Second World War. In the late sixties Cziraky spent three years as an undercover cop buying drugs in Yorkville. He was as loquacious as the staff sergeant was reserved. But underneath Cziraky's breezy manner and wry sense of humor was a shrewd and penetrating mind. The two partners were responsible for the successful solution of another savage and baffling murder which only recently had come to court. On 7 June 1985 Maureen Fiaschetti, married only a few weeks, was sexually assaulted and murdered on a waterbed in her Scarborough home. Cziraky and Stewart eventually traced the crime to Wade Wright, a fellow employee at a Toronto computer firm who belonged to the same baseball team as Maureen and her husband, Terry. "We knew who murdered her," said Ed Stewart, "but it took us eleven months to pin it on him. It was like going fishing. We had to throw him a hook and then reel him in very slowly."

During the drive to Toronto, exhausted by the events of the past twenty-four hours, Andrew slept; and on waking he was cool and collected. Cziraky asked him whether he knew Erin Gilmour, wondering whether Andrew might have been in any way connected with that recent unsolved killing. Erin was a beautiful girl, the child of wealthy but separated parents, the mother the granddaughter of the former lieutenant-governor of Ontario, Colonel Henry Cockshutt; the father, David Gilmour, a younger son of a rich family. David Gilmour had teamed up with a Hungarian emigrant, Peter Munk. Profiting from the highly successful Clairtone Sound Company which they had set up, both became wealthy. Peter Munk's twenty-four-year-old son, Anthony, who was dating Erin at the time, discovered her body in her apartment at 37B Hazelton Avenue. Erin was lying on her bed, stabbed in the left chest and sexually assaulted. The homicide squad took fingerprints and questioned Erin's friends, but the case remained a mystery. Who killed Erin Gilmour and why, remained unsolved questions. There were similarities between the murders of Nancy and Erin; but Andrew replied that he did not know any girl of that name.

By 7:30 A.M. the police had taken Andrew to Nancy's apartment which was being thoroughly searched, its contents listed and all pertinent exhibits photographed. He was then led outside so that he could identify the garage at the rear corner of the apartment where she normally parked her car.

About 8:15 A.M. Andrew arrived at No. 53 Station where he was booked in and given breakfast. When he was asked whether he wished to phone his parents, he said no. At midday he was removed from the station and taken to the court to be formally remanded. There was a second hearing afterwards, which ordered that he be placed in protective custody at the Don Jail until the further procedures for dealing with his case had been determined.

Later that day Constable Thorpe found Nancy's cat, Tinkerbell, hiding under the bed and handed it over to Kristi Morrison; it subsequently found a safe refuge with Mrs. Eaton, though for some months it lost its appetite and fled from male company.

The Don Jail is a forbidding fortress of squalid sights, foul smells and menacing sounds. Inmates are housed in dingy and claustrophobic cells starkly furnished with steel bunks and soiled mattresses. A hole in the floor serves as a toilet and there is a pervasive stench of urine. Muscular bodies and tattoos abound. The air is charged with tension. Time passes like a record stuck in the same groove, a hypnotic routine of misery and squalor that dulls the senses and drags out the tedium of doing time.

Andrew was placed in protective custody, in a special block consisting of two groups of eighteen cells, each housing two inmates, so located that the detainees are safe from attack by other inmates who might be provoked by the antisocial nature of their crimes, such as child molestation and rape.

His stay in the jail was unremarkable, free from surges of energy which had led to the many violent and disturbing episodes of the past. This restraint was the more surprising in that there must have been much about life in the jail which he found unappetizing and anger provoking. In a disciplined and structured setting he was better able to control the impulses which were said to be uncontrollable. It was almost as if, away from his family and the irritations of school life and work, he lapsed into unimpassioned apathy. One of the prison guards described him as a "spoiled brat," but neither he nor the other guards thought that he was crazy, at least in the accepted sense of the word. "Next time I fly off the handle," a guard said, "I'll plead insanity!"

He had a number of visitors, apart from his family, who were allowed to talk to him by telephone through a glass partition. Lisa Orsatti called, weeping copiously, but Andrew remained stoical. He was more moved when Tami Mori came to see him some three days after his detention, the first of five such visits.

Tami was a girl with her own problems. "During the period of time that you corresponded with him [Andrew], do you recall writing a letter telling him you'd been thrown out of the house?" Tami was asked at the trial. "Yes," she replied. "And that, indeed, you wanted to commit suicide?" "It was," she admitted, "a silly thought at the time. But yes, Andrew told me, 'Why commit suicide today when there's always tomorrow?' He was telling me not to do it, it was pointless, it was stupid."

Worried by rumors that young men in prison were sometimes the object of sexual advances by other men, she asked Andrew if he had had problems in this respect, but he was reassuring.

When she visited Andrew in the company of another friend, Anna Ludwig, she told him that many people cared for him, and they could hardly believe that he had actually murdered Nancy. "Did you do it?" she mouthed. Andrew nodded affirmatively. Tami began to cry and walked from the room while Anna stayed behind. About a week later Tami went by herself. She did not use the telephone but mimed, making a round hole with finger and thumb and inserting another finger in the orifice. "Did you have sex with her?" "Yes," he mouthed in reply. "Were you high?" she enquired. He shook his head. "Do you think there is something wrong with you?" Andrew simply shrugged his shoulders.

Another girl who became deeply interested in Andrew was Sherri (not her real name), an English girl from Bournemouth who had a rose tattoo on her left ankle. She had come to Toronto with her mother, who was separated from her husband, when she was a child of four. Like Andrew she had had a troubled childhood and became involved in the drug scene. With a friend she once tried to set fire to the "goddamned school" at London, Ontario, which she attended, and as a result was placed on probation for six months. Later she took courses in training as a mortician, while working on and off as a waitress in a strip joint in Toronto's red-light district. She took some time to make the grade, but eventually gained employment as an undertaker's apprentice.

Sherri met Andrew through Norman Nault whose brother, Noel, was dating Sherri's friend. She had come across Andrew at Toby's where he was playing a video game and later joined the group of friends who went nightly to the Connection Club on Yonge Street. She went back to Noel's where Andrew was then staying, and she and Andrew smoked a few joints together. On another occasion she took Andrew back to her house, but having drunk too much he passed out on the bathroom floor and after that they lost contact. It was only on the bus with her mother, going to her temporary job at the Red Cross Centre, that she saw Andrew's picture in the newspaper and, to the astonishment of her mother and other passengers, shouted out, "Holy fuck, I know that guy!"

So she wrote to him and soon afterwards made a visit. "I was scared stiff," she admitted. Believing that only close friends were allowed to visit prisoners on remand, she described herself as "Andrew's girlfriend." This soon became a realistic description of their relationship. She began visiting him every week, winning his confidence, so that friendship developed into romance. She signed her love letters to him "Pussy Cat," and Andrew rather pathetically ended his letters with "Teddy Bear." He was at first reticent, but eventually he did talk a little about the murder. It was something, he told her, which he could not stop himself from doing. But whatever brainstorm caused the incident, he did not seem to her to be crazy. Indeed, she thought that he was a "very caring person." She wanted to marry Andrew and bear his children, no matter how long she had to wait.

The tedium of prison life was broken by visits from Brother Basil McCormick, a novice who had taken an interest in Andrew. The police reports had described Andrew's "religious beliefs, debts and income," strangely combined together, as "none," but under instruction from Brother McCormick, who maintained contact with him for more than a year, Andrew at length expressed a desire to repair yet another defect from his childhood — baptism and confirmation. The ceremony was carried out in the presence of his parents, Brother McCormick, Robert Greene, vicar of the neighboring St. Bartholomew's parish, and by the archbishop of Toronto, Dr. Lewis Garnsworthy, in the prison chapel on the fifth floor, a room only recently consecrated to religious purposes.

The comforts of religion could not assuage the feeling of hopelessness about the future which from time to time assailed him and, in a moment of acute depression, Andrew swallowed disinfectant and had to be rushed to the prison hospital. Like the earlier attempt that he had made on his own life, this seemed more probably a cry for help than a genuine attempt at self-destruction.

Since Andrew was only seventeen and a half, it seemed possible that his case might be heard before a juvenile court. A hearing was held on 28 May at Old City Hall. The dingy hallways of the Victorian edifice resembled a scene from Dickens: tattooed prisoners manacled to each other on their way to the holding area in the bowels of the building; fuming relatives of the accused huddled in dark corners with lawyers from Legal Aid; weedy looking vagrants asleep on benches; robed judges and counsel jostling through noisy crowds on their way to one of seventeen courtrooms. Here, outside the court for juvenile offenders, Mrs. Eaton momentarily came face to face with her daughter's murderer. "Are you all right?" she asked. "Yes," Andrew nodded.

The hearing was over in less than an hour and Andrew was again remanded and, at the request of his defense counsel, Clayton Ruby, he was sent for assessment to the Syl Apps Campus at the Thistletown Centre for Children and Adolescents. He arrived there on 24 June 1985 for a thorough psychiatric assessment under the Secure Treatment Program. Dr. Richard Meen reported on 17 July that he had found Andrew cooperative and polite, but emotionally flat. He was, he said, "quite hopeless and down," for there was no way in which he could plan for the future until the court reached a verdict. Andrew blamed his problems less on his own lack of effort than on the inability of other people to help him resolve them. "He was not," Dr. Meen reflected, "totally free with sharing his thought process." Dr. Meen could detect no feelings of warmth, commitment or involvement. Andrew would, he surmised, "impulsively respond in a very violent fashion" and his style was "somewhat suspicious, cautious and ungiving."

Dr. Kenneth Keeling, who provided a psychological report, also intimated that Andrew had been "quite cooperative," but he felt that Andrew very understandably was getting tired of the number of tests to which he had had to submit in the last few years. There was a "hint of suspiciousness," and once he flashed anger when Dr. Keeling asked him what he thought of a staff member's description of him as a "con artist." Andrew told the doctor that he was depressed and anxious about his situation. He wondered whether there was any point in existence, so much so that he often contemplated suicide. He lacked any real sense of identity.

The social worker at Syl Apps, Joy Freeman, interviewed Andrew on three occasions, and like his other interviewers found him cooperative and comparatively forthcoming, even if there were periods when he seemed withdrawn and stared silently into space. At times he seemed upset and on the brink of tears but at others he was flat and unemotional. Nor did he display any feeling of guilt, though he felt "ashamed and embarrassed."

> He identified his anger and inability to connect with people as his main problem as well as a sense of literally not knowing who he is. Andrew's desire to find out more about himself, at least superficially, is clear. However, his fear of finding "nothing" is overwhelming.

Joy Freeman commented that Andrew, nihilistic in his approach to life, was "a good candidate for long-term psychotherapeutic treatment in a secure long-term psychiatric facility." The reports showed plainly that the outcome of the trial would depend very largely on the evidence of the experts, and the extent to which the court would be swayed by their arguments.

The court for the preliminary hearing was convened on Friday, 25 October before Judge C. Scullion. It was to meet for seven days, 25, 28 and 29 October, and 6, 7 and 8 November, with a final session on Friday, 29 November. Paul Chumak appeared as counsel for the Crown as he was to do in the final trial, and Marlys Edwardh, Clayton Ruby's partner, as

counsel for the defense. All witnesses were excluded from the proceedings apart from Nancy's mother, who was accompanied by her friend,
Cicely Bell.

The first witnesses to be called were the attendants at the two
gasoline stations to which Andrew had gone in the hope of seeking help
when Nancy's car had begun to seize up. Tate Passer and Jeffrey Plouffe,
who worked part-time while he was studying fire prevention technology
at Seneca College, told how Andrew had called at the Petro-Canada
gas station on Highway 400 just before 9:00 P.M. that Monday evening,
asking for help with his car. They advised him to drive to the all-night
Husky station further up the road. "He seemed fine . . . He just seemed
to be in a hurry."

Two other attendants, Dan Reynolds and Kirk Griffith, from the
Bradford Husky station located between highways 88 and 400, related
how the car which was obviously in its last stages had come to a halt
about 10:45 P.M. Andrew, who seemed glassy eyed, as if he were stoned,
"was sort of just wandering around, didn't really care about nothing,
just a laid-back type of fellow. . . . He wasn't jumpy at all . . . just clued
out." They said that the car would have to be towed; but before the tow
truck came, as Andrew went to try to move the car himself, the Ontario
Provincial Police arrived on the scene.

The police constables, John Madden, Ken Dolan and Taylor Hunt
described Andrew's apprehension and arrest:

> He seemed very calm . . . wasn't agitated in any way, almost as
> though he was expecting it, resigned. He said "Look, I'm cool,"
> as though he wasn't going to make any problem . . . emotionally
> flat, neither sad nor happy . . . coherent. He responded normally.

When Andrew blew, as requested, into an Alert, a roadside screening
device, the results were negative. His clothes were all removed but after
they had been searched and investigated, they were given back. He was
allowed to smoke a cigarette, the last in his pack, and then seemed to
go to sleep, his head covered by a blanket. P.C. Hunt looked into the
cell nineteen times between 11:30 and 2:00 A.M., when Andrew was
taken to be interviewed by the homicide officers, Staff Sergeant Stewart
and Sergeant Cziraky, who took him back to Toronto shortly after six on
the Tuesday morning.

The next batch of witnesses were friends who also stressed the apparent normality of Andrew's behavior both on the weekend preceding the murder and on the Monday after it. Norman Nault spoke of how they had spent the weekend until Andrew left them and of his seeing Andrew twice at Toby's the following day. He seemed to Norman "very calm, very normal, a little depressed." Andrew had asked him if he liked the new sweatsuit which he was wearing — it belonged to Nancy — which he said he had just bought. He told Norman that he would probably meet him that Monday evening after his shift ended about 7:00 P.M.

Lisa Orsatti, Frank Panos and Tami Mori gave evidence. Lisa said that she got along with Andrew "really good" but she was confused and vague. "I really don't know. I don't remember that well," she kept on saying. Andrew had never discussed his problems with her, nor had he ever mentioned his "angry feelings" to her. "We didn't really talk intimately about our problems or hang-ups." Before she had gone with him to the Mental Health Centre on Friday, 18 January, he had been "high-strung" but he was "more relaxed" after the group-therapy session.

When Frank Panos saw him on Monday evening Andrew "seemed perfectly fine like I mean, he was relaxed, he didn't seem uptight or anything." Frank and he saw each other often, meeting nearly every weekend, but they had never been close. "We used to go out all the time and stuff but he never discussed his problems with you." Frank thought that Andrew was really a "bit of a loner," sometimes very quiet and withdrawn, at other times pretty bossy. "He wanted his own way all the time."

Tami Mori told of their early friendship, and of Andrew's last visit when he had so strangely asked her if she would go for a drive with him in Nancy's car. Marlys Edwardh was very interested in her account of the visits which she had paid to him in the Don Jail. She pressed Tami to explain why and how she had asked Andrew if he had murdered Nancy and later had sex with her, and how he had responded. "Tell us what occurred during this conversation. What did you ask him and what did he say, as best you can recall? Tell us the exact words."

On 6 November, Nancy's mother told of her telephone conversations with Nancy on the Sunday evening, and of the discovery of her body the following day. She mentioned incidentally that Nancy had told her how surprised she had been the previous Wednesday when Andrew had asked her to be sure to take her purse and car keys with her to the bedroom; but nothing was then said of the knife which the defense was later to say had been confined to Nancy's care that evening for fear that he might harm himself or someone else.

There followed evidence of the routine communications which had passed between Andrew and his probation officers, Dana Somers and Catherine Anest, and the officials with whom he had made contact on Monday, Mrs. Cowling at the Rosedale Medical Centre, Miss Miller at the Royal Bank and Mrs. Jean Pepperdene at the National Trust. In their brief meetings with Andrew there had been nothing in his attitude to suggest any abnormality, let alone that he had just committed a brutal murder.

That left the court to consider three significant and, in some respects, more controversial blocks of evidence, since these were to have some bearing on the arguments which the counsel for the defense was to develop: evidence of the forensic scientists, Dr. Sepp and Mr. Kelder; of the psychologists from Penetanguishene, David Vinegar and Paul Henry; and that of Sergeant Ed Stewart and his colleague Joe Cziraky, who had interviewed Andrew after his arrest.

The scientists' language was often highly technical. Dr. Sepp, chief pathologist at Toronto East General Hospital, gave detailed evidence of the stab wounds and the general condition of Nancy's body. He could not say in what precise order the wounds had been inflicted, nor how long after their infliction Nancy had remained alive. "Maybe half an hour, maybe forty-five minutes. It is very difficult to say. But we know from past experience that it is not an instantaneous death." An examination of the vaginal swabs suggested that the sperm "were deposited very recently *before* death," a view which was to be modified by Keith Kelder's evidence, and certainly proved unacceptable to the psychiatric experts called by the defense.

Kelder, a forensic biologist from the Centre of Forensic Sciences, investigated in detail samples of blood from Nancy and Andrew, of semen, of textiles and hairs from Nancy's apartment. Much of the dialogue was again of a highly technical nature and the court's attention was riveted on the sexual aspect of the case. Traces of Andrew's semen had been found on his shirt, cast aside after he had a shower, on the bath towel (on which Kelder also found one of Nancy's pubic hairs) left in the living room, and on the inside of the fly area of Andrew's undershorts. "My findings," Kelder told the court, "are consistent with the semen [which, he said, was in "high concentration"] having been deposited at or near the time of death."

Counsel for the defense pressed him on this statement, and Kelder at length admitted that he could not say for certain how long the semen had been in Nancy's body. It might have been there "an hour *before* death" or even "two hours *after* death." Was this, Edwardh enquired, "entirely consistent with an act of necrophilia some hour and a half later?" "I could not," Kelder replied cautiously, "exclude the possibility." Earlier he had said that he supposed that sexual intercourse had occurred when the body was in a stationary position, face up, with no opportunity for draining. He also established that Andrew had so successfully washed the blood from his black pants that the stains would not have been visible to the naked eye, which explained why he had been able to wear them (but not the white shirt with the blue trim) on his visit to the Royal Bank shortly after 11:00 A.M. on the Monday morning.

The evidence given by the psychiatrists at Penetang was subjected to a penetrating and rigorous examination by Edwardh. She was already aware that the defense would argue that Nancy's murder was the result of Andrew's deep-seated psychiatric problems which the authorities at Penetang had conspicuously failed to discover or even satisfactorily investigate.

Dr. David Vinegar was called first to discuss Andrew's visit to Penetang on Friday, 18 January. He had come to the conclusion, he told Marlys Edwardh, that Andrew's mental state was:

> ...in the relative sense, normal; in the sense of not suffering from anxiety, not appearing to be under undue stress, not being obviously psychotic, not suffering from illusions, hallucinations...paranoid ideas...not suffering from depression or any major mood disorder, not suffering from any major psychiatric disorder....

Edwardh then asked Dr. Vinegar to outline his qualifications. His response showed that while he had medical degrees, his training in psychiatry had been cursory, confined to a series of brief courses, a one-week course in neurology at the Albert Einstein College of Medicine, two two-day seminars in cognitive therapy and manic disorders at the Clarke Institute, apart from those courses in psychiatry and neurology which had been a part of his general training in medicine. "You've pointed out," Vinegar commented somewhat sadly, "the limitations of my training."

Indeed it soon became apparent that Edwardh's intention, if expressed in the politest manner, was to discredit Dr. Vinegar's assessment of Andrew's personality and problems, and to question the treatment, or lack of it, which he had received at Penetang. The Mental Health Centre, she maintained, had made insufficient effort to secure the reports which had been made at the Institute for Living at Hartford, Connecticut. Then she asked Vinegar why the EEG conducted at Penetang had not been carried out on Andrew while he was asleep as well as when he was awake. "We decided against it," Vinegar replied, "because his observable behavior was not suggestive of temporal-lobe epilepsy during his hospital stay." Edwardh responded: "I take it though you appreciate, sir, that epilepsy patterns can appear in sleep EEGs and they do not appear in waking EEGs?" "Oh, yes," said Vinegar. "Oh, yes." At this stage it seemed likely that the defense would suggest that Andrew's conduct could be explained by epileptic factors, which would exempt him from criminal responsibility.

> I take it [Edwardh continued] from your description of your decision whether to give Andrew anti-convulsant medication or not, in terms of whether there may be some kind of temporal-lobe epilepsy that the absence of any specific behavior in the hospital was really the thing that stayed your hand, as well as your concern about whether he was the kind of patient who could be relied on to take these drugs responsibly?

Like the psychiatrists, the lawyers were not notable for the clarity or crispness of their comments. "Are you going to be much longer, Ms. Edwardh?" the judge sighed. "Yes, Your Honor," the lawyer said stoutly. "We'd better give the court reporter," the judge commented, "a chance to get some air."

When Dr. Vinegar was recalled to the stand the direction in which the defense was likely to advance became clearer still. Edwardh pressed him on the "possibility of temporal-lobe epilepsy being present in this young man," and the advisability of using anti-convulsant drugs such as the Institute for Living had suggested. "It is ridiculous," Dr. Vinegar answered, "to give medications where there's no behavior to control."

Finally she passed to the reasons for Andrew's discharge from Penetang, arising in part from his own wish to leave and from Dr. Vinegar's realization that he seemed no longer to be benefiting from the therapy and might reasonably be better off if he lived under probationary supervision in Barrie or Toronto. "So," defense counsel commented, "his failure to progress satisfactorily in the group and his unwillingness or whatever to abide by things like curfew rules, led to the decision on your part at this time that he leave the hospital."

Dr. Vinegar seemed to be suggesting, Edwardh added, that Andrew's problems were simply those of a "spoiled teenager who was having trouble accommodating with his parents." "In my opinion," the doctor replied, "that's a totally idiosyncratic interpretation that you're making." But she insisted that Dr. Vinegar and his colleagues at Penetang had failed dismally to trace the source of Andrew's "assaultive aggressive behavior."

"I'm not sure," the judge interrupted, "that this whole exercise has to do with the preliminary hearing at this stage." Dr. Vinegar was then asked to withdraw temporarily, so that Ms. Edwardh could address the judge.

> Your Honor, [she said] I believe, from my conversation with Mr. Chumak, that it will be the theory of the Crown that there was a sexual assault that occurred primarily as a result of a pass taken and rejection made that precipitated the eventual assault and murder.

For that reason the psychiatric evidence was of the greatest relevance to the case. "I agree," Chumak intervened, "with Your Honor that the questioning by my friend might be somewhat overextensive. . . . I realize that Your Honor has been most patient." "I don't see how it can possibly get completed today, the way she's going," the judge commented with a touch of mild acidity.

Marlys Edwardh took the hint and speedily concluded the cross-examination by asking Dr. Vinegar whether Andrew's conduct could have been prompted by a sense of rejection. "No," Dr. Vinegar replied. "Thank you. Knocking on the door," she observed, "sometimes obviously works faster, Your Honor."

The demolition of Dr. Vinegar had been carried out with such resolution and success that his colleague Paul Henry had a comparatively smooth and brief cross-examination. Henry, who had graduated from

Guelph University in 1971, had worked as a psychologist at Millhaven Penitentiary in Kingston for two years. He had then become executive director of St. Leonard's Halfway House for released offenders before moving to Penetang in November 1976. He had also been a trainer for the Canadian National Hockey Team. He described his relationship with Andrew as good, explaining that the principal treatment he had received had been through the medium of group-therapy sessions. He detailed his short interview with Andrew on 18 January and the subsequent reassuring phone call with his step-grandfather, Mr. Patterson. "After receiving the telephone call from Mr. Patterson, did you go out and try and contact Andrew?" "No," Henry replied, remarking that, in spite of the alarm bells ringing in Andrew's mind, there seemed no immediate reason for concern about what might happen.

The final evidence presented to the court came from Staff Sergeant Edward Stewart. He spoke of going to Nancy's apartment on the Monday evening and of ordering photographs of the exhibits to be taken, and of his finding the white T-shirt with the blue trim "blood soaked and wet to the touch when I was there that evening." Then, accompanied by Joe Cziraky, he had gone out to Bradford and taken a statement from Andrew about the murder and his subsequent activities that Monday. At a critical moment the recording machine in the courtroom broke down, and it was not until three weeks later on Friday, 29 November 1985, that the court resumed its last session.

Once more the sergeant described Andrew as very calm and detached, only once expressing irritation when he was asked about the cut on his hand. "I cut myself when it happened." "Are you right-handed or left-handed?" "I would have to be right-handed," he snapped. "How the hell would I get cuts on my left hand?"

Marlys Edwardh concluded by drawing attention to the fact that in his first statement Andrew had said nothing about what had happened between his entry into Nancy's room on waking at 8:10 A.M. and the phone ringing at 10:30 A.M., suggesting that it was an episode perpetrated in a moment of aberration which he wished to forget. "I am," he had said of the intervening period, "refusing to remember. I am trying to block it out of my mind. She was on her side facing the TV. Her eyes were closed."

Whatever the variations in detail, the facts of the case had now been established. What was at issue was the interpretation to be put upon them. The judge came to the conclusion that:

... there is more than sufficient evidence that a reasonable jury properly directed could convict on first-degree murder. The fact that this girl was lying in bed. The fact that she was in sleeping clothes. The fact that her clothes were torn. The fact that her underpants were torn. The positions of the stab wounds. The fact that there was an actual act of intercourse. I am more than satisfied that there is sufficient evidence and he will be committed for trial on the charge of first-degree murder....

The court was not to meet until ten months had passed, on 15 September 1986. In the intervening period the defense had ample time to work out its strategy. At the end of February, Ann Taylor, Bill Jephcott's sister, wrote to the legal partner of Clayton Ruby, Marlys Edwardh, giving her impression of Andrew's mental state which, so she believed, suggested that there was an organic basis for his "increasingly regressive behavior." She expressed the hope that he would be able to undergo an exhaustive neurological assessment. Meanwhile Taylor would consider the names of possible experts in the brain and behavior domain whose testimony could be invoked in the coming trial.

Two outstanding names were to be brought out of the hat, those of Frank Ervin, professor at McGill University, and Basil Orchard of the University of Toronto, both of whom had unrivaled experience in Canada in dealing with the criminally insane. Orchard was to interview Andrew's parents on 12 December 1985 for some three hours and ten minutes, and Andrew himself some months later, on 3 and 8 March 1986 and again on 9 May, on all three occasions for two or three hours.

He was to comment that Andrew did not have a complete or continuous memory recall.

He would tell me something and there would be other things he could remember in connection with that. And then he would tell me something else and it didn't just follow the previous bit. ... For instance he told me that he stabbed her and he told me that he had sex and I had to ask when these things occurred and he had to place it in some kind or order.

Dr. Orchard had to create a pattern out of these "memory blobs" which would make sense. It seems obvious that Andrew's memory, not for the first time, was able to play tricks, and that there was a strong element of unreliability as well as an element of fantasy in some of his recollections. It was, however, on this somewhat unsatisfactory foundation, supported by the massive reports compiled by psychiatrists and others at earlier dates, providing in all over six hundred pages of evidence, that Basil Orchard, in collaboration with Frank Ervin, was to build his case. It was a case which Clayton Ruby was to present with great skill to the court in mid-September 1986 in justification of a plea of not guilty because of insanity.

IX

MURDER, MADNESS ___ AND THE LAW ___

El sueno de la razon produce monstruos.
[*The sleep of reason produces monsters.*]

GOYA, *LOS CAPRICHOS*

The law hath not been dead, though it hath slept.

SHAKESPEARE, *MEASURE FOR MEASURE*

As crimes do grow, justice should rouse itself.

BEN JONSON, *CATILINE*

THE TRIAL OF ANDREW LEYSHON-HUGHES attracted attention throughout Canada, not merely because the killer and the victim both belonged to two of Canada's best-known families but because of the bizarre nature of the murder itself.

It would be reassuring to believe that murder was a gross abnormality [Brian Masters wrote in his fascinating study of the British murderer, Dennis Nilsen], a dramatic departure from respected ethical standards which restrain civilized man from surrendering to his baser instincts....Far from being an

125

aberration which despoils civilized man, murder *belongs* to civilized man more than it does to primitive peoples or to other species which inhabit this planet. As man has become more civilized, intelligent, creative and dominant, so he has become more murderous.[1]

By and large, there is not a great diversity of motives for murder: gain, jealousy, revenge, sex. Very few murders are premeditated. Most arise out of a blazing argument, or are the outcome of a situation such as an armed robbery or burglary in which murder may be part of the scenario, whether originally intended or not. The majority of murders are domestic crimes, a third of the victims killed by husbands, wives or lovers. If the highway is the most dangerous place to be, then the bedroom, or wherever human passions flare up, is not far behind.

In the summer of 1986, nineteen-year-old Robert Chambers confessed to strangling eighteen-year-old Jennifer Levin to death, in New York's Central Park, in a fit of passionate rage.

> She said I looked really cute and that I would look cuter tied up. She wrapped her underwear around my wrists and they were locked behind my back, because I was leaning on my hands. And she just pushed me back...and then got on top of my chest and she was facing my feet. She was just having her way and then she squeezed my balls and I could not take it. And I managed to get my left hand free and I grabbed her and yanked her as hard as I could and she just flipped over me and landed right next to the tree. And then she didn't move.

The court found Chambers, a handsome prep school graduate and former altar boy who came from a rich family, guilty of manslaughter. Murder is not exclusive to the poor, the moronic or the insane, as another recent case involving a Canadian businessman illustrates.

Joseph Robb, the wealthy president of Northern Fine Foods in Toronto, discovered that his wife of twenty-five years, Sheila, was having an affair with Michael Horton, for whom she had worked at the Toronto office of Burson-Marsteller, a New York-based public relations firm. Having found love letters from Horton to his wife in her briefcase, (one of which read, "What I would have given for an obscene phonecall from you"), Robb decided, in May 1987, to fly to London to confront Horton and try to persuade him to break off the affair.

He arranged to meet Horton at the Churchill Hotel in London where he was conducting an international management seminar. The conversation began amicably enough but as Horton got up, saying that he could not consider Robb's proposal and that he had a dinner date, Robb lost his temper, took hold of Horton's lapels, broke two bottles, one of mineral water, the other of gin, over his head and stabbed him in the throat with a penknife, used for sharpening pencils, no less than twenty times. "I just exploded. . . . Then, somehow the knife was in my hand and I started stabbing."

He then rang the police. When he was brought to trial in London early in 1988, his counsel pleaded that Robb, said even by his estranged wife to be normally of a quiet and gentle disposition, had been "provoked beyond the limits of his endurance. He was mindless. . . a man out of control, perhaps not even a man." Mr. Justice Miskin sympathized with Robb's predicament and the jury brought in a verdict of manslaughter rather than the one of murder which the prosecution had demanded. He was sentenced to three years imprisonment, a sentence which, in spite of the provocation, seems curiously lenient, given the savagery of the attack.

But what is it that makes a man or a woman into a murderer? What elements in their personalities drive men and women to take the life of a fellow creature? Some scholars have suggested that there could be a link between certain types of physique and crime. "Yon Cassius has a lean and hungry look — he thinks too much — such men are dangerous," was Julius Caesar's comment on his would-be assassin. When George Cruickshank set out to illustrate Charles Dickens' *Oliver Twist*, he depicted Fagin and Bill Sykes as unprepossessing criminal types. A French prison doctor declared that criminals had faces "stamped by a seal of brutish and impassible instinct." The nineteenth-century Italian psychiatrist Cesare Lombroso believed it was possible to deduce criminal tendencies from the shape of a person's cranium or head. People of the so-called mesomorphic type, that is those in whom mesoderm or bone, muscle and sinew predominate, were said to be peculiarly prone to aggressive activity.

More recently, in the mid-1960s, it was suggested that chromosomal abnormalities could give rise to delinquent tendencies, and that violent offenders were likely to possess an extra Y, or male chromosome. But there is little evidence to support the XYY theory.

Outbursts of violence have also been associated with damage to the limbic system, that is, the area, primitive in impulse, nearest the brain stem. It has been shown that gross structure lesions in parts of the limbic system promote aggressive behavior. This was to be one of the conditions to which the psychiatrists were to draw attention in the trial of Andrew Leyshon-Hughes.

The invention of the encephalogram (EEG), which measures the rhythms of the brain, has helped in the detection of mental disorders resulting from brain damage. Yet an analysis of murder fails to establish that there is a criminal type or that murder has basic physiological roots. Although physical characteristics and genetic causes in combination with environmental factors may help to shape criminal behavior, behavior patterns are not necessarily genetically or physically determined.

How normal in any case is the murderer? The husband who kills his wife to marry his lover, the lover who kills the husband to marry his wife, the thug who kills a security guard to rob a bank, the man who kills a policeman to make a safe getaway, seem to be acting in a rational way. They know what they want and they are determined to get it.

There are murders, unhappily common in the late twentieth century, where the ingestion of alcohol or drugs disturbs the reasoning process of the mind, so leading to an abandonment of normal restraints. On 20 December 1983 two youths from Toronto, seventeen-year-old Adam Graham and twenty-year-old William Stoddert, bludgeoned a pal to death with a bottle and a ten-pound shock absorber. They cut up the corpse, threw the limbs into a neighboring ravine and consigned the trunk to a bank of snow. His parish priest described Graham as "one of the finest young men in the parish," but on the day of the murder he had absorbed six or seven hits of LSD and half a bottle of hard liquor.

There are some murders, horridly spectacular in character, which seem so motiveless or irrational as to be the acts of madmen, though whether or not the instigators are insane is a debatable matter. In 1924, two rich American youths, Nathan Leopold and Richard Loeb, who had become lovers, seized Bobbie Franks, a friend of Loeb's younger brother, and killed him because they wanted to commit the perfect murder, "murder for fun."

There are others who seem to kill simply for the pleasure of killing.

"Every man has his passions," said the German Rudolf Pleil, condemned for rape and multiple murders who took his life in his cell in 1958. "Some prefer whist. I prefer killing people."

A murderer of similar kind was the notorious Peter Kürten, the so-called monster of Dusseldorf, who felt an irresistible urge to kill, experiencing orgasm at the moment he knifed his victims or seized them by the throat. Deprived of affection in childhood, he began his career of killing by pushing two boys into the river Rhine and watching them drown, his imagination spurred on by frequent visits to a waxwork show, a local chamber of horrors. When he was thirteen he found satisfaction by stabbing sheep as he sodomized them. If he was in the vicinity of a road accident, he ejaculated. On another occasion he slit the neck of a swan and sucked its blood to achieve orgasm. He showed neither pity nor remorse. He was convicted on nine counts of murder in 1930 and sentenced to death nine times. Before he was executed, he enquired whether he would be able to experience the flow of blood as his own head was being severed.

As bizarre was the Hungarian Sylvestre Matuschka, who could only find sexual satisfaction by causing trains to crash. In August 1931 the Vienna express was derailed near Berlin; the next month the Budapest-Vienna express was derailed by an explosion, killing twenty-two people. Matuschka was tried for causing the train crashes, which served to give him an orgasm. Sentenced to life imprisonment he managed to escape, making his way to America. He joined the army and, in 1953, was posted to Korea as chief of an army unit for blowing up trains. Or, even more macabre, Fritz Harrmann, the homosexual butcher of Hanover, who killed off his young victims by biting through their windpipes, later selling their bodies for meat.

The Italian town of Verona was startled early in 1987 by the arrest of two young men, students at the local university, for the murders of fifteen people. Marco Furian was the son of a well-known plastic surgeon; Wolfgang Abel's father was the former president of a West German insurance company. They had become self-appointed executioners of those whose sinful lives, they deemed, deserved death; among them a homosexual waiter hacked to death in Venice, a gypsy, a prostitute, a homosexual priest in Trento (into whose forehead they had hammered a nail, then inserted a chisel with a wooden crucifix glued to it) and five people who died when they burned down a pornographic cinema in Milan. "Death," they wrote in Italian runic characters, "will come to those who betray the true God." The psychiatric report, which described their family lives as spoiled but without affection, diagnosed partial insanity with pronounced schizophrenic tendencies.

The borderline between madness and sanity is, however, so thin that there is a no-man's land where the signposts are obscure. The Greek tragic dramatist, Euripides, told the story of Heracles who returned home triumphant, having fulfilled successfully the tasks imposed upon him by the goddess Hera. His wife greeted him warmly, but then suddenly and dramatically Heracles went mad and killed his wife and two children. Awakening from his compulsive action, he realized the horror of what he had done. Euripides purposely brought Madness — Lussa — onto the stage to stress the inexplicability of the event. This is not an unfamiliar story. Today we might describe it as a psychotic episode and would probably expect a successful insanity defense.

But in cases where the accused pleads not guilty because of insanity, judge, counsel and jury may well find it difficult to weave their way through what can seem an impenetrable thicket as they seek to measure the madness or sanity of the accused's behavior. Robert Burton, in the *Anatomy of Melancholy* (1621), exclaimed:

> But see the Madman rage distraught
> With furious looks, a ghastly sight
> Naked in chains doth he lie,
> And roars amain, he knows not why.
> Observe him: for as in a glass
> Thine angry portraiture it was
> His picture. Keep still in thy presence:
> Twixt him and thee there's no difference.

What exactly constitutes insanity is a complex subject; and even more difficult to define is the extent to which it may deprive an individual of responsibility for his actions. In past centuries insanity was for the most part adjudged to be "raving lunacy," what today would be termed an acute psychotic disorder.

The law seems early to have taken madness into account.[2] The ancient Hebrews and the Greeks held that lunatics and young children could not be held responsible for their actions. Aristotle argued that free and rational desire was a prerequisite which was lacking in animals, young children and madmen. Similar notions found some expression in

Roman and Byzantine law. In England, as early as the reign of Henry III, the jurist Bracton applied what was termed the "wild beast" test for madness; a man whose behavior and mentality resembled that of a beast was held to be mad. In 1278, a man who had murdered his daughter was released on the grounds that he was insane.

By the early seventeenth century lawyers were concerned with the phenomenon of temporary insanity as a plea. In his *Institutes of the Laws of England*, Sir Edward Coke commented that "a lunatic that hath sometimes his understanding, and sometimes not... is called *non compos mentis*, so long as he hath not understanding [when the crime was committed]." If a man liable to temporary insanity committed a crime during a "lucid interval" he should be found guilty. Sir Matthew Hale, who was chief justice of the King's bench in 1671, argued contrariwise that only total insanity "where there is no free act of the will" could be put forward as a justifiable plea in criminal cases.

It was not effectively until the eighteenth century, the so-called age of reason, that in England the law began to take heed of the plea of insanity as a defense in criminal cases. In a case in 1724, the judge declared that, "if a man be deprived of his reason, and consequently of his intention, he cannot be guilty." In 1760 a plea of insanity was entered, though unsuccessfuly, in the case of an English nobleman, Earl Ferrers, who had shot his steward in a bout of rage.

Some twenty or so years later, on 2 August 1786, Margaret Nicholson, a deluded spinster in her forties, tried to stab King George III as he alighted from his carriage, but her thrust was feeble and the king was unhurt. "No," said George, "I am not hurt — take care of the woman. Do not hurt her, for she is mad." When Margaret was apprehended, she was "totally unmoved by any representations of the atrocity of her crime." Curiously enough there was some suspicion that she simply had been *posing* as a woman "to facilitate her crime," and she was subjected to a physical examination by "three elderly matrons" to make sure that she was of the female sex. A Dr. Monro, who gave evidence that "he never in his life had seen a person more disordered," asserted that "she app...ed to have a consciousness of what she had done, but did not seem sensible of having committed any Crime." Subsequently she was ordered to be taken to the hospital of St. Mary of Bethlehem (Bedlam) "to be confined for life" and there she died forty years later, in May 1828, "a sprightly, deaf old woman addicted to snuff."

When four years after Nicholson's murder attempt, another lunatic,

John Frith, who suffered under the delusion that he was the Apostle St. Paul, threw a stone at the king, the presiding judge, Lord Kenyon, declared that "the humanity of the law of England...has prescribed, that no man shall be called upon to make his defense at a time when his mind is...not...capable of doing so."

From the legal point of view an even more significant case, also involving an attack on King George III, occurred in 1800. When the king entered the royal box at the Drury Lane Theatre in London, a man in the pit, James Hadfield, discharged a pistol at him. Hadfield was arrested and interviewed by the king's son, the Duke of York, who recognized him as one of his own orderlies who had been on campaign with him in the recent war in Flanders. When Hadfield was asked why he had committed the crime, he replied that he had tried to kill the king because he himself "was tired of his life" and "thought that he should be certainly killed if he were to make an attempt upon his majesty's life."

In many ways Hadfield appeared to be a normal, sane man, but his mind had become obsessed by a delusion that "the world was coming to a conclusion; and that, like our blessed Saviour, he was to sacrifice himself for its salvation...that he must be destroyed, but ought not to destroy himself." This delusion, which was attributable to head wounds that he had suffered on active service, possessed his mind to such an extent that he had tried to kill the king for an irrational motive. He was no raving maniac but he was suffering from what would today be called a paranoid psychosis. "We found," the foreman of the jury told the judge, "the prisoner is not guilty; he being under the influence of insanity at the time the act was committed." He was to survive for nearly half a century more, dying in 1849 in custodial detention in Bedlam.

Hadfield's case, which may well have been the first case in which it was argued that brain damage caused diminution of responsibility, led a Dr. John Johnstone to write Medical Jurisprudence, which was the first English book published on the psychiatric aspects of crime. Lawyers were, however, far from persuaded that a plea of insanity exculpated a man guilty of murder. On 1 May 1812, John Bellingham, a forty-two-year-old merchant and the father of twelve children, shot and killed the British prime minister, Spencer Perceval, in the lobby of the House of Commons. Bellingham had come to the deluded conviction that the government of which Perceval was the head was responsible for his imprisonment as a bankrupt in Russia. "It is a private Injury," he shouted, "I know what I have done. It was a denial of justice on the part of the government." Did Bellingham, the court had to decide, really know at the time he committed the murder, what he was doing or was his understanding impaired? He was convicted and executed.

There the issue rested until, in1843, Daniel M'Naghten, a Scot who suffered from paranoid delusions, decided to kill another British prime minister, Sir Robert Peel. He did not know what Peel looked like, and by mistake shot and killed his secretary, Edward Drummond, instead. His case was naturally compared to Bellingham's but, as his defending counsel exclaimed, "in the opinion of the most scientific men who have considered it, there now exists no doubt at all that Bellingham was a madman." Medical evidence was given to support M'Naghten's plea of insanity, and he was found to be "not guilty, on the grounds of insanity." Starting from the same ground as in Bellingham's case, the law in M'Naghten's had reached a diametrically opposed conclusion.

The verdict caused a public outcry in which even Queen Victoria joined. Indignation was expressed that a man who could be shown to be suffering from mental disease "could get away with murder," whereas offenders in their right minds would be hanged. But how could the sheep be separated from the goats, the responsible from the irresponsible? To provide some guidance for the future, the Lord Chancellor asked a panel of judges to answer five questions which would at least clarify the legal tests for insanity.

The M'Naghten Rules provided the basis for the law as it related to insanity throughout Britain and the British Empire. They remain with some significant modifications the foundation of law in the United Kingdom and in Canada:

> Every man is to be presumed sane and to possess a sufficient degree of reason to be responsible for his crimes, until the contrary be proved to their satisfaction; and to establish a defence on the ground of insanity, it must be clearly proved that, at the time of committing the act, the party accused was labouring under such a defect of reason from disease of the mind, as not to know the nature and quality of the act he was doing; or, if he did know it, that he did not know what he was doing was wrong.

"A man deprived of all power of reason," as Lord Chief Justice Mansfield put it in 1812, ". . . could not certainly commit an act against the law." The Canadian, Mr. Justice Martland, echoed his words in 1976. "If," he said, "a person who has committed a crime did not by reason of disease of the mind know what he was doing, he is not to be convicted, because it was really not his act."

Similar language threads Section 16 of the Canadian Criminal Code which defines the law relating to murder and madness:

> Where [it states] a person kills or is party to the killing of another he shall not be convicted of murder if he was suffering from such abnormality of mind. . . as substantially impaired the mental responsibility for his acts. . . .
>
> No person shall be convicted in respect of an act or omission on his part while he was insane. . . . A person is insane when he is in a state of natural imbecility or has disease of the mind to an extent that renders him incapable of appreciating the nature and quality of an act or omission or of knowing that an act or omission is wrong. . . . Everyone shall, until the contrary is proved, be presumed to be and to have been sane.

The Canadian Criminal Code had modified the M'Naghten Rules in two significant ways. The words "defect of reason" had been replaced by "abnormality of mind," a change which allowed for a psychological interpretation in the legal test of insanity rather than as the words "defect of reason" might suggest, a purely intellectual test. The other change was more momentous since on it the verdict, in cases where a plea of not guilty because of insanity was entered, effectually depended. Where the M'Naghten Rules state that it is an essential ingredient of mental disease "not to *know* the nature and quality of the act," the Canadian Criminal Code substituted the word "appreciate" for "know." "Appreciation," as the McRuer Report worded it, "embraces the act of knowing, but the converse is not true."

Such changes to the M'Naghten Rules have sometimes baffled lawyers and provided a field day for psychiatrists.

> The day of epilepsy [Ralph Partridge commented in 1953] as the stock defense to a charge of murder is now done. The great merit that it used to possess was inscrutability; no doctor could tell, by

observation, whether a man was epileptic or not. That advantage has vanished with the invention of the encephalograph. . . . . Unless their client has the right EEG, the lawyers for the defense have shifted their dubious cases of insanity to unchartered territory, where the EEG has so far not been able to follow them.[3]

It is less, however, with the *definition of insanity* than with the application of the law that we are more immediately concerned since what was to be applied in Andrew's case as in other cases was the *legal test of insanity*. "In many, if not most cases involving the defense of insanity," as Mr. Justice Martin put it in 1977, "the question whether the accused suffered from a disease of the mind is not the critical issue, the pivotal issue is whether a condition which admittedly constitutes a disease of the mind rendered the accused incapable of appreciating the nature and quality of the act or of knowing that it was wrong."

A friend met a neighbor. "How are your children?" she asked. "Dead," the neighbor replied. "You must be mistaken." "Oh, but it is so. I have hung [sic] them." Sure enough, when the neighbor went to the laundry room she found the four children hanging there. The mother *knew* what she had done but the mental disease from which she suffered made it impossible for her to *appreciate the nature and quality* of the act which she had committed.

Here the evidence was crystal clear, and in a number of relatively recent cases which have come before the Canadian courts the verdict of not guilty because of insanity has been upheld for this reason, though sometimes only after an appeal to a higher court. In July 1975, Judith Irwin stabbed to death her seven-and-a-half-month-old son, Jason. She told the police that the deed was probably done by a stranger who had asked her if he might use her phone, but their suspicions were aroused, she was brought to court and found guilty of murder. When, however, the Ontario court of appeal ordered a psychiatrist to examine her, he reported that she had been suffering from a personality disorder for at least ten years, and so was unable to "appreciate the nature and quality of the act when she killed the child."

That very summer, a month later, a young man, Mr. Simpson, was charged with two attempted murders. Shortly after midnight he had accosted an eighteen-year-old student, as she left the Village Pump at Simcoe, Ontario, grabbed her by the neck, pushed her to the ground and stabbed her, shouting, "All I want is my knife back," and, "All I want to do is to fuck"; but fortunately a passing car heard her screams and she escaped. Only a few weeks later, at the same tavern, Simpson met another woman who proved more accommodating than his first victim, for she went back to his apartment and had intercourse with him. When she was leaving he grasped her by the throat and she felt a sharp stab in her back as he muttered, "You'll never talk." She managed, however, to stagger down the stairs and make her way to a taxicab. At the ensuing hearing the court produced two psychiatrists, Dr. Arnold and Dr. Fleming, who bore witness to Simpson's "impulsiveness, explosiveness and tendency towards antisocial behaviour," and testified that he must have been insane at the time he committed these offenses, and did not "appreciate the nature and quality" of what he was doing.

A similar case which occurred in Hamilton in 1980 was not so easily concluded. Cooper, an outpatient at the Hamilton Psychiatric Hospital, approached an inpatient, Denise Hobbs, after a social function, asked her to strip, grabbed her by the throat and killed her. A psychiatrist, Dr. Sim, agreed that Cooper might well have intended to harm the girl but his mental capacity was such that he may not have believed that by choking her he would kill her. Prosecution counsel showed some skepticism. "I put it to you, aren't you really splitting hairs, Dr. Sim, when you say the accused had the capacity to form the intent to choke, to cut off the airway of an individual, yet didn't have the capacity to form the intent to kill?" The court concluded that Cooper was not insane. He was convicted of murder, and a subsequent appeal was dismissed. When, however, the case reached the Supreme Court, a new trial was ordered. Since his arrest, Cooper had given clear signs of personality disorder, mental retardation and schizoid, antisocial and inadequacy features, which may have affected his capacity to appreciate the crime.

In other cases where the circumstantial evidence provided by the expert witnesses seemed strong, the outcome was even less predictable. A taxi-driver, Glenda Ferster, picked up a Mr. Kjeldsen at the Calgary airport and he ordered her to drive to Banff. He raped her, bound her up and then got into the car intending to dump her body by the roadside, but she managed to break free. In the ensuing struggle he killed Ferster, by striking her several times with a rock and stuffing a stocking down her throat. His defense argued that Kjeldsen suffered from a mental disease which made it impossible for him to understand the consequences of his action.

The dialogue which took place between the prosecution and a defense witness highlights the problem implicit in trying to distinguish between *knowledge* and *appreciation* of an act:

DR. WAYNE (defense): At the time of the offence the accused did not appreciate the nature and quality of his act.
PROSECUTION: He did not know he was killing her?
WAYNE: Know is a very small part of appreciate.
PROSECUTION: Well answer that little tiny point then. Did he know he was killing her?
WAYNE: I really don't know.
PROSECUTION: Did he know she was a human being?
WAYNE: He didn't treat her like a human being.
PROSECUTION: I am not asking that, doctor. Did he know it? Did he know this was a live woman that he started to hit over the head with a rock?
WAYNE: Probably.
PROSECUTION: And so then I submit to you that he also knew that he was killing that woman.
WAYNE: I will accept that.

The judge commented that if Kjeldsen "had an appreciative awareness of striking with a stone, that it might cause death or injury, that has brought us within the meaning of Section 16 [of the Canadian Criminal Code] regardless of what his emotional attributes might be." So he was convicted of murder, a verdict that was later upheld by the Alberta court of appeal.

It is plain that what was at issue in these trials was the extent to which the accused could be shown that he or she had failed to *appreciate* the nature and quality of his or her act. This point is well illustrated by a strange case which occurred in Vancouver in January 1977, when a Czech emigrant to Canada, Vladimir Adamcik, was charged with armed robbery. Adamcik suffered from religious delusions and was convinced that he was the reincarnation of a Czechoslovakian Robin Hood who had lived some four hundred years previously. He was an inmate of the Riverdale Mental Institution. Without permission he wandered downtown in Vancouver and was horrified to see a wooden crucifix, surrounded by gaudy tinsel, for sale in a shop. He thought this so blasphemous that he decided that he must buy it, to rescue the image of the Lord from sacrilege, but found that he did not have the requisite cash. So, he went to a local bank with a toy gun and demanded money, some 3,200 dollars, and with this returned to the shop to buy the crucifix. After he had made the purchase, he noticed that the saleswoman was "shaking and breathing heavily" and, imagining that she might be possessed of the devil, he took her money. The experts were somewhat in disarray. The psychiatrist Dr. Whitman argued that knowing was the same as appreciating, and that Adamcik not only knew but appreciated what he was doing. The court concluded otherwise. Adamcik *knew* that he had a toy pistol and that he was performing a robbery, but as a result of schizophrenia he was incapable of *appreciating* what he was doing.

Adamcik's case discloses another feature of the trials where insanity is the accused's defense — the frequent divergence of expert opinion. In Kjeldsen's case the Crown's psychiatrist insisted that the accused did not suffer from an actual mental disease but from a temperamental disability which did not prevent him from appreciating what he had done.

A similar division of opinion occurred in the case of Wayne Rabey in 1974. A third-year student at the University of Toronto, he attacked a girl with whom he had been associating but who had rejected his advances, hit her over the head with a piece of galena rock which he was taking home to study (he was a geology major) and tried to strangle her. One expert, Dr. Rowsell, held that Rabey had done what he did in an extreme state of rage and that he appreciated the nature and quality of his action. Another, Dr. Orchard, declared that his rejection was a psychological blow which had induced a dissociative stage, "a disorder of consciousness which occurs as a result of part of the nervous system shutting off," which meant that his actions were unconscious and involuntary while he was in this condition, an argument which Dr. Orchard was again to advance in the case of Andrew Leyshon-Hughes. Eventually a majority in the Supreme Court concluded that if Wayne Rabey had been in a dissociative state, he was suffering from a disease of the mind and, therefore, was not responsible for his actions.

Rabey's case was interesting in another way. The judges agreed that valuable and essential as is expert evidence, the science of psychiatry is still too inexact to be able to recognize all forms of mental disease, and so far as the legal test of what constitutes insanity is in question ordinary persons trained in the law may be better able to reach a right decision than the experts. It is thus possible for judges and juries to virtually ignore expert opinion.

This happened in the case of the British murderer, Peter Sutcliffe, a truck driver nicknamed "The Yorkshire Ripper." He murdered thirteen women between 1975 and 1980, at first prostitutes — whom he stabbed repeatedly in the stomach or the vagina, either with a knife or screwdriver — but later girls whom he picked up at random. He rarely sexually assaulted his victims, the killing itself apparently affording him sexual satisfaction.

Both prosecution and defense psychiatrists agreed that Sutcliffe was suffering from paranoid schizophrenia. Sutcliffe declared that from a tombstone in a graveyard where he was working, God had instructed him to rid the streets of prostitutes. When his brother, Carl, visited him in jail, he told him he had acted as he did because there were too many "dirty slags littering the streets" and he was just "cleaning up a little." Mr. Justice Boreham refused, as he was entitled to do, to accept the verdict of the psychiatrists and reduce the charge from one of murder to one of manslaughter. The case went to a jury who, by a majority of ten to two, found Sutcliffe guilty of murder. He was sentenced to imprisonment for life, to serve a minimum of thirty years. Somewhat ironically, his mental condition later deteriorated to such an extent that in March 1984 he was transferred to a mental hospital.[4]

How far is the judicial process in Canada and other English-speaking countries attuned to dealing with those suffering from mental disorders and acute behavioral problems? A general reform of the Canadian Criminal Code, formulated in 1893, and partly revised in 1955, is in fact long overdue. With that object a Law Reform Commission was set up in 1970; but where it made recommendations they were generally ignored. When it presented two critical reports *Evidence* and *Mental Disorder in the Criminal Process* to Parliament, the federal justice department responded simply by setting up study groups. The commission suggested that the question of incompetency should be resolved by consultation with at least three experts before a trial starts, and it recommended the abolition of the lieutenant-governor's warrant, though as yet without effect.

The commission is thought likely to recommend that the plea of not guilty by reason of insanity should be replaced by a plea of non-responsibility by reason of mental disorder. If this were to happen it would have the effect of introducing something similar to the concept of diminished responsibility which the UK, following the example of Scotland, introduced by the Homicide Act of 1957. This act provided that a killer should not be convicted of murder "if he was suffering from an abnormality of mind" which "substantially impaired his mental responsibility for his acts," and permitted a charge of manslaughter to be substituted for a charge of murder. The judge was empowered to send a person guilty on such a charge to prison with a recommendation for medical help there. In 1978, Mr. Justice Kaufman, in a dissenting judgment in the case of *Regina v. Theriault*, argued forcibly for the introduction of the concept of diminished responsibility into Canadian law. Yet in spite of the flurry of concern which the reform of the law relating to pleas of insanity has long caused, and the promise that positive proposals would be presented to Parliament before the end of 1987, everything remains in limbo.

In the United States the situation is much more complex because of the differences between federal and state laws. The most important change was made in 1954 by the judgment of Judge Dave Bazelon in the case of *Durham v. the United States* in which he declared that "an accused is not criminally responsible if his unlawful act was the product of mental disease or mental defect," the latter defined as "any abnormal condition of the mind which substantially affects mental or emotional processes and substantially affects behavior controls." This judgment opened a veritable Pandora's box, for it could be fairly argued that any of the abnormalities listed in the handbook of the American Psychiatric Association, such as drug abuse, alcoholism and even heart disease, could be put forward under the cover of this plea.

The Durham judgment was modified in 1972, with the approval of Judge Bazelon himself, by the Brawmer ruling (so-called after Archie Brawmer who had been charged with a shooting affray at a party). This declared that a man was devoid of responsibility if, as a result of mental disease or defects, he lacked a substantial capacity to appreciate the wrongfulness of his conduct and so was unable to conform his conduct to the requirements of the law.

The call for further reform and clarification of the law relating to the insanity defense was a sequel to the acquittal of President Reagan's would-be assassin, John R. Hinckley, Jr. in June 1982. Hinckley, the son of a wealthy Denver executive, was a university dropout who had become obsessed with the film *Taxi Driver* which he saw some fifteen times. In the movie, the loner, Travis Bickle, turns from an attempt at a political assassination to the rescue of a young prostitute, Iris, played in the film by Jodie Foster. Hinckley modeled his lifestyle on that of Bickle, and professed to have fallen in love with Jodie Foster, who naturally did not respond to his overtures. [5]

It was Hinckley's apparently insensate motivation which swayed the judge and jury to favor a verdict of not guilty because of insanity. He had tried to kill the President for no identifiable political reason but because, so he asserted, he wanted to divert the attention of his loved one to himself by an action which she could not overlook.

Contrariwise, the prosecution argued that Hinckley wanted to make a niche for himself in the hall of fame. "Actually," Hinckley said, "I feel good because I accomplished everything on a grand scale." He boasted that his life seemed like a "movie starring me," with the President and Mrs. Reagan in supporting roles and a cast of directors, lawyers and hangers-on.

In a trial which lasted eight weeks, several high-priced psychiatrists were locked in combat. Even the prosecution agreed that Hinckley suffered from a dysrythmic disorder and various personality disorders; but it argued that, in spite of the 628 pages of psychiatric assessment, there was no evidence to suggest that Hinckley was mad. He knew what he was doing at the time of the shooting, had been planning it for some time and was aware that it was against the law. "John," as one of the prosecution's expert witnesses said, "was never so disturbed or distraught that he was unaware of what he was doing or why he was doing it."

Hinckley was found not guilty because of insanity and dispatched to St. Elizabeth's Hospital in New York for treatment. The verdict sent a shock wave through the United States, in part because it seemed inconceivable that a man who had shot and seriously wounded the President and three others should go virtually scot-free. Even some of the jurors admitted that they had had doubts. "Even though we had the doctors and professors there," juror Maryland T. Copeland said, "they did not prove anything either with all their knowledge and degrees. They couldn't prove him insane, they couldn't prove that he was sane — how can we laymen do it?" The insanity defense itself seemed on trial. The concept of mental illness had been widened, to use the words of the British judge, Lord Devlin, "at the expense of the concept of moral responsibility."

In the aftermath to the verdict in the Hinckley trial attempts were made to tighten up the federal law on the insanity defense. In practice many states had already changed their procedure, and others were to follow suit. Montana had abolished the insanity defense altogether in 1979 and had been followed by Idaho. Some dozen or so states have introduced the plea of "guilty but mentally ill." Where this is the verdict, the defendants are ordered to be treated in mental institutions until and if they recover. On their recovery they spend the rest of the term for which they are sentenced in prison. When, for instance, drama student Paul de Witty stabbed his teacher to death with a pair of scissors, the Illinois court sentenced him to a term of twenty years. Initially he was to be treated in a mental hospital but if he recovers he will finish his sentence in prison. "The effect of this plea," said Georgia's attorney-general, "is to say that the defendant is not absolved from responsibility for criminal actions."

Many object to the insanity defense on the grounds that it favors the rich against the poor. "The insanity defense," in the opinion of Senator Larry Pressler of South Dakota "is a rich man's defense. A poor man can only use it successfully if he is a cause célèbre or somebody else finances it."

There is the further objection that the psychiatrist is selected because he is known to favor the arguments of the defense and is, therefore, little more than a hired adjunct who is paid a large sum to tailor-make a psychosis to fit the counsel's needs. As Dr. Alan Stone of Harvard, a former head of the American Psychiatric Association said, the court is like a "three-ring circus, in which lawyers are the ringmasters and the psychiatric witnesses are the clowns, and if they are carefully trained, then they will be trained clowns."

Psychiatrists must, however, have a place in the scheme of things, but what weight should be given to their evidence? In 1975 the British judge, Lord Justice Lawton, declared that justice would be better served if psychiatrists were removed from center stage and placed in the wings. He expressed the fear that:

> ... trial by psychiatrists would be likely to take the place of trial by jury and magistrates. ... Psychiatry has not yet become a satisfactory substitute for the common sense of juries and magistrates on matters within their experience of life.

Disease of the mind, as Mr. Justice Dickson observed, "is a legal concept and has to be interpreted and applied by the court in accordance with legal concepts, not by doctors in accordance with medical purposes."

It is plain from Professor Elliott Leyton's study of six American multiple murders[6] that the psychiatrists are often at sea. When Edmund E. Kemper murdered his grandparents just before his sixteenth birthday in 1963, the California Youth Authority, disagreeing with the prosecution's argument that Kemper was a danger to himself and others, found him simply a sufferer from "personality trait disturbance, passive-aggressive in type." He was sent to the Atascadero Mental Hospital for sex offenders where the authorities were so impressed by his behavior that he was let out on parole. While on parole, he strangled a fifteen-year-old girl, Aiko Koo, dissected her body, and put the head in the trunk of his car, which he parked outside the psychiatrists' office. Here, after examination, he was pronounced unlikely to be a "danger to himself or any other member of society." He was thus given the green light for a campaign of murder, with distinct necrophiliac tendencies, which subsequently claimed a dozen or so victims.

A similar conflict of opinion between the experts occurred at the trial of the youthful Charles Starkweather who, with his girlfriend Caril, had gone on a murderous rampage in early 1958. "Brain tumor or pressure on the brain," said one psychiatrist. "No trace of organic brain disease," said another. "Suffering only from a minor personality disorder." The defense argued that he was "dangerously sick" and did not know the difference between right and wrong at the time of the murder. Starkweather, like members of his family, did not wish for the "taint of insanity," disowned the counsel put forward by his own defense and was sentenced to death for first-degree murder.[7]

David Berkowitz, who, between July 1976 and August 1977 specialized in attacking and killing young women and courting couples in New York, was thought by one set of psychiatrists to be so insane as to be unable to stand trial and by another to be sufficiently competent to take part in his own defense. During an intense argument it was said that Berkowitz was "as normal as anyone else. Maybe a little neurotic [he had killed seven and seriously wounded eight people]." He was sentenced to 365 years in jail.

Professor Leyton argues strongly and perspicaciously that the crimes committed by these murderers, and indeed by delinquents in general, are rooted in social rather than in psychological disorientation. Their motives, he writes, "are neither insane nor random but buried deeply in the social order."[8]

Where the defense rests its plea on insanity, judge and jury are inevitably placed in a quandary. "The basic question," Dr. Orchard, who was to be a key witness in Andrew's defense, has said, "is... into which category does the person who did the offending act fall? Is he bad or mad?" Unfortunately the categories into which criminals with mental problems fall are much less clear-cut than Dr. Orchard's statement would imply. A person can be bad at one time and mad at another or even mad *and* bad at the same time. "The degree of mental abnormality or mental illness," the British psychiatrist Anthony Storr, has observed shrewdly, "is no more easily measured than love in a marriage."

When, as in Leyshon-Hughes' case, the murder is particularly disgusting and bizarre it is easy "to confuse what is sick with what is sickening; that is, to base a decision regarding the [insanity of the] accused on the repulsiveness of his act rather than on his mental state at the time he committed the offense."[9] This misconception is the "he-killed-her-so-he-must-be-crazy" syndrome.

"The problem with this argument is its circularity: killing is crazy; therefore, anyone who kills must be crazy and ought to be found innocent by reason of insanity. By this faulty logic, no one who commits a heinous crime can be found guilty of murder."[10] On the contrary, insane minds and insane acts do not necessarily go together.

Such then were the issues with which judge, counsel and jury were to be concerned when Andrew's trial opened in September 1986. If the plea of not guilty by reason of insanity was to be put forward successfully, then Andrew's defense would have to show clearly that even if he knew what he had done, he was yet unable to appreciate its nature or quality, or fully to comprehend the legal consequences of his action. If the plea failed, and Andrew was held to have been of a sane mind when he committed the crime, then he would be found guilty of first-degree murder and sentenced to life imprisonment.

X

REGINA V. ANDREW LEYSHON-HUGHES

He reminds me of the man who murdered both his parents, and then, when sentence was about to be pronounced, pleaded for mercy on the grounds that he was an orphan.

ABRAHAM LINCOLN
(GROSS, *LINCOLN'S OWN STORIES*)

The world is still deceived with ornament
In law, what plea so tainted and corrupt
But, being season'd with a gracious voice,
Obscures the show of evil?
What damned error, but some sober brow
Will bless it and approve it with a text,
Hiding the grossness with fair ornament.

SHAKESPEARE, *THE MERCHANT OF VENICE*

And oftentimes excusing of a fault
Doth make the fault worse by the excuse.

SHAKESPEARE, *KING JOHN*

"ERNEST JOHN ANDREW LEYSHON-HUGHES, you stand indicted...that on the twenty-first day of January 1985, at the Municipality of Metropolitan Toronto in the Judicial District of York, you unlawfully did kill Nancy Eaton and thereby commit first-degree murder.

"How do you plead?"

Andrew murmured, "Not guilty by reason of insanity."

So on 15 September 1985, there began in the Supreme Court of Ontario a trial which was expected to last all of three weeks. The cast of characters was gathering. Down the hall from the courtroom dozens of potential jurors were waiting, somewhat impatiently, to be called for examination. Eyeing the scene, from seats along the wall, was a group known as the 'regulars,' old people or vagrants who came to the courthouse every day to watch the trials. They knew all the cases, all the gossip, all the lawyers and all the judges. A bag lady with a cast on her arm announced that she was waiting to see Andrew. "Who's Andrew?" asked an old man sitting next to her. "The boy who killed that rich Eaton girl," she replied.

Andrew's parents, grandparents and his Aunt Amy attended the trial. So, too, did Nancy's mother, accompanied every day by her friend Cicely Bell, and sometimes by her brother David and cousin Brenda McCarthy. Mrs. Eaton would arrive in a chauffeur-driven limousine, elegantly dressed and always wearing a big hat and dark glasses. She, Cicely and other friends would eat lunch across the road from the Supreme Court at the exclusive University Club. When Clayton Ruby asked Mrs. Eaton why she attended the trial, she replied, "Don't forget, I come from a long line of lawyers. You don't think that I'm going to stay at home doing needlepoint when you're discussing my daughter. It's the last business of Tiger's life." Throughout the trial, when the going got tough, Mrs. Eaton would visit her daughter's grave as if she could derive strength from this.

The trial was presided over by Associate Chief Justice Frank Callaghan of the Ontario Supreme Court. Married with four sons, Callaghan had been a judge in the Supreme Court since 1978. He had had a distinguished legal career, both in private practice and as deputy attorney general and deputy minister of justice for Ontario. Throughout the trial he wore a permanently pained expression.

The counsel for the Crown was Paul Chumak, a tall, academic-looking man of forty. Brusque in manner, but not discourteous, he made it plain that, even if Nancy *was* an Eaton, he was running the

Mrs. Eaton, with Edward on her left, at Nancy's funeral, Friday, 25 January 1985 (The Toronto Star)

Nancy Leigh ('Snubby') Eaton leaving the courthouse after the verdict (Canada Wide Feature Services Limited)

Sarah Leyshon-Hughes
(Canada Wide Feature Services Limited)

Ernest Leyshon-Hughes
(Canada Wide Feature Services Limited)

Clayton Ruby
(Canada Wide Feature Services Limited)

Paul Chumak
(Canada Wide Feature Services Limited)

Dr. Frank Ervin
(Canada Wide Feature Services Limited)

show. Serious minded and conscientious, he had earlier put off a holiday to Greece in order to concentrate his attention on the case.

After Andrew's trial, Chumak resigned from the office of the Crown and became involved in the case of John Demjanjuk, a Ukrainian immigrant living in the United States who was extradited in 1986 to Israel to stand trial as a war criminal. He was accused of being "Ivan the Terrible," one of those responsible for the atrocities at the appalling Treblinka extermination camp in Poland where nearly a million Jews died in the gas chambers. Chumak argued strongly that it was a case of mistaken identity, that Demjanjuk was the unfortunate victim of Russian spite and Jewish fanaticism. He told the court that Israel itself was on trial. The judges did not take kindly to this remark. "Are you threatening the court?" Judge Dorner asked. At the end of the fourteen-month trial Demjanjuk was found guilty and sentenced to death.

Chumak's legal opponent was Charles Clayton Ruby, a skillful criminal lawyer with a reputation for getting his clients off. He is said to enjoy cases which attract high media visibility and particularly likes to defend accused who *prima facie* seem to have little chance of proving their innocence. He was assisted in the case by Peter Clarke.

In legal circles, Ruby has been a controversial figure. After Andrew's trial he was to champion the cause of accused found not guilty by reason of insanity. He rejected the notion that a person sent to a hospital for the criminally insane has a soft time of it: "It is not easy time," Ruby said in the *Toronto Star*. "They can shoot you full of drugs, for example." According to *The Star*, Ruby will appear before the Supreme Court of Canada, using the Charter to protect the rights of the insane. He will argue that when someone is found not guilty of murder because insane, a warrant of the lieutenant governor, which places him in a psychiatric institution, should not be issued automatically. If Ruby is successful it could result in a system in Canada whereby there is no automatic incarceration following a verdict of not guilty by reason of insanity. An accused who is found to be insane at the time he committed the murder but who, by the time of sentencing has recovered his sanity sufficiently not to require custodial treatment, could virtually walk out of the courtroom a free person, considered innocent of the murder he had perpetrated.

The first two days of the Leyshon-Hughes trial were largely given over to the choice of the jury. It had to be ascertained whether any potential jurors knew anything about the case which would interfere with their judgment or prevent them from approaching the case impartially. Clayton Ruby requested that they might be asked whether they felt "a latent bias in relation to the insanity defense and the evidence proffered by psychiatrists and psychologists," given that in this case there was inevitably going to be a "high degree of subjectivity and emotional response." But the judge did not think it necessary to put this question. Jurors were, he said, better educated and more intelligent than they had been twenty years ago. The selected jury consisted of seven men and five women, whose occupations ranged from college student to retired manufacturer of jewelry.

When the jury entered the courtroom the judge addressed them on their responsibility to the court.

> As jurors it is your exclusive responsibility to decide all ques-
> tions of fact in issue in this case, and then, governed by my
> instructions on the law, to bring in a verdict based upon the
> facts and the law as I explain it to you.

He cautioned them to use their common sense in weighing the evidence of witnesses, some of whom might appear to be unduly nervous in the witness box, and to perform their duty "in a manner uninfluenced by pity for any person or animated by passion or prejudice against any person." He warned them not to discuss the case, even with members of their own families, and to refrain from listening to reports on radio and television which "may be unwittingly distorted," and if, by chance, they used an elevator in which there happened to be lawyers involved in the case, he reminded them that "charming gentlemen that they are, it becomes embarrassing to them if you start asking them questions and try to speak to them."

The preliminaries complete, Paul Chumak opened the case for the prosecution. Before, however, he started his speech, two procedural points had to be settled. The Crown's case depended in part on exhibiting some sixty-nine photographs of the apartment, and of the deceased, which the judge and Clayton Ruby agreed constituted admissible evidence.

> This is not a tea party so they [i.e., the jurors] will just have to
> look at them and assess them. . . . Although they may be inflam-
> matory, it is in the interest of justice they go in.

Yes, Ruby agreed, "this is a case where the bizarre nature of the crime and the number of wounds is part of my argument for the defense of insanity."

The other exhibit consisted of three volumes of psychiatric, medical and other reports made on Andrew. The judge called on Basil Orchard, who was to be a witness for the defense, to explain the nature of this evidence. Orchard testified that these reports were like hospital records, reliable, impartial and scientific. He vouched for the high reputation of the consultants concerned, more especially for those at the Institute for Living at Hartford, Connecticut, which he described as "one of the foremost institutions of its kind on the continent." Paul Chumak questioned the relevance of some of the material and the comprehensibility of the handwritten notes, especially those made by Dr. Solursh, which were "like a tape recording which is gibberish. . . . For a lay person, it's more confusing than helpful" and could be easily misconstrued. But the judge ruled that in a plea of insanity such evidence was admissible. The weight to be attached to the evidence was a matter for the jury to decide.

Paul Chumak made it plain that it was the Crown's case that Andrew "murdered Nancy Eaton by stabbing her repeatedly while committing a sexual assault." He did not even allow for the possibility that the murder was an act of insanity; rather, Andrew knew what he wanted and was determined to get it. Chumak's opening address was in the main a recital of the events of the week preceding the murder, starting with Andrew's visit to the Mental Health Centre at Penetanguishene and leading stage by stage to the murder itself and his subsequent arrest. In fact neither the prosecution nor the defense disagreed about the events themselves, though in his evidence Dr. Orchard was to add some significant, if questionable, detail. What was at issue in the main was the question of interpretation. Was Andrew's attack a sexual assault, as Paul Chumak was to contend, or was it an arbitrary and involuntary action over which Andrew had no real control?

In support of the Crown's argument, the first witness, Constable Mark Thorpe of the identification unit, produced pictures of Nancy's apartment on Farnham Avenue, together with a large number of grisly photographs which were handed to the jury: the left leg and foot of Nancy Eaton, the foot resting on a blue-and-white-striped man's shirt with a certain amount of staining on it, a small portion of torn pink panties, the large white planter lying on its side, the victim lying on her back showing "five large rents in the chest and abdomen," the blood-splattered wall, the yellow stain of the broken egg on the bathroom floor, the kitchen knife, the handle and blade bloodstained with the tip of the blade bent, and photos taken at the autopsy showing the stab wounds.

At one point Clayton Ruby asked Thorpe, "There was no explanation for the eggs?" "No," he replied. Nor was Thorpe able to explain why the potted palm had been placed on the bed. He gave evidence that Andrew's fingerprints were found on many of the objects, including the murder weapon itself. While the photos of these exhibits were being handed round the jury, Andrew stared into space and showed no emotion.

Nancy's mother was the next witness called by the Crown. The packed courtroom suddenly became still, rapt in attentive silence, as Mrs. Eaton, in a voice numbed by the pain of recollection, relived the most excruciating and shattering hours of her existence. Her voice broke with emotion and, for a moment, it seemed that she might not be able to continue; but she quickly regained her composure and, with extraordinary dignity, finished her testimony.

Other witnesses called by the Crown included the friends upon whom Andrew had called on that Monday evening, who, by and large, repeated the evidence they had given at the first hearing. Norman Nault agreed that Andrew had earlier talked of suicide, but had seemed perfectly normal when he last saw him. Tami Mori broke down temporarily as she described the visit she had made to the Don Jail in the course of which she had asked whether he had killed Nancy and had had sex with her. Chumak asked how she had reacted to Andrew's affirmative answer. "I ended up crying," she said. Andrew had looked "ashamed. He had his head down and nodded." Frank Panos thought that Andrew seemed sane enough when he called at his house at 6:45 P.M. that Monday evening.

The pathologist Dr. Sepp then described the twenty-one stab wounds which Nancy had suffered, but he admitted again that he could not establish the exact time of her death nor the order in which the wounds had been inflicted. He told Chumak that it was possible for a victim in such circumstances to "live for quite a number of minutes" and that he had even known of a case where a person with a single stab wound in the heart had still been able to walk out on to the street after it had happened. He also gave evidence of the semen deposited in

Nancy's vagina. Clayton Ruby, seeking to refute the Crown's arguments that Nancy's murder had been primarily a sexual attack, questioned Sepp to establish that Nancy was dead when Andrew had intercourse with her — an integral ingredient in the case he was putting forward to prove that Andrew was insane when he committed the murder.

Lisa Orsatti talked of her relationship with Andrew and her last visits with him to Penetang and to Toronto. She agreed with Ruby that she had realized that something was bothering Andrew but she did not know what it was. "You don't know why these two gentlemen," Ruby asked, referring to Dr. Vinegar and Paul Henry, "let him leave?" "No," she replied. "To everyone's regret," Ruby reminded the jury, "he [Henry] didn't keep him."

At this stage Chumak called no psychiatric evidence. The Crown's case seemed to rely in the main on a description of the murder and its sequel, Andrew's own statement following his arrest and the witnesses' testimonies that Andrew seemed to them completely normal the day of the slaying.

At the conclusion of the Crown's case, in spite of the strong objections from Paul Chumak, Ruby asked for the charge to be reduced from first- to second-degree murder on grounds that the Crown had failed to show that the killing was planned and deliberate or that it was incidental to a sexual assault. Judge Callaghan reserved judgment and ultimately, because of the way in which the trial was to be concluded, the matter was not raised again.

It was now up to Clayton Ruby to prove to the satisfaction of judge and jury that Andrew was not guilty by reason of insanity, having failed absolutely to appreciate the nature and quality of what he had done. Ruby had no difficulty in establishing the bizarre character of the major crises in Andrew's life. In deeply emotional tones Andrew's mother, Sarah, told of the attempts that she and her husband had made to get to the root of his personal problems. She referred to the manner of his birth which suggested, only recently as it seemed, that this might provide a clue to the subsequent difficulties of his life. She described her son's disturbed educational records and her own difficult relationship with him, giving rise to the dramatic encounters which in cyclical fashion seemed to dominate his life.

Later, other relations and friends — Peter Elcombe, Bill Jephcott, his wife Amy, and Andrew's father — were to supplement Sarah's account of Andrew's seeming mental instability, and of the attempts, fruitless as they turned out to be, which he had made to get help when the "surges of energy" threatened to engulf him. When Paul Chumak asked Ernest Leyshon-Hughes if he knew why his son had sometimes hit him, he replied, "I don't know."

All this was hardly in doubt. What Ruby had to show was that these outbursts of ill-temper and what some might call wickedness stemmed from a mental disease, not from evil intention nor even sexual desire. In his opening address for the defense Ruby criticized the authorities at Penetang for not having reacted more rigorously and more intelligently to Andrew's feelings the week before the murder when things were getting out of control, and the Toronto General Hospital for not having made a deeper investigation of Andrew's problems when his uncle took him there in the course of the week. "One story I want to bring out," he told the jury, "is the failure of the Ontario health system to help Andrew when he needed it."

Whatever testimony the other witnesses for the defense had given, it was the expert evidence which was to count. Ruby warned the jury that the arguments were likely to be complicated and they might have to "face a week of very hard work." He stressed the apparent normality of Andrew's behavior to which the Crown's witnesses had testified before and after the murder, which he believed to be nonetheless consistent with the mental disease from which Andrew was suffering. The murder of his "best, his closest friend," was not a normal or a rational act. Andrew, so these experts believed, suffered from an organic brain dysfunction, a very likely result of the problems at birth to which his mother had alluded in her evidence. Symptomatic of this mental disease was an apparent confusion and lack of response when waking. As a child Andrew responded so poorly in the early mornings that his mother suspected that he might be deaf. He was so confused that he found difficulty in pouring milk into a glass without spilling it. Some at least of the major crises in his life had been initiated in the early morning as Nancy's murder was to be. Andrew's aunt had described him as "a machine that hadn't been turned on."

The first major witness for the defense was Dr. Basil Orchard, a psychiatrist of wide experience in dealing with the criminally insane. A doctor of medicine at the University of Toronto where he graduated in 1961, he had been subsequently director of the regional division at Penetanguishene and consultant to the division for the criminally insane before joining the university as assistant professor in 1971. For

nineteen years he had been a member of the staff of the Clarke Institute
of Psychiatry and more recently staff psychiatrist at the Credit Valley
Hospital in Mississauga. He was a member of the Law Reform
Commission to consider law and insanity, and was the author of a
number of learned articles. Orchard estimated that he had treated some
three or four hundred cases clinically, a majority of which had been
concerned with homicide, and had served as an expert witness in a
number of murder trials in the Canadian courts.

Dr. Orchard had no doubt as to the verdict. Andrew "was insane, in
my opinion." He went on to justify this assertion in a series of
wide-ranging arguments in the course of which he was to refute
vigorously the critical questions with which the Crown's counsel
assailed him.

First he commented at some length on the volumes of medical and
psychiatric reports which had been submitted to the court, beginning
with the records of Andrew's birth. This was, in his opinion, the crucial
incident, providing the foundation on which a massive scaffolding was
to be erected. He drew the court's attention to items from the medical
reports which suggested that there might have been some abnormal
features about Andrew's birth. The newborn baby had been "slow to
breathe"; "the placenta [which was providing nourishment for the
infant in the womb] was infarcted [i.e., dead]"; "the first breath [took]
two-and-a-half minutes," which he described as "very slow." These
features, together with references to shortness of breath, led him to the
conclusion that Andrew's birth had not been a normal delivery.
Orchard believed that loss of oxygen and low blood sugar had caused the
brain dysfunction which lay at the root of Andrew's personality
problems.

He admitted that it was difficult to detect the damage and to measure
its volume. The damage had been diffuse, "a cell here and a cell there,"
"not the kind of damage that one would get with a tumor," a condition
caused by "antenatal and postnatal asphyxia" which, though organic in
character, was not yet a "localized lesion." It was something difficult to
pick up, even by using an encephalogram, since the damage was not
confined to a specific area emitting abnormal spiking or epileptic
discharges.

Nonetheless this organic brain disease was, as Dr. Orchard and his
colleagues were to emphasize, the operative factor in giving rise to the
many violent episodes in Andrew's life and to Nancy's murder in

particular. It accounted for the "episodes of explosive behavior which [were] somewhat pointless." In such incidents the higher control centers, located in the cortex where judgment and rational thinking are located, had ceased to function. Action became directed by impulse, desire and feeling "without any judgment or consideration or concern. . . . It is a sort of high-drive state."

But this was not all. As a result "there is a personality disorder present." Dr. Orchard diagnosed this as a borderline personality disorder, which was not episodic but continued all the time, "a disorder in thinking, feeling and behaving." This behavioral disorder, Dr. Orchard supposed, helped to explain the many strange features of Andrew's character, such as his learning disability, his inattentiveness and inability to concentrate, which had been such a source of worry to his parents.

The presence of a borderline personality disorder naturally strengthened the defense's case, explaining Andrew's potential for irrational and insane behavior. "A borderline personality disorder with a psychotic state," was how Dr. Orchard diagnosed Andrew's problems, the first continuing the whole time, the other sporadic, but both in combination giving rise to violent episodes of which Nancy's murder was the culmination.

With his thesis in mind, Dr. Orchard reviewed the reports which psychiatrists had made on Andrew. Although none of the many eminent psychiatrists who had previously examined Andrew had reached a diagnosis similar to Dr. Orchard's or, with one exception, even approached it, Orchard sought to incorporate their arguments into his general presentation. He suggested that while they had a partial view, he had the benefit of a full picture, despite the fact that Andrew's earlier psychiatrists had observed and treated him for many years, while he himself had only seen Andrew alone for less than six hours over a space of just two months.

The prolix and even at times obscure arguments rolled on, leaving, it would seem, the judge as well as the lawyers somewhat bored and a little baffled. "I just wonder," the judge commented, "if it is necessary for the doctor to read all these reports to the jury. Whether he could draw their attention to the conclusions and explain his opinion in the light of that." Paul Chumak thought it was regrettable that summaries had not been made of the opinions, and even Ruby said that he was trying to find a medium between going over everything and being so sparse that the jury didn't know what to do.

Dr. Orchard passed then to the heart of the matter, the working or non-working of Andrew's mind at the time of Nancy's murder. Although, he said, Andrew had a memory and was able to recall what had happened, he was mindless at the time or rather the mind that was operative consisted of animal drives unrestrained by the reasoning will, the cortical activity. Nancy, he repeated, "would be the last person it would be appropriate for Andrew to destroy. . . . I am unable to find any reason that Andrew knew of why Nancy Eaton should have died."

Orchard added that the early morning — because there is a diminution in cortical activity at the approach of sleep or in waking — was the prime time for Andrew's episodic psychotic activity to erupt; sleep lessens resistance to control.

Even if Andrew remembered what he did, Orchard believed he had no real conception of what had happened.

> He had no memory of feeling anything. It is not empty of memory. It is just blank about feelings. There is a memory of striking her with a glass thing and a memory of starting to stab her with the knife. I am not sure whether he remembers all the stab wounds. He could remember, he thought, four or five. He couldn't remember any more, but also he said it was really painful to remember.

The juggling with the eggs, Dr. Orchard held, "was a fogged, aimless, driven function — brain stem function." That and placing the potted plant on the bed "tells me that the mind is not functioning in any way at that time." As bizarre and inexplicable, in Dr. Orchard's view was the sexual intercourse with Nancy's corpse which he believed had occurred some hours after the killing.

Under examination from Paul Chumak, Dr. Orchard stood his ground firmly, insisting that the murder was mindless and motiveless. It was not necessarily automatic, but it was involuntary:

CHUMAK: When he stabbed Nancy the cortex was not functioning, but what is going on? What is in his head?

ORCHARD: Very little except an enormous urgent drive to act. It is as if the cortex is turned off so the reasoning function, the judgment function, the control functions which normally play half or more of the influence that goes into any behavior we have is not there.

CHUMAK: At the time, does he know it is a knife in his hand?

ORCHARD: He might or might not.

CHUMAK: Does he know that he is killing this young lady when he stabs her?

ORCHARD: I don't think — I don't think he can focus on that, that he is killing somebody. He is merely acting. It is as though there is no mind and only drives like a lower animal. There is no mind or thought. It is as though that part is shut off at that time or it is not able to work. . . . It's just wild explosive activity.

CHUMAK: Would he have available to him. . . the ability to know whether or not killing someone was against the law or not against the law?

ORCHARD: No.

CHUMAK: Would he be able to intend to kill or intend to cause a sexual attack or to intend to cause bodily harm?

ORCHARD: No.

JUDGE: You were just asked whether or not he intended to kill. Did you mean that he didn't intend to kill or he didn't have the capacity to form the intention to kill?

ORCHARD: I don't think he had the capacity to form that intent.

Dr. Orchard parried Chumak's thrusts with skill, stonewalling where it seemed necessary. From time to time, sometimes at Ruby's prompting, the judge cut the questioning short to keep Chumak from straying from the direct path.

Chumak questioned Dr. Orchard on Andrew's capacity to recall the events, suggesting that if his memory had been operating distinctly, then he should have realized what he was doing and consequently bore some responsibility for his action. Andrew had told Sergeant Stewart that he was trying to forget it. "I am refusing to remember. I am trying to block it out of my mind." That surely implied that he had been aware of his actions. Dr. Orchard replied that Andrew was trying to forget because it was "very painful and awful," underlining the argument that was pivotal to his diagnosis of Andrew as a borderline personality, someone who is capable of caring, rather than an antisocial personality, devoid of all conscience. "He had," he told Paul Chumak, "an ability to care. . . ."

CHUMAK: He did not care about Nancy, in terms of what he did to her?
ORCHARD: Yes, he did care for her.
CHUMAK: He murdered her.
ORCHARD: Yes.
CHUMAK: Is that caring about somebody if you murder them?
ORCHARD: That isn't at that time.

But Dr. Orchard went on to suggest that Andrew's contemplation of suicide as a way out did imply that he knew "how inappropriate that behavior had been." "He killed somebody that he cared about and he knew he killed her," but at the time of the murder his mental faculties were so disorientated that he lacked "the capacity to care or think or judge or even to know much." Orchard admitted that Andrew's capacity for care was intermittent. "He didn't have an incapacity to feel what others feel, but at times he was incapable. . . . I found the capacity to care about other people; I found the capacity to recognize other people's feelings, but it was not a constant thing." Dr. Orchard said later in the cross-examination:

> [Andrew] would feel something coming on and go and ask somebody for help, would always be trying to keep a relationship going. He tried with his family, no matter how up and down that went and how difficult it was. He tried with Nancy Eaton and that went over a period of years. And when things started to go wrong, he would be looking for help.

Paul Chumak then turned to his principal plea, that Nancy's murder was a straightforward sexual attack or a sadistic psychopathic killing, implying that Andrew was responsible for his actions — both arguments which Dr. Orchard, and later Dr. Ervin and other psychiatrists, strongly resisted.

CHUMAK: So you are not even prepared to concede that it is a sadistic killing?
ORCHARD: No. Sadism is in the person doing it. For instance if one wants to make a really sadistic killing then one might do a great deal to threaten and frighten and terrorize the victim prior to actually removing the life with a lot of near actions that would never take the life and not quite take it.

CHUMAK: Such as hitting a person over the head and causing a depression
in the skull, stabbing a person in the head and these stab wounds not
being fatal in themselves, that would all be consistent with sadism?

Dr. Orchard replied that this was a possible scenario but he would
not agree with Paul Chumak that the superficial wounds in the breast
were inflicted for sadistic or sexual ends. "It doesn't look like trying to
torture. It looks like a lot of stab wounds and some that are deep and
some that are not." He added that he was not a pathologist. Earlier
Clayton Ruby had got Dr. Sepp to testify that he "would not expect
to find the pattern of stab wounds found in this case if it was a planned
and rational killing."

Feeling perhaps a little like Sisyphus, Paul Chumak came more
directly to the sexual aspect which was the heart of his argument.

CHUMAK: When you say the killing was pointless, I suggest to you that
to him it was not pointless. This was a girl that he had a crush on.
ORCHARD: I suggest then that that would be pointless.
CHUMAK: If he was interested in having sex with her. . . that appears to
be what he said to the police and he wanted sex with her and he
wanted to force sex with her, then it would not be pointless I suggest
to you.
ORCHARD: No. Pointless to kill her because he could only have sex
with her body. It would be more pointless than to force a sexual act
with her.
CHUMAK: There is a motive for this killing. It is basically a sex killing I
suggest to you.
ORCHARD: I would think then he didn't do it very well. Because if it is
going to be a sex killing, usually it is sex and then kill, and so he
couldn't really bring an effective sexual relationship around by killing.
CHUMAK: There are various components to sex. He obviously touched
her private part or parts while she was alive. For instance with the
knife, those particular injuries to the breast did not penetrate the
shirt. . . the whole scenario is one of sexual assault.

Orchard admitted that Andrew had been sexually attracted to Nancy
but vigorously maintained that the murder was both senseless and
motiveless. "So, in your testimony," Chumak asked Orchard, "you

would have the court and jury believe that he was so removed in this psychotic state that even the presence of a policeman would not deter him from doing what he wanted to do?"

ORCHARD: I think it is likely. In fact the policeman would have got stabbed.

CHUMAK: What would be in his mind... when he is killing her and stabbing her, during the murder?

ORCHARD: His memory is there and basically there is very little feeling.

CHUMAK: Feeling for what?

ORCHARD: Feelings. Not particularly for anybody. Feelings that he thought should be there. It was a high level of activity and drive but he remembers the events... so there is a pretty clear memory.

CHUMAK: At that time would he have the capacity to know, for instance, that he was holding a knife, as opposed to a baseball bat or a glass of water?

ORCHARD: That is very hard to say but I think he may not have known it was a knife.

CHUMAK: Did you ask him about that?

ORCHARD: Yes. He knew afterwards it was a knife.

But Dr. Orchard could not ignore the rape. He took Andrew's word that it had occurred some time after the killing.

CHUMAK: Did he tell you how long after Nancy was dead that he had intercourse?

ORCHARD: He did not give me the time, but it was after he had been out and back. And he saw the body and wanted to put it up on the bed, because it was on the floor. And he tried to put it up on the bed and the panties ripped, and he had the idea of intercourse. It was a period of time. I have no idea how long.

CHUMAK: What do you make of the fact that there is nothing in any of the psychological records that would indicate sexual disturbance that would lead him to want to have sexual intercourse with someone who is dead?

ORCHARD: I would say... it is way out of the ordinary.

CHUMAK: When he was in intercourse with her, is he psychotic then?

ORCHARD: He may be again. I think this is a very inappropriate act, and a dead body is not an attractive sexual object.

There were many other questions which Paul Chumak could have put to Dr. Orchard concerning this bizarre incident, but he contented himself with asking Dr. Orchard why he so readily accepted Andrew's word, given that Andrew was a compulsive liar.

CHUMAK: Have you considered that what much of what he told you could in fact be lies?
ORCHARD: Yes. When I am examining somebody I look for that. I often find it. I think he was fairly truthful in the things that I could see that I could check against.

When Dr. Orchard intimated that the psychotic episode probably lasted an hour or even less, Paul Chumak, who seemed to miss the opportunity to push the question of times further, asked him how he viewed the events which followed the murder. When, in fact, did the psychotic episode cease and Andrew return to normality?

CHUMAK: What happens after the attack?
ORCHARD: Then reality begins to return or the cortical function begins to work again — begins to be active again and then he knows what he's done.
CHUMAK: When it is over, he starts recovering the cortical function?
ORCHARD: Yes. When he starts to recover his cortical functions, then he is likely to get very depressed and to feel hopeless.
CHUMAK: What do you make of the fact that he starts committing antisocial acts after he ransacks the place, he forges the check. When he forged the check, he can't make the number and the figures coincide. What do you make of that?
ORCHARD: I think it might mean that he is not able to function very well at the time. . . . It may mean that he is not in good contact with reality, but he is not in the same loss of content as he is in the midst of the explosive behavior.

Clayton Ruby must have been pleased with Dr. Orchard's evidence. Orchard had never given way to Chumak's, at times, penetrating questioning. He had insisted that Andrew had lacked the capacity to appreciate that he was killing Nancy Eaton.

CHUMAK: Dealing with the physical nature of the act, that is, the use of the knife to inflict the stab wounds, the sexual assault, ripping open her shirt, cutting her on the breast, was he able at that time, when those acts were being done, did he have the capacity at that time to know what he was doing, that is the physical notion of what he was doing?...Did he have the capacity to know that he was stabbing Nancy Eaton at that time?

ORCHARD: No...I don't think that he would be able to appreciate...what he was doing.

JUDGE: In other words, he couldn't appreciate that he was killing her?

ORCHARD: That's right.

CHUMAK: Did he know right from wrong on that occasion?

ORCHARD: I think he couldn't even turn his mind to right or wrong, or any of those higher judgments.

The defense had another equally strong force to bring up the rear in the person of a heavily bearded guru from Montreal, Dr. Frank Ervin, a sixty-year-old psychiatrist of international repute. Born in Little Rock, Arkansas, Ervin had had, as Clayton Ruby was very keen to stress, a long and distinguished career. He became closely associated with the Harvard Medical School where he specialized in psychiatry, with a particular interest in the functions of the brain. In 1969 he was appointed associate professor of psychology. In 1979 he took a chair in the department of psychiatry at McGill University. Apart from a long and impressive list of articles contributed to learned journals, well over a hundred in number, Ervin was, with V.H. Mark, the author in 1970 of *Violence and the Brain*.

In introducing him, Ruby allowed himself a glint of humor. "You are a visiting scientist at the Instituto Nacional de Neurologia in Mexico. Is my accent terrible?" "Pretty bad," the professor said. "You are also the director of primate laboratories in St. Kitts? Aside from its attractive location, I don't know about that outfit?" "It's a laboratory," Ervin replied, "which utilizes the monkey who is indigenous on St. Kitts to study the role of social process and brain dysfunction in behavior as a model for human conditions." "I have rarely had the privilege," Ruby said with a touch of complacency, "of putting forward such a distinguished scientist."

Though Ervin was, in many respects, a witness of star quality, he had in fact only seen Andrew for less than an hour two weeks before the trial. He called for a blackboard to illustrate his points and lectured fluently and learnedly as if to one of his university classes. The lecture was largely a précis of some of the research in which Ervin had been engaged for the past twenty years, and an attempt to apply it, where relevant, to Andrew's case. For Ervin, Andrew was a classic example of his theorizing and the invitation to testify must have seemed a heaven-sent opportunity to air his hypotheses. He was to prove an impressive witness.

Dr. Ervin argued that as a result of his brain dysfunction, Andrew was in a "dissociative" state when he killed Nancy.

> Critical to my thinking about him is the evidence that he started life with a somewhat damaged brain and that every experience thereafter had to be filtered through that disordered brain and the environment was always responding to the consequences of that disordered brain.

Fundamentally, Ervin contended, the limbic system, which directs a person's basic drives, was hyperactive, freed from the controls that direct reason, knowledge, awareness and judgment governed by the cortical system.

> Let me say in a word what is going on. The state has been described... as a limbic ictus... not a layman's term. It's a state in which part of the brain is hyperexcited. It's hyperactive.... It is not diagnostic of a specific disorder, but it is not working right.

Ervin showed that if in an experiment a part of the brain could be stimulated by an electrode, it would react aggressively — "focusing on a target that is appropriate... physically assaultive behavior." In such a situation the "crocodile brain," a phrase which greatly attracted the attention of the media, was dominant.

> This is the oldest part of the brain.... It's all of the brain that simple vertebrates like the crocodile, which is a successful

animal, have — that part that is important for the survival of
the species: feeding, fighting, reproductive activity... necessary
activity; both predatory and defensive aggression.

It was, Ervin believed, this poorly organized crocodile brain, unhind-
ered by the higher part of the brain, which regulates the emotions, morals
and the ability to judge reality, which prompted Andrew's reactions
when he killed Nancy. Like other witnesses, Ervin stressed Andrew's
apparently dissociated state at the time of waking and in the early
morning.

Difficult time period for him. He gets up... and this... crocodile
man carries out this heinous act which Andrew must perceive
as being totally alien to his whole relationship with Nancy...
and he is an aghast observer of that scene.

Andrew, Ervin said, was probably suffering from limbic seizure at the
time of the stabbing which made his inner drives hyperactive, providing
electrical activity in the brain that cut off control and restraint. "There
is a disruption of function, a rush of fear, anger, violence jumbled out of
control."

Dr. Ervin compared the mental disease from which he believed
Andrew to be suffering with that found in a rabies victim, where the
sufferer has emotions, and full motor control as well as a recollection of
what is happening, but is in the grip of a disease which he or she cannot
control.

Rabies is a virus disease of the brain characterized by attack
behavior. The victim has waves of attack behavior and knows
they are coming on. If he is not tied down, he will attack, bite
— a mad-dog syndrome. He can feel them coming on and
clearly has dissociated the awareness of the internal state from
the state itself, knows this is about to happen but cannot
prevent or control it. And then in the midst of the attack, once
with it, perhaps has memory of it and is extraordinarily
apologetic, ashamed and so forth.

In response to other queries by counsel, Ervin said that so far as
Andrew's behavioral problems were concerned, he was "most comfortable
in thinking of him as a borderline personality disorder with a parallel

and second diagnosis...of attention deficit disorder which covers his childhood abnormalities." Questioned about the length of time of the explosive episodes, Ervin supposed that it was possible for them to wax, wane and then wax again, which might account for Andrew's supposed rape of Nancy some hours after the murder. "I am sure he is in this same kind of strange dissociated state. He is aroused by all the excitement...but the act is bizarre, dissociative, unlike any fantasy preoccupation that I have seen any evidence of in this boy." That is all done by this "other state." Asked about the juggling of the eggs and putting the plant on the bed, he had no definite opinions:

> He may have done that as a symbolic act of some sort. It's the appropriate thing to do. You have a dead person that you care for. It's symbolic to plant a tree....I don't know.

When Paul Chumak tried to draw Ervin out further on some aspects of Andrew's personality problem, the judge intervened somewhat petulantly.

> You have [he told the Crown prosecutor] been putting assumptions to him which is not the way he sees things. I think you're just wasting the court's time with the type of question you have been putting to the doctor for the last half hour.

Orchard and Ervin had done their work well. Other experts for the defense would be called, among them Dr. Fred Jensen, an Australian, who had emigrated to Toronto in 1970. He had become an associate professor at the University of Toronto in 1980 and for thirteen years, between 1973 and 1986, was a staff psychiatrist at the Clarke Institute of Psychiatry. Jensen had also been the deputy director of the Metropolitan Toronto Forensic Service. His evidence was interesting, since it showed some degree of variance from what was rapidly becoming the establishment line.

Jensen had seen Andrew when he was in the Don Jail. At his first appearance Andrew had been dressed in "baby-doll clothes," overalls made of a stiff material which could not be used for a suicide attempt.

> His first appearance was quite dramatic. He was extremely rumpled. His eyes were suffused. His face was expressionless,

and yet he was able to give a coherent account of the circumstances that led up to his being where he was.

When Jensen saw him three weeks later, Andrew seemed a changed person. His voice was higher, but he seemed more like an automaton than a human: "There was hardly any eye contact." Another three weeks passed and Andrew was so transformed in appearance that Jensen did not recognize him. "He was presentable, well groomed and looked quite a different person."

He believed that Andrew was suffering from a severe personality disorder, a character disorder of a mixed nature in which there were antisocial features; but in reply to Chumak he did not deny that there were also present some borderline features to which Orchard had drawn attention. He seemed, however, less happy to subscribe wholeheartedly to Dr. Orchard's theory, and much of what he had to say in evidence would have sustained the argument that Andrew suffered from an antisocial personality disorder and was a psychopath:

> ...a narcissistic person, egocentric, demanding and difficult, but there was a great deal of inadequacy and the crying need for assistance underneath that rather unappetizing exterior of narcissism, egotism and eventually antisociality in his behavior.

Dr. Jensen had an interesting reflection on the murder itself:

> I think [he told Ruby] there is a blind rage to kill someone, to act violently, to destroy. I think it's an act of destruction rather than killing...an act of destruction that the person feels compelled to express.

Jensen had seriously considered whether there might be evidence to suggest that Andrew did in fact suffer from temporal-lobe epilepsy, and was not ready to lose sight of this possibility. But he agreed with Paul Chumak that if Andrew was suffering from the personality disorder alone, he would have had the capacity to appreciate the nature of the physical acts that he was doing and the capacity to know right from wrong. Andrew would have been conscious that he was stabbing Nancy with a knife and that she might die as a result of what he did. "Would he," Chumak asked Jensen, "lack any appropriate emotional feelings at that time?" "The antisocial features in his personality," Jensen replied, "would tend perhaps to make him a little unaware — less aware of the feelings of others and he might be unemotional about it." All this would certainly support the Crown's contention that Andrew was indeed a psychopath.

Ruby was evidently disturbed by Dr. Jensen's evidence.

> I want you to assume, just to make it clear for the jury, that you are wrong in your characterization and Dr. Orchard is correct that there is a borderline personality disorder together with unspecified brain damage. Would you agree with Dr. Orchard's conclusions or disagree with them?

Jensen gave a cautious reply. It depended on the severity of the personality disorder. If it was slight then Andrew's ability to appreciate what he was doing was not impaired.

> If the borderline is so severe that he is psychotic, or if that brain damage to which you referred involved specific discharge to the temporal lobe which involved rage, then he would be unable to appreciate what he was doing at the time.

Ruby must have given an inward sigh of relief. "In the state that you thought he was in, he would not be conscious of legal right or legal wrong?" he asked. "No," the doctor responded. Dr. Jensen's evidence was mixed, but at the end the defense seemed to have won through.

Dr. Lionel Solursh followed. He had left Toronto to become a professor of psychiatry at the Medical College of Georgia in May 1986, and had had considerable experience with Andrew as a private patient. It was Dr. Solursh who had suggested to Andrew's parents that they should consult the Hartford Institute for Living. He blamed the authorities at Penetang for not having picked up the cause of Andrew's problems. Solursh strongly disagreed with the notion that the murder was sexually motivated. "I'm making a definite assumption that it was not a sexual assault, and I see no reason to consider it is."

In summing up, Ruby returned to his old theme. The murder of Nancy Eaton, he told the jury, was not a crime, but a tragedy. Andrew Leyshon-Hughes had killed the one person he loved because the system had failed to help him. Ruby, who handled the judge and jury with equal insight, had made the best of a legal argument and had played a game of legal chess with discernment and penetration. In securing his services, Andrew's family had made a shrewd and ultimately successful move.

At 2:45 P.M., on the ninth day, the trial ended abruptly with the Crown conceding the case. The decision followed a lunch at which Chumak met the Crown psychiatrists who heard the evidence that the accused was insane at the time of the killing, evidence which had been in many instances given to them for the first time at the trial. "I am prepared," Chumak told the judge, "to accept the plea of insanity." "His aunt's testimony was pivotal," Chumak commented later.

> She was an unquestionably truthful witness. During the [loaded gun] episode, she said that over a nothing incident [Andrew] appeared to go into a trance-like state.... He looked like the devil. He had this horrific expression on his face and, mind you, this was triggered by nothing. Now, that evidence was very critical in terms of how he functioned or misfunctioned as a human being. This was a genuine instance for a psychiatrist to examine a past instance of his break with reality. The gun incident was not something that was made up by the family. The weight of psychiatric opinion — not only of defense psychiatrists but of psychiatrists who were objective, fair-minded straight shooters — testified that he was insane. And I couldn't get around that hurdle.

It was a decision with which the judge evidently sympathized.

> I want you [Judge Callaghan told the jury] to know that the psychiatric evidence that you have heard has been overwhelming...the accused at the time of the killing of Miss Eaton, was incapable of appreciating the nature and quality of the act or of knowing that this act was wrong — by that we mean legally wrong.... The accused suffered from a borderline disorder with an organic brain dysfunction going back to childhood.

"I usually," the judge added, "don't express my view of the case but, in the light of what I have heard here, I am satisfied that that is the appropriate verdict. But it is not my decision. It's yours." After such a direction it would have been a brave or foolhardy juror who would have challenged the opinion of the court. Whatever the individual members of the jury may have felt, they were left with no option. After consulting for seventeen minutes they returned, at ten minutes past four, and delivered a verdict of "not guilty because insane."

In a short address, Judge Callaghan said Andrew "may never go free."

> He will be sent to a mental hospital — a hospital for the criminally insane where he will live in very restricted and confined circumstances. He will be detained for an indefinite period until such time as it's found by the appropriate authorities that the illness has been cured or controlled to the point that he no longer poses a danger to our society. That may be never!

Callaghan ordered Andrew to be detained in "strict custody" in the Oak Ridge Unit at Penetang. Ruby, commenting that "Andrew had finally found out what is wrong with him," was ecstatic. He clutched Andrew's hand in a triumphant salute and then gave a thumbs-up sign to Andrew's parents; his mother, Sarah, hugged the lawyer and wiped away her tears.

Ruby caught Mrs. Eaton's eye after the verdict. Snubby waited for the defender of her daughter's murderer to make his way across the crowded courtroom and, as he was about to extend his hand, she said, "Congratulations," and walked head high out of the courtroom.

XI

THE PSYCHOPATHIC MURDERER

Mala mens, malus animus.
[Bad mind, bad heart]

TERENCE, ANDRIA

The disease of an evil conscience is beyond the practice of all
the physicians of all the countries in the world.

W.E. GLADSTONE, SPEECH,
PLUMSTEAD, 1878

Mad, bad and dangerous to know.

LADY CAROLINE LAMB ON BYRON,
JOURNAL

AS ANDREW LEYSHON-HUGHES LISTENED to the verdict his sullen face
lit up, showing some degree of relief and pleasure that the trial was over.
The Crown counsel, Paul Chumak, had conceded that the evidence
which the psychiatrists had brought forward was so convincing that he
no longer thought that it was worthwhile to continue with the case.

The detached observer might wonder whether the expert evidence was as overwhelming as it was claimed to be. The defense counsel had fired both barrels to defeat the enemy, and their arguments, complex and technical in character, had persuaded the court that Andrew was indeed insane at the time he killed Nancy Eaton.

Yet he was not proved to be suffering from any precisely defined mental disease. Can he or should he — as had been suggested three years earlier — be described as a psychopathic murderer? It raises a possibility which requires a more detailed investigation of what constitutes the psychopathic killer.[1]

Although there appears to be substantial evidence to the contrary, Orchard held strongly that Andrew was not a psychopath, that he suffered instead from a borderline personality disorder. But his colleagues were less sure. Dr. Ervin said that he was "most comfortable in thinking of him as a borderline personality disorder, with a parallel second diagnosis...of attention-deficit disorder." Dr. Jensen said that Andrew had a "mixed character disorder with antisocial features," in which there were also ingredients of a borderline personality disorder. Dr. Orchard refuted Paul Chumak's suggestion that the borderline personality disorder was a "very vague category." Yet an eminent British psychiatrist, Dr. Patrick Gallwey, has said recently that the diagnosis:

> [covers a] wide range of different conditions and does not effectively represent a closely defined psychiatric disease category.
> It is a generally descriptive term that may be used of those who have ego deficiencies resulting from early prolonged infantile deprivation.[2]

When Chumak put forward the symptoms associated with the antisocial personality disorder, characteristic of the psychopath, Orchard agreed that Andrew fitted ten out of the twelve criteria, but he objected that the fundamental difference between the two types of disorders was that Andrew recognized that he needed help and showed, if intermittently, signs of caring for others.

This is surely an over-simplification, for there is in fact no hard and fast frontier between these disorders as the *American Diagnostic and Statistical Manual*, the so-called psychiatrists' bible, makes abundantly clear. One disorder may merge into the other. In any case, even if Dr. Orchard saw in Andrew signs of caring, it could be argued that it was less because he cared for others than because he cared for himself. His main concern, as his treatment of his parents, of his aunt and uncle and his manipulation of Nancy all showed, was to promote his own interests.

> The borderline personality [according to Dr. Jacqueline Masson of the University of Toronto] would tend *not* to stab another person; rather, in an effort to discharge tension he would be more likely to slash himself. The painful nature of his life is reflected in repetitive self-destructive acts, such as wrist-slashings and other such self-mutilation. Violence, for the borderline personality, is usually directed towards *self*, not others.

Andrew seems to fit most appropriately into the category of the antisocial personality, commonly called a sociopath or psychopath. The psychopath is not insane in the accepted sense of that word. His mind may work abnormally but he is not mentally deranged and he does not suffer from a specific mental disease. His judgments, if occasionally ill-balanced and sometimes disordered, are not based on delusions or hallucinations. He does not lose contact with reality, nor does he suffer from mental imbecility; rather he is often a person of good intelligence. Indeed, the principal difference between the psychopath and the normal person may be described as quantitative rather than qualitative.

What marks the psychopath is that he or she has a personality problem, which leads to abnormally aggressive or seriously irresponsible conduct of a distinct and violent antisocial character. The symptoms of a psychopathic disorder, difficult to diagnose and define, are, however, less specific and less easily measurable than those associated with mental illness and, whatever it is from which the psychopath may suffer, it falls short of madness.

An illuminating dialogue between prosecuting attorney Gerard Sullivan and Dr. Harold Zolan, a forensic psychiatrist, at the trial of Ronald DeFeo, Jr. — the Amityville, Long Island man whose massacre of his family inspired the film, *The Amityville Horror* — crystalizes the distinction between the legally insane psychotic and the psychopath, who is evil but not crazy. Dr. Zolan was first asked to define psychosis:

DR. ZOLAN: A psychosis is a form of mental illness in which the patient has lost the capacity to deal with reality, to distinguish between reality and fantasy.

ATTORNEY SULLIVAN: Now, are there some forms of mental disorders, Doctor, which are not as grave or serious as a psychosis?

DR. ZOLAN: Yes.

ATTORNEY SULLIVAN: And is antisocial personality one of those?

DR. ZOLAN: Antisocial personality is a personality disorder, as opposed to a mental illness.

ATTORNEY SULLIVAN: What was your diagnosis of Ronald DeFeo, Jr.?

DR. ZOLAN: My diagnosis was that of an antisocial personality.

ATTORNEY SULLIVAN: What were its characteristics?

DR. ZOLAN: The antisocial personality runs a fairly wide gamut including people who appear different but actually basically are the same. And that gamut extends from a smooth persuasive con artist to the aggressive, destructive, rather obviously criminal activity that we are more apt to identify as an antisocial personality. The characteristics, the basic characteristics of all antisocial personalities are that they are people who have not been socialized into the society in which they live. They pretty much have a code of their own. They are people who are grossly selfish and callous, who are extremely egocentric, who have no capacity to experience or to feel guilt. They have a low frustration tolerance. They are easily aroused and at times often explosive. And their main purpose in life is self-gratification generally regardless of the cost to others. I should add one other important thing, and that is that the antisocial personality fails to benefit from experience or punishment, and therefore is found to repeat antisocial acts despite the fact that they have been punished or warned or admonished. They probably constitute one of the largest groups of recidivists in our penal institutions.

ATTORNEY SULLIVAN: Now, Dr. Zolan, can you tell us how these or any of these characteristics of antisocial personality affect the ability or capacity of one to know and appreciate the wrongfulness of his conduct?

DR. ZOLAN: They do not affect it in any way at all.[3]

The psychopath knows and appreciates that he is committing a wrongful act. He simply does not care about his human prey.

We are all born as greedy babies [commented the British psychiatrist Anthony Storr] unable to appreciate the needs or feelings of other people. Only gradually, through affectionate dependence on those who care for us, can we attain the capacity to identify with our nearest or dearest, and the wish to do unto them as we would be done by. It is this capacity to put ourselves into the shoes of other people which makes us behave even reasonably decently. The fear of punishment is not the chief deterrent. Rather is it this fear of the loss of approval of and rejection of our fellows. Psychopaths have been unable to develop this kind of conscience, which enables ordinary human beings to regard others as themselves. For them, other people are merely obstacles in the way of their desires, or else means by which they can obtain gratification.[4]

Psychopathic disorders have existed since the beginning of man, but it is only in recent times that lawyers and psychiatrists have begun to recognize them. Even now there remains an acute measure of disagreement about their nature and treatment. There could be no difficulty in recognizing that the crazy loon who imagined that he was the Emperor of China or the man who thought that he was a poached egg were persons void of natural wit and so mad. But what of the others whose conduct at first sight suggested insanity, but who, on closer investigation, did not suffer from a specific mental illness? For long, society esteemed that they were mad whereas, in fact, they were the progeny of antisocial personality disorders, now conveniently, if often too vaguely and indiscriminately, described as psychopaths.

The case of the nineteenth-century French psychopath Vacher well illustrates the difficulty of making a correct diagnosis. Self-pitying and resentful of rough treatment, he was liable to explosions of temper which led to violence. He placed the responsibility for his actions on a mad dog that had bitten him, so he alleged, at the age of eight. At one time he entered a monastery, but was thrown out for trying to seduce the novices. Vacher proposed to a young girl after his discharge from military service (in the course of which he had tried to cut his throat for failing to be appointed a corporal) and when she refused, he tried to shoot her, only wounding her and making himself deaf in one ear. He was placed in a lunatic asylum, discharged and at once began a campaign of murder. He cut a young girl's throat and had intercourse with her dead body.

Ten more victims followed, five of them boys. Violating girls as he slit their throats, Vacher asserted that he was acting as an instrument of

divine vengeance, punishing sinners through the killing of their off-
spring. He was arrested but was not identified as the murderer, being
simply sentenced to three months for indecent assault. In prison he
confessed to the murders. Vacher's defense was insanity, but the doctors
did not support his plea and in December 1898 he was sentenced to
death. Vacher was certainly a psychopathic murderer.

Historically, it was only slowly that the concept of the psychopathic
condition was accepted by doctors and psychiatrists, even more hesitantly
by lawyers and judges and, eventually but reluctantly and far from
whole-heartedly, by the general public. As early as the opening years of
the nineteenth century, the French psychiatrist, Philippe Pinel, drew
attention to a young man who seemed normal but, when moved by
passion, became violent to the extent that, when a woman spoke
roughly to him, he pushed her down a well. Pinel had identified a case
of mania, as it seemed to him, which lacked the mental confusion
characteristic of lunacy. It was a case of what he called *manie sans délire*
(mental derangement without delirium), in which there appeared "no
sensible changes in the functions of the understanding, but perversions
of the active faculties, marked by an abstract and sanguinary fury with a
blind propensity to acts of violence." In 1835, the English physician,
James Pritchard, observed there seemed to exist a type of "madness"
which lacked the clinical features of insanity. Its chief features were:

> . . . a morbid perversion of the natural feelings, affections, incli-
> nations, temper, habits, moral dispositions and natural impulses,
> without any remarkable [i.e.: observable] disorder or defect. . .
> [of the] knowing and reasoning faculties, and particularly without
> any insane illusion or hallucination.

The law was slow to recognize the psychopathic condition and was
less sure of how to deal with it, as it still is, while public opinion
remained skeptical. In 1885, the Russian lawyer, Belinsky, defending a
client in St. Petersburg, correctly described the psychopath as "an
individual whose every mental faculty appears to be of the normal
equilibrium. He thinks logically, distinguishes good and evil, and he
acts according to reason. But of all moral notions he is entirely devoid."
The British newspaper *Pall Mall Gazette* reacted to the report of the
case by commenting briskly:

...the short and long of it seems to be that if egotism is fully developed in a human being, he becomes "morally irresponsible," a very convenient doctrine, to which, however, mankind will have to add a corollary that wherever a fully developed psychopath is discovered he shall be immediately hanged.

It was a verdict agreeable to opinion of the day which applauded the execution in 1892 of a psychopathic doctor, Neil Cream, who poisoned prostitutes. "Nobody," *The Times* commented pontifically on hearing of the verdict:

...who had read the evidence can doubt the justice of his doom: all right-minded persons, as we believe, must experience a feeling of satisfaction that a villain so inhuman is soon to meet his deserts. . . there does exist amongst us a certain number of moral monsters whom it is the first duty of society to hunt down and to destroy.

But even the law has to adapt itself to changing conditions and new knowledge. In Britain, the Gowers Commission of 1949-53 allowed that psychopathic disorders could be a "necessary and legitimate" ingredient in the defense of criminals, making a caveat, however, that the concept of a psychopathic disorder was still so loose as to "provide a wastepaper basket for cases otherwise difficult to identify," an opinion which might be thought to be as applicable today as in 1950. The Canadian courts had also come to recognize the concept of psychopathic disorder as a legitimate defense, the Criminal Code Amendment Act of 1948 requiring two qualified psychiatrists to give evidence in such cases.

But it is important to observe that, although psychopathic disorders may be put forward as an ingredient in the defense of criminal cases, such disorders do not necessarily remit the accused's responsibility for his actions, nor *per se* should psychopathic disorder be identified with insanity. The psychopath's legal responsibility is not abolished, though in some cases it may appear diminished or impaired, yet not sufficiently to justify a verdict of not guilty by reason of insanity.

Outwardly psychopaths may well appear extraordinarily ordinary; they are nonetheless deeply disturbed individuals, unwilling to behave in accordance with accepted social norms. What is even more disturbing for society is the fact that there is no real treatment or cure for their condition. Their's is a disease of the mind — call it an antisocial personality disorder or what you will — which cannot be easily diagnosed, let alone cured. "Like a cancer, it grows in the dark. It grows in the inner recesses of the mind, its roots imbedded in early childhood. It is the AIDS of the mental health world."[5]

The psychopath does not necessarily become a criminal. He or she is a natural denizen of all societies, so much so that one African tribe, the Ik in mountainous Uganda, appear to be a psychopathic people, made so when in 1934 a game preserve was created which robbed them of their main source of livelihood, the hunting of animals. "They could not adjust and, within three generations, had turned into a group of cold, relatively isolated, selfish psychopaths."[6] Psychopaths can be the most dangerous of criminals, the most predatory of politicians or the most unscrupulous of businessmen. They can also be highly respected members of the community, whose psychopathic tendencies are for the most part screened from the public.

In a recent study of the film star Peter Sellers by his son Michael, Sellers appears as a man with psychopathic characteristics, a man with a deep sense of inferiority in spite of his fame, who gave way to savage tantrums when he failed to get what he wanted, sometimes with devastating effects on his private life. On one such occasion after a row with his children's nanny, he refused to stay in the house and left to spend the night at his club. "What the hell am I doing here?" he phoned his wife. "If anybody is going to leave, it's that bloody nanny." He returned home, took hold of a carving knife and thrust it into the nanny's bedroom door, shouting, "I'll kill you, you cow." The nanny, terrified by her employer, made her escape through the window.

The psychopath is a supreme con artist. A striking example of this is afforded by the career of Ferdinand Waldo Demara, Jr. After running away from a difficult home he tried first to become a Trappist monk and then a schoolteacher. He then faked his own death, took on the identity of a Dr. French, whose degrees and credentials he assumed, and became dean of a small Canadian college where he taught abnormal psychology before obtaining a commission in the Royal Canadian Navy. When he was a ship's doctor on the destroyer *Cayuga* during the Korean War, Demara was called on to perform surgical operations, which apparently he did with some success. Later he became a minister of religion.

The psychopath is a product of infancy and childhood. Although the hand of an adult may hold the gun, it is the mind of the child that pulls the trigger. Feeling no love as a child, the future psychopath develops only a warped capacity for affection. He will take what he wants, irrespective of other people, for he lacks any real sense of caring. Not all deprived children become psychopaths, though most psychopaths have a deprived childhood.

In Western societies it is generally assumed that children need the continuous loving care of both their parents if they are to fulfill themselves; in other societies such affection may be generated by a much wider family circle. But affection is nonetheless an essential ingredient for a child's future happiness. There are some examples of children, such as Itard's Wild Boy of Aveyron (in 1797), who have been reared by wild animals and have been wholly unable to communicate. Other children, kept for long periods in close confinement, have emerged mentally and emotionally retarded.

These are rare cases, but experimentation has shown that separation from parents or deprivation of affection can have catastrophic results in later life.[8] Children under three appear liable to feel later the effects of separation from their parents, especially if their relationships with their parent substitutes are unsatisfactory. The death of a relative who has shown affection, such as a father or grandfather, also has the effect of making a child especially vulnerable to delinquency. Recent research has shown that if a child experiences, for any length of time, the real or even the imagined hostility of parents, school or other authority, even those who seek to help him, he may well be disposed to become a violent delinquent. Such environments form the breeding ground for the future psychopath, as a case involving a Canadian youth, Vaughan Pollen from Winnipeg, clearly illustrates.

The boy's father left home when Pollen was fifteen, his mother neglected him, his elder brother bullied him. So he withdrew more and more into a world of his own, comforted by the loud and raucous heavy metal of the rock band KISS, the Knights in the Service of Satan. He cut out newspaper items on crime and violence and even compiled a log book of the insects he had killed. He found it exceedingly difficult to make school friends, and when one of the few he had made, Kenneth Maitland, appeared to reject him, Pollen went to school in October 1978 and shot him dead. Pollen's troubles were self-evidently rooted in his childhood and bleak upbringing.

After the child leaves the womb, he needs to replace his original biological roots by new affection, which provides him with protection and security. He needs a loving, warm relationship which will enable him to create a community of feeling with other people. If this is unavailable, he will live only to himself, evoking a life-thwarting syndrome. Socially inadequate, he will find it difficult to obtain or to keep a job. He will be unreliable and untruthful. He is apt to become self-centered and so narcissistic as to be incapable of giving people affection or of showing love.

Aggression becomes the release valve for the psychopath's pent-up emotions. Some of the crimes which he perpetrates will seem motiveless. In Bisbee, Arizona, in 1972, a sixteen-year-old student, Bernard J. Roth, shot his parents, both high-school teachers. When he was asked why, the boy — described by the county attorney as the "nicest boy you would want to meet" — replied, "The people are getting old. I'm not mad at them. I have no hostilities." However senseless the murder may appear to be, for the killer himself it has meaning, even if the meaning is symbolic and even unconscious.

The case of this boy killer may be compared with another psychopathic youth, Billy, a tiresome, ill-tempered boy who had tried to kill his sister with a butcher's knife when he was eleven because she refused to give him a ride in her car.[9] When he was at school in North Carolina he tried to kill a schoolteacher who had accused him of smoking in the toilet. The family moved to Maryland where a teacher tried to separate Billy from a girl with whom he seemed to be getting too intimate. So he went back home, grabbed a loaded rifle, returned to school, killed one teacher and shot and wounded two others. "I don't think," Billy said, "there is anything wrong with me. But when I get mad I'm nuts. I just want to kill." He showed some, but very few, signs of regret for what he had done. The encephalogram revealed no abnormalities in his brain pattern. The Rorshach Test did produce some explosive patterns, such as violent ink blots, but there seemed to be nothing fundamentally wrong. Eventually he was declared an antisocial delinquent and sent to an institution for psychiatric treatment.

In childhood and adolescence, we acquire ways of responding to the world, in thinking, feeling and reacting, in the light of our social experience. We are molded by the traditions, values and standards of behavior of the group to which we belong. Even in matters of deep individual impulse, such as sexual conduct, we are disciplined by society. The psychopath, however, operates according to a different set of values, if values they are, from those of the normal person, though he is not unaware that such values are both socially and legally unacceptable. What appears to be a perversion of the norm becomes, for him, a desired end, an ultimate objective, the only means by which his inner tensions can be released. In pursuit of a single desire or impulse, without conscience, he disregards everything except the object of his passionate need, and allows aggression to triumph over natural reason.

The annals of North American criminal history are replete with case histories of psychopathic killers. These murderers cause serious legal and medical dilemmas as to how to judge correctly the nature of their problems and how to distinguish between those who are responsible for what they do and those who are not. The cases which follow demonstrate the difficulties which confront lawyers and psychiatrists. They show also how the insanity defense has failed in cases of psychopathic murder, perhaps simply because, to use old-fashioned language, the psychopath is not a madman but a wicked person without a conscience.

A classic case is that of Dr. Holmes, born in 1860 in New Hampshire as Herman Webster Mudgett. A student at medical school involved in defrauding an insurance company by faking a patient's death, Holmes practised for eight years as a doctor in New York State. He also married. Then he moved to Chicago and graduated from petty crime to murder. His house had a chute down which his victims could be tossed into the basement, his rooms equipped with pipes by which they could be gassed. Holmes' killings, at least twenty-seven in all, were motivated by the desire for money, sex or for self-preservation, but there were even darker forces at work in his mind. Attracted by Cesare Lombroso's theory that it was possible to detect a criminal by his physical features, Holmes became convinced that one side of his face and body, the side governed by the right hemisphere of the brain, was, like Dorian Gray, showing signs of degeneracy, a theory which, in spite of the fact that Lombroso's ideas have been long discredited, seems actually to be borne out by Holmes' photograph.

There were peepholes in Holmes' rooms through which he could watch his victims die a painful and lingering death. One, Benjamin Pitezel, was tied up and burned with benzine. Then Holmes persuaded Pitezel's wife to let him take three of her children "to join their father" which, in a manner of speaking, was what they did. Holmes admitted that he had done what he did "for the pleasure of killing my fellow beings, to hear their cries for mercy and pleas to be allowed even sufficient time to pray."

Half a century later, William Heirens[10] of Chicago appeared on the scene. He was the pathological victim of a sexual obsession. He burgled houses to steal women's panties to help him masturbate, and came so to associate burglary with sexual satisfaction that even breaking into a house was sufficient to induce an orgasm. But if he found a woman in the room, he became violent, hitting and stabbing his victim. He was so aware of his passion that he once locked his clothes in his bathroom and threw away the key, but desire remained so strong that he crawled along the gutter of the roof to retrieve them. "For heaven's sake catch me before I kill more. I cannot control myself," he wrote on one of his victim's walls. Fortunately he was caught. In sentencing him, in 1946, the judge said that he was never to be released.

Another American psychopath of more recent date was the notorious Ted Bundy.[11] His antisocial personality disorder was rooted in early childhood, for he was born out of wedlock and until he went to college was led to believe that his elder sister was his mother. Charming and intelligent, Bundy won high praise from his professors, under whom he had studied psychology at the University of Washington, as a "very responsible and emotionally stable young man," a judgment made in 1972 within months of his first of some thirty or so murders. Between 1972 and 1978 he inveigled young girls into his possession by putting his arm in a sling or walking with crutches and, by pretending an injury, got them to unlock his car and induced them to get inside. Having abducted them, Bundy sexually assaulted and then killed them. In some cases he kept the corpse for some days, renewing the makeup and even shampooing the hair. After his sixteenth murder he was arrested for attempted kidnapping and sentenced to prison, but managed to escape through a hole in the ceiling. Bundy settled in Tallahassee where he claimed to be a graduate student at Florida State University. Within a few weeks of his arrival he had decimated the dormitories of a university sorority house. The body of his last victim, twelve-year-old Kimberly Leach, was discovered in a pig barn, half-eaten by predators. After his arrest,

Bundy, who once described himself as "the most cold-hearted son of a bitch you will ever meet," was astonished at the public outrage prompted by his murders. "What's one less person on the face of the earth anyway?" he asked.

The psychologists' reports were mixed. Professor Jorgenson of Utah University, where Bundy had been a law student, had earlier described him as a normal, intelligent young man with a "good, solid presence" and "positive self-identity." The encephalogram was "completely unremarkable," and there was no trace of any organic brain disease. At most Bundy was suspected of having some traits of an antisocial personality disorder. His defense argued that the evidence against him was circumstantial, until a dentist was able to demonstrate that the teeth marks on one of the buttocks of his victims corresponded with Bundy's own dental impact.

Bundy talked of having another self inside or apart from himself which was the responsible agent, "a disordered self." When he was sentenced to death, he observed, "I cannot accept the sentence, because it is not a sentence to me... it is a sentence to someone else who is not standing here today." "Take care of yourself, young man," the judge said in sentencing him to death, "you went the wrong way, partner." In practice there was an indefinite stay of execution; and Bundy turned to the study of Buddhism and oriental mysticism while he dictated, using the third person, his autobiography.

For reasons which are obscure, but which may be sociological in origin, the United States seems to be more commonly the hunting-ground for the psychopath, but there are ample examples in European and British criminal history.[12]

The Alsatian, Jean Baptiste Troppman, born in 1869, bullied by his father, became a homosexual and a loner, though so handsome and strong that he was admired by the Russian novelist Turgenev, who accompanied him to the scaffold in 1889. Troppman had made the acquaintance of a rich businessman, Monsieur Kinck. He dosed Kinck's wine with cyanide and buried him in a neighboring forest; his son, whom he stabbed, joined his father. Troppman then asked Madame Kinck, with her five other children, to go with him to meet her husband. Outside Paris, at Pantin where Monsieur Kinck was supposed to be staying, Troppman killed off the remainder of the family. He was arrested at Le Havre, where he was hoping to take a boat to sail to America with the money which he had managed to extract from the

Kincks. The murders showed a strong element of sadism, but what was the most astonishing thing about them was Troppman's obsession with a contemporary novel, Eugene Sue's horrific tale of the underworld, *The Wandering Jew*, which seems to have much influenced his outlook. Nearly a century later, another psychopath, David Mark Chapman, shot John Lennon in New York, in part because of his obsession with J.D. Salinger's novel, *The Catcher in the Rye*. Salinger stressed the naiveté of childhood imperiled by the spurious, adult world. In Chapman's mind Lennon stood for the loss of innocence and the triumph of phony adulthood.

An intriguing combination of greed and killing for killing's sake drove a Swedish doctor, Sigvard Thurnemann, to a career of murder in the 1930s. Specializing in nervous diseases, he was bisexual and a student of the occult. Superficially his motive was robbery, from the proceeds of which Thurnemann hoped to emigrate to South America. In some instances he had availed himself of information from the patients whom he counseled in order to attack them. Under hypnosis, a patient, Mrs. Blomqvist had told him where she kept her jewelry. Thurnemann made a hole in her bedroom wall — the house was built of timber — into which he placed a rubber hose. The hose was then attached to the exhaust of his car, so that Mrs. Blomqvist was gassed while she slept. After her jewels had been abstracted, the house was set on fire. Thurnemann was sentenced to imprisonment for life, but later went mad.

Finally we may take the cases of four British psychopaths, perhaps the more interesting because in each case it was strongly argued that they were insane, and in each the defense failed to establish its case. The courts ruled that, though psychopathic, these murderers appreciated the nature and consequences of their crimes and were, therefore, guilty of first-degree murder.

In June 1946, Neville George Heath,[13] a personable young man with fair, wavy hair, who had long been involved in petty crime and who for various offenses had been court-martialed and dismissed from the armed services, murdered a prostitute, a Mrs. Marjory Gardner, at a London hotel, the Pembridge Court. It was a particularly vicious attack. When the chambermaid discovered Mrs. Gardner's body the next day, she was lying on the bed savagely maltreated, the body whipped, the buttocks lashed with a plaited thong, the nipples practically bitten off and the private parts brutally lacerated. She had been suffocated with a pillow.

Heath left London for an English south-coast resort, Worthing, where he took rooms at a hotel as Group Captain Rupert Brooke. From there he wrote a curious letter to the police headquarters at Scotland Yard in London, admitting that the room in which Mrs. Gardner had been found was his, but alleging that he had let it out to a client of the woman, and had only returned at three the next morning to find her "in the condition of which you are aware." Much worried, as he said, by his compromising position, he had left the hotel. He had already met another lady friend, a Mrs. Doreen Marshall, who had come to recuperate at Worthing from an attack of flu. Heath offered to accompany her back to her hotel which, however, she was never to reach, for her body was found under some rhododendron bushes in Branksome Chine, naked except for her left shoe, maltreated like that of Mrs. Gardner, slashed at least four times with a knife.

Heath's defending counsel, J.D. Casswell, put forward a plea of partial insanity. The psychiatrist, Dr. Hubert, argued that although Heath knew what he was doing, he did not know that what he was doing was wrong, and in consequence Dr. Hubert believed him to be certifiable as morally insane. This led to a crisp and illuminating dialogue between Dr. Hubert and the prosecuting counsel, Anthony Hawke.

HAWKE: At the time he was inflicting those injuries he thought it was right.

HUBERT: Yes, he thought it was right.

HAWKE: Did he think it was right, in your opinion, because he is a perverted sadist?

HUBERT: Yes.

HAWKE: Because he could only obtain his sexual satisfaction by inflicting cruelty, you say he thought it was right, do you?

HUBERT: Yes, I do.

HAWKE: Are you saying, with your responsibility, standing there, that a person in that frame of mind is free from criminal responsibility if he does grievous bodily harm?

HUBERT: At the time, yes.

As in so many other cases there was a clash of medical expert opinion, for the senior medical officer at Brixton Prison argued that although Heath was self-evidently a pervert and a sadist, neither sadism nor sexual frenzy were themselves sufficient evidence for insanity. Heath was sentenced to death and hanged on 20 October 1946. While everyone agreed that he had suffered from "abnormality of character and temperament," this did not exculpate him from responsibility for the murders he had committed. Heath had felt a powerful need to assert himself, expressed, for instance, in his calling himself an air force officer and in his alluding, without any basis in fact, to his noble connections. Concentrated egocentricity ultimately had led to sadistic killings.

Prima facie John George Haigh[14] murdered for gain, but the method of his murders and his general attitude towards them suggest a deeply disturbed personality. He was strictly brought up; his parents were members of an exclusive religious sect, the Plymouth Brethren, who banned newspapers and the radio, and would not allow him to take part in any sport or entertainment. He became a chorister at Wakefield Cathedral, but reacting against his background, Haigh entered into a life of petty crime and served a number of prison sentences for obtaining money on false pretenses.

After his release from prison, Haigh met William Donald McSwan in a pub and invited him round to his apartment at 79 Gloucester Road, Kensington. There, he killed him with a blow to the head and lifted his dead body into a water-butt which he had previously filled with sulphuric acid. After the body had decomposed, Haigh poured the residual fluid down a manhole. He was to rid himself, in a similar fashion, of McSwan's parents the following summer, appropriating their property to the value of four thousand pounds. Haigh now believed that he had found the clue to the perfect murder, for if there was no body there could hardly be a crime.

Haigh made the acquaintance of Dr. Henderson, a retired Scots doctor (in the purchase of whose house he showed interest), invited him down to Crawley in Sussex where he was employed, shot him in the head and placed him in a barrel of sulphuric acid. Henderson's wife, Rosalie, was persuaded to come to Crawley on the pretense that her husband had been taken ill, and suffered the same fate. Haigh, who marked these various occasions in his diary by making a little red cross on the appropriate day, then disposed of the Hendersons' property to the value of eight thousand pounds.

He soon frittered the money away gambling and was pressed by the Onslow Court Hotel, where he was staying, to settle his bill. Haigh had made friends with Mrs. Durand-Deacon, a fellow hotel guest and an elderly widow, who happened to mention to him that she had thought of a scheme for manufacturing plastic fingernails and wanted to find someone who might be ready to promote the idea. Haigh leapt at the proposal and invited her down to his factory at Crawley where she suffered the same fate as the Hendersons and McSwans. When, after breakfast the next morning, a friend of Mrs. Durand-Deacon's told Haigh that she was worried by her non-appearance, he went with her to Chelsea police station to report it. Mrs. Durand-Deacon's jewelry, of which he had disposed, led the police to Haigh himself, and so to the factory at Crawley where they dredged the sludge from the barrels of sulphuric acid and recovered the few remains of the unfortunate widow, her false teeth and some bits of bone.

After his arrest Haigh decided that it would be in his best interest to plead insanity. "Tell me frankly," he asked a police officer, "what are the chances of anyone being released from Broadmoor [the English criminal lunatic asylum]?" He pretended that he had been carrying out God's orders, that the nightmares of blood which he experienced could only have been placated by the sacrifice of his victims. To support his plea of insanity he behaved in such a way as to persuade others that he really was mad, gloating over his murders, adding a certain number of imaginary victims and boasting of drinking their blood as well as his own urine.

It is an open question as to how much of this was artifice, but there was much to suggest that Haigh was a calculating criminal rather than a creature of impulse. His early murders were motivated by greed, but greed seems ultimately to have become subsidiary to the act of killing as the motive force. In Mrs. Durand-Deacon's case all that he had actually acquired as a result of murdering her was a Persian lamb coat, a watch, which he subsequently sold for ten pounds, and some odd trinkets. His attitude towards his victims was cold and callous, without a trace of remorse. In the process of disposing of Mrs. Durand-Deacon he had interrupted his horrid work to enjoy an egg on toast at a local restaurant in Crawley. The expert psychiatrist who was called on his behalf, Dr. Henry Yellowlees, claimed that early formative influences on Haigh's life had led to the development of a paranoic condition which meant that he was not wholly responsible for his actions.

The prosecution rebutted the arguments strongly. "I am asking you," Sir Hartley Shawcross said, addressing Dr. Yellowlees, "to look at the facts and tell the jury whether there is any doubt that he must have known that, according to English law, he was preparing to do, and subsequently had done, something which was wrong?" "I will say yes," Dr. Yellowlees replied, "to that if you say 'punishable by law' instead of 'wrong'." "Punishable by law," Shawcross responded triumphantly, "and therefore, wrong by the law of the country." "Yes," Yellowlees agreed reluctantly, "I think he knew that." The admission was enough, for it demonstrated by the M'Naghten Rules that Haigh was not insane, but a psychopath who appreciated the nature and consequences of his actions, and he was accordingly executed at Wandsworth prison on 6 August 1949.

Like Heath and Haigh, Reginald Halliday Christie seemed to live an outwardly normal life.[15] Like Haigh he had been strictly brought up and like them both he had a number of police convictions, mainly for larceny, but also one for maliciously wounding a prostitute with whom he had been living. But, unlike the others, he had a mental history, marked by severe headaches and depressions, which resulted in a nervous breakdown. It was after returning from the hospital that Christie strangled his wife. He explained that she had been suffering from convulsions and that he decided to bring her life to an end. "So I got a stocking and tied it round her neck to put her to sleep." He disposed of her body by placing it under the floorboards which seemed, he said, to be the best place "to put her to rest." In the course of time she was to be joined by three other women. Christie brought his victims home, got them drunk, strangled them and masturbated over their dead bodies. He then put them under the floorboards. After he had killed one of the women, he put her in a deck chair in the kitchen, left her there all night, washed and shaved and had his breakfast while she was sitting there the next morning. It was only after Christie left his home at 10 Rillington Place in London, that the new tenant, tapping the walls to fix a radio, found an alcove in which some of the grisly remains rested.

At the subsequent trial, in 1953, Christie, who said he would have continued to murder had he not been caught, pleaded insanity. The psychiatrists were divided. The defense psychiatrist, Dr. Hobson, thought that Christie suffered from a hysteric condition which, under the M'Naghten Rules, would have qualified as a mental disease. He did not, Dr. Hobson thought, know that what he was doing was wrong. Christie's memory seemed impaired as though he found it unpleasant to recall the details, nor did his stories always add up. Dr. Matheson, for the Crown, held that Christie had an inadequate personality and behaved abnormally under stress, showing some signs of what would later be termed a dissociated personality. Dr. Curran agreed that Christie was an "inadequate psychopath with hysterical features" but did not regard him as insane. Perhaps the psychiatrists' evidence was irrelevant, for he was found guilty and hanged.

The death penalty had been abolished in England before Dennis Nilsen came before the English courts in 1983. He was a multiple killer whose crimes were peculiarly sordid and unpleasant, some of the details of which, repellent as they are, help to explain the complexities of the psychopathic personality.[16] On Thursday, 4 February 1983, one of the tenants of a rooming house at 23 Cranley Gardens in the London suburb of Muswell Hill, found that the toilet was blocked. As all efforts to liberate the drains proved futile, she called in a firm of experts, Dyno-rod, who came the following Tuesday evening. Their representative was appalled by the stench from the sewer, very different from that of excrement, and was puzzled by a kind of layer of porridge at its base, which seemed to be composed of pieces of discolored flesh. As it was getting late, he decided to leave a closer inspection to the next morning.

The tenant of the third-floor flat, Dennis Nilsen, a quiet, thirty-eight-year-old loner, was distinctly put out by this piece of news, as indeed he had need to be, for at the same time he had been sedulously seeking to rid himself of the remains of his last victim, Stephen Sinclair, whom he had strangled a few days earlier. He was boiling his head in a large pot on the gas stove and severing his body into segments for disposal down the toilet. In the night Nilsen walked softly down the stairs, opened the manhole and removed some of the sludge which he dumped over a hedge. He planned to go to the supermarket to buy chicken pieces so that they could be substituted for the human flesh. Time, however, was running short, and closer investigation made it possible to retrieve just sufficient human remains from the sewer to justify the arrest of Nilsen. When he arrived at Hornsey police station, P.C. McCusker asked him, "Are we talking about one body or two?" to which Nilsen replied, "Fifteen or sixteen, since 1978. I'll tell you everything. It is a relief to be able to get it all off my mind." If it was a relief, neither then nor later did Nilsen show any real sign of remorse.

Dennis Nilsen was a Scot by birth, son of a Fraserburgh woman and her Norwegian husband. He grew up a very lonely child, fond of his grandfather whose death, when he was six years old, apparently made a profound impact on his mind. He never had a close relationship with his mother, resenting her marriage to a second husband, and liked nothing better than to wander off by himself. At fifteen Nilsen enlisted in the army and served overseas where he first found an outlet for his homosexual inclinations. He ended up in the Army Catering Corps with the rank of corporal. When Nilsen came out of the army in 1972, he served for a year with the police force, but finding it less companionable than the army, he resigned. In any case, his private life, as he drifted from one gay bar to another, from the Coleherne in Earl's Court to the King William IV in Hampstead and the Salisbury in St. Martin's Lane, was hardly suitable for a member of the constabulary. Eventually Nilsen found a position in the civil service at the Job Centre on Denmark Street where he worked industriously, though any sort of promotion was slow in coming, in part because of his quick temper, his active involvement in the civil-service union and rumors of his homosexuality.

Basically, Nilsen was a very lonely man, his mongrel dog Bleep, the only real outlet for his emotions. An attempt at companionate living with a younger man proved too fragile to last. What Nilsen wanted was companionship, but a companionship that was passive rather than active, something to look at, an article to be possessed.

On 30 December 1978 he picked up an Irish youth and took him home to 195 Melrose Avenue.

> I was afraid to wake him in case he left me. Trembling with fear,
> I strangled his struggling body and when he was dead, I took his
> young body back to bed with me and it was the beginning of the
> end of my life as I had known it. I had started down the avenue
> of death and possession of a new kind of flat-mate.

The nameless Irish youth was the first of some eleven or so victims whom Nilsen strangled at Melrose Avenue, and there were three others at Cranley Gardens, apart from seven attempts where he either failed or the intended victim got away. Most of the victims were young men, often homeless drifters; only one was very different, a young Canadian tourist, Kenneth Ockenden, from Burlington, Ontario, who had been due to fly back to Canada the next day.

What were the driving forces behind Nilsen's actions? Clearly he had necrophiliac tendencies. Even as a young man he would spend hours contemplating his own naked body in the mirror, his face painted white, his lips blue, modelled as a corpse. Yet, though Nilsen was a homosexual whose murders were associated with sexual fulfillment, he did not kill his victims because he wanted to have sex with their dead bodies. Rather, he seems instead to have killed for company; he wanted to keep his human prey with him as passive companions in his power and possession. Indeed, after the act of murder, Nilsen became gentle. He washed the bodies carefully, laid them on the bed or sat them in a chair and even talked to them. He only attempted sex with six of them, either intercrurally or by masturbating on their stomachs, apparently never by penetration. He kept his dead companions until they began to putrefy, forcing him to consign their rotting corpses, so he thought, to oblivion.

Nilsen disposed of the bodies in the first instance by putting them under the floorboards, sometimes steaming off the flesh in a giant cauldron on the stove, dismembering them and, at Melrose Gardens, burning them in huge bonfires in the garden, countering the objectionable smell by burning rubber tires. At Cranley Gardens he flushed the remains down the toilet, and it was the blocking of the drains which led to the discovery of the murders and Nilsen's subsequent arrest.

At his trial the defense counsel argued that Nilsen was suffering from a severe but unspecified personality disorder, identified, however, by one witness as a borderline personality disorder. The psychiatric evidence proved, however, to be confused and contradictory and the prosecution had no difficulty in showing that within limits Nilsen was intelligent, cunning and deliberate in his actions. It was a case of human wickedness. "I probably," Nilsen confessed later, "did enjoy those acts of killing." He knew both what he was doing and its potential consequences. By a majority verdict of ten to two he was found guilty of murder six times and of attempted murder twice. He was sentenced to life imprisonment with a recommendation that he should serve a minimum of twenty-five years. Nilsen, so the court concluded, had killed in cold blood to satisfy his perverted desires. Mr. Justice Croom-Johnson commented, "Is a cold-blooded killer not responsible for his acts?...A mind can be evil without being abnormal. There are evil people who do evil things. Committing murder is one of them."

Where in this horrific gallery of psychopathic murderers does Andrew Leyshon-Hughes stand? The more conventional psychopath is a much lesser figure than those we have been considering, like Harry,[17] the son of a brutal father and a young ineffective mother, who found it difficult to make friends and whose life was punctuated by acts of mindless violence. Harry courted a girl, and when she refused his date he bought a knife to kill her, but the plan miscarried. He went in and out of prison and eventually died at a youthful age by swallowing five open safety pins.

Andrew is not a multiple murderer nor is he as pathetic a figure as Harry but many of the features which are characteristic of the psychopathic murderer certainly seem to appear in him. Heath's brutal murder of his victims bears comparison with the vehement stabbing of Nancy. The necrophiliacs, Christie and Nilsen, carried on their daily lives in the presence of their dead victims, as did Andrew, with apparent detachment and no sign of remorse. Andrew is much younger than most of those we have been describing. But what of his personal makeup and motives? To what extent do these fit the description of the psychopath? Was Nancy's murder as motiveless as it was made out to be, or were there tendencies, psychopathic in character, which were not wholly irrational or completely outside Andrew's control, which reappeared that grim Monday morning on Farnham Avenue?

XII

—— A QUESTION OF GUILT ——

Were such things here as we do speak about?
Or have we eaten on the insane root
That takes the reason prisoner?

SHAKESPEARE, MACBETH

Piece out our imperfections with your thoughts.

SHAKESPEARE, *HENRY V*

THE TRIAL OVER, THE COURT HAD dispersed, satisfied that it had done its work well. The prosecution had crumpled, evidently convinced that its acquiescence with the defense's arguments was justified. Professor Ervin returned to Montreal, doubtlessly convinced that his theories had now been vindicated in practice. Clayton Ruby, an acknowledged master of the insanity defense, became the focal point of congratulations for his Ciceronian performance. His defense of Andrew, a masterpiece of jurisprudence and trial preparation, had procured the verdict which his clients had been eager for him to obtain. Andrew himself expressed his gratitude for having finally found out what was wrong with him. His family, shamed as they had been by Nancy's murder, could escape the stigma of having produced a first-degree murderer. Andrew, so the court ruled, was a sick young man, not responsible for his actions, who could be expected to respond to treatment, and with good conduct, whatever the judge said in his summing-up, might well resume a place in society within a few years. It was a satisfaction which the media, too, by and large shared.

But was there any real justification for such satisfaction? When the case opened Paul Chumak had argued strongly that Nancy's murder had been a sadistic psychopathic killing, sexual in its motivation. The defense countered this charge by contending that it was a murder without a motive which could only be accounted for in terms of a severe mental aberration rooted in a brain dysfunction and its sequel, a personality disorder. "That," Mr. Justice Callaghan observed, "is a disease of the mind, rendering him incapable of appreciating the nature and quality of the act, or knowing that the act is wrong."

But how deeply, in fact, had the problems of Andrew's personality been probed? Is Andrew Leyshon-Hughes really insane or, rather, is he someone without a conscience, what in old-fashioned terms might be described as evil? Was justice sidetracked? We will let the reader decide.

Much of the evidence placed before the court were matters of opinion rather than matters of fact. "Some of the material here," Clayton Ruby put it to Dr. Orchard, "is not factual observation but opinion." Orchard agreed, adding that it was customary in the field of psychiatry to study others' opinions.

> You as a juror [Mr. Justice Callaghan said in his opening address to the jury] must bear in mind that what is being adduced is a psychiatric opinion and the doctor will be asked what he looked at and what he relied on, and that will be taken into consideration by you in arriving at your conclusion. . . . you are the judges of the facts and how much weight you attach to a psychiatrist's [opinion] will be for you [to decide].

In some instances opinion seemed closer to speculation. Much was made of the trivial fact that Andrew was hard to wake in the morning, got up unwillingly and seemed for some time in a semi-dazed state. "He would," his father told the court, "go through the dressing process in a cloud to the point that when he came downstairs for breakfast, we would point out that shirt doesn't go with that sweater." As persuasive as this might be in the context of counsel's argument, such teenage behavior is familiar to many a household.

Fundamental to the defense's case was the hypothesis that Andrew suffered from brain damage which could give rise to personality problems and violent behavior. It was so central to the defense's case that, as Dr. Jensen said in his evidence, if there was no brain dysfunction the diagnosis of a personality disorder would not in itself prevent Andrew from having the capacity to know what he was doing and to distinguish right from wrong. In Andrew's case it was argued that there had been brain damage at birth, even though it was eighteen years before any attention was drawn to this as a possible explanation for his behavioral problems. It was never proved and there was no hint of real trouble at birth. Although Dr. Orchard was entitled to speculate on the meagre information in the hospital records, actual evidence for the brain damage was sparse and inferential. Contrariwise, the "maternal result," according to the Obstetrical Summary Sheet, was "good" and on the Newborn Nursery Chart the "diagnostic impression" was listed as "normal newborn." When, minutes after Andrew was born, Mrs. Leyshon-Hughes asked the doctors if "...everything was okay...they said 'Yes, yes, don't worry about anything'." Some years later Dr. Hackney ruled out the possibility that Andrew had suffered brain damage. "He had," she said, "a normal birth." Another medical record dated 10 August 1976, stated that the "condition at birth [was] good." Dr. Vera Bril reported that Andrew's EEG was perfectly normal and that it revealed nothing that would suggest any grounds for organic brain dysfunction or impairment. It seems fair to say that brain damage — and Andrew showed no signs of temporal-lobe epilepsy — had not been absolutely authenticated. Even if some slight damage had occurred, it is impossible to measure either its incidence or significance.

For all the research done by neurologists and psychologists the brain still remains a mystery, a continent that is only partly mapped, on which theologians and philosophers, doctors and other scientists have planted flags to denote the areas of the territories they claim. But, like the distant planets of the universe, there remain impenetrable tracts where only a glimmer of light from time to time illuminates the obscure terrain. Like the universe itself, for all the unprecedented progress in exploration made in the twentieth century, much of the brain remains virgin territory. "Many of the facts about the brain," Professor Ervin has written, "are unknown or just beginning to emerge after years of intensive research."

There is a deeper, even insoluble problem:

> "The mind," according to Dr. Patrick McGeer, professor of neurological sciences at the University of British Columbia, "is abstract, and the brain is physical. We can tell what parts of the brain and what biochemistry of the brain lead to the abstract, but I don't think we can probe the mysteries of the abstract at all..." That is because the human mind and personality arise out of the awesomely complicated interplay between an individual's brain cells and his or her experience of life — the teeming flow of sounds, shapes and colors, of promises, pleasures and pain that impinge on the human organism from the moment of birth.... "The brain is seemingly put together in a rigid way," says Vincent Castellucci, director of neurobiology and behaviour at the Clinical Research Institute of Montreal. "But the quality of the brain's connections is modified by experience.... Just by talking to someone, I am modifying some of that person's synapses."[1]

The human brain has evolved through many millennia. It incorporates three features: the reptilian, the mammalian and the neo-cortex, which came with the development of man. In reptiles such as the crocodile — hence the press' attribution of the term "crocodile man" to Andrew — the primitive brain, the limbic brain, is dominant. Violence and impulsive action are likely to be governed by the structure of the limbic brain. In normal conditions such impulses are controlled and regulated by the human brain or neo-cortex. But the brain is so delicately poised an instrument that its mechanism can be easily disturbed. The writer Arthur Koestler observed that mankind was a "naturally unbalanced species" in whom the rational faculty could be very easily put at risk.

For some years there has been increasing interest among neurologists and criminologists in what has been termed a "dyscontrol syndrome," basically a disordered impulse, rooted in a brain dysfunction, which gives rise to behavioral abnormalities. A survey of 105 murderers carried out in 1952 showed that half of them had abnormal EEGs. Injuries or illnesses which produced special lesions in the brain, damaging the cerebral cortex, clearly gave rise to acts of aggression. In the 1920s, following an epidemic of sleeping sickness, children suffering from this brain infection became disturbed and violent.

In 1970, Professor Frank Ervin, then director of the Stanley Cobb Laboratories for Psychiatric Research at the Massachusetts General Hospital, with Dr. Vernon H. Mark published a study, *Violence and the Brain*. The authors argued that violent and irrational behavior were a very likely sequel to brain damage, the symptoms of which could not be easily detected. In such cases the limbic brain, activated by events within the victim's environment, took over, causing mindless violence.

Dr. Ervin illustrated his argument by referring to the case of a young patient, Julia,[2] who as a two-year-old had had a brain infection as a result of an attack of mumps. She became prone to explosions of seemingly unprovoked violence, of which, however, she seemed to have had some forewarning. Accompanying her parents to the cinema, she felt she was going to have another of what she called her "racing spells." She went to the ladies' room, automatically taking a knife out of her handbag. When she looked at herself in the mirror, the left side of her face seemed to her disfigured and "evil." When another girl came into the room and accidentally bumped against her, Julia plunged the knife into the girl's heart. Fortunately help arrived to save her life. At the hospital where Julia was taken for psychiatric treatment she told the nurse who was writing a report, "I feel another spell coming on, please help me." "I'll be with you in a minute," the nurse replied but before the minute had passed, Julia had taken a pair of scissors from the nurse's pocket and driven them into her lungs. Medical tests showed difficulties with her memory structure and her brain scan indicated some abnormalities. She also had epileptic features. She was operated upon, a neural surgeon removing her amygdalae (limbic nerve tissue involved in aggression), and afterwards she suffered only from mild outbursts of rage.

Violence and the Brain made wide claims, suggesting that brain damage was a significant factor, not merely in unprovoked violence, but also in hard drinking, impulsive sex and reckless driving. "It is likely," Ervin and Mark wrote, "that more than ten million Americans suffer from an obvious brain disease, and the brains of perhaps another five million have been subtly damaged." Which one of us is safe? Clayton Ruby described the book as an "absolutely seminal and crucial work for everybody in this field," but a critic wrote of its main theme that "it was not a clearly defined syndrome because most of its manifestations are in part socially determined," and that "the data to support these hypotheses are as yet rather flimsy."[3]

More specifically, in attributing attacks of unprovoked and sporadic violence to brain damage the authors had alluded to the damage which could be sustained at birth through loss of oxygen[4] (sometimes due to excessive anaesthesia) and prolonged reduction in blood sugar, endangering the limbic system. Such damage might be later expressed in an inability to control bowels and bladder, in "impulsive hyperactivity resistent to social control," making the child "indiscriminately aggressive and impulsively violent."

Whether or not the authors had overstated their case, Andrew Leyshon-Hughes must well have seemed to Professor Frank Ervin a classic textbook example of the thesis which, with Dr. Mark, he had developed nearly two decades earlier. It can hardly be denied that many of the features which characterized Andrew's life seemed to fit their theory. But as Ervin admitted, it is extremely difficult to establish scientifically that damage has been done to the limbic system.[5] The diagnosis has to be based on behavior patterns which give rise to apparent "dyscontrol" or "ego rupture." So, in Andrew's case, it was impossible to prove beyond question the hypothesis of a brain dysfunction.

Two questions can now be fairly put, both fundamental to Andrew's guilt. Did Andrew know what he was doing that Monday morning? Why was he doing it? Was the crime, in other words as motiveless and as pointless as it was made out to be? A psychopath, who is responsible for his actions, has a motive, however warped it might appear.

Did Andrew know what he was doing? On this point the defense witnesses did not seem to be absolutely sure of their answers. Fundamentally they agreed that even if Andrew knew how he was behaving, he did not know that in plunging the knife into Nancy he was killing her. Professor Ervin compared Andrew's action to that of a small child stabbing at his mother, saying as he did so, "'I hate you, I hate you. I want you to die.' A two-year-old doesn't know what that means. . . . The kid seems to know what he is talking about. But, it is too complex. They don't know what they are talking about." Andrew, Ervin observed, might or might not have known that he had a knife in his hand, but, "I don't think he thought it was a carrot." Dr. Orchard went even further to say that Andrew definitely knew that it was a knife. Both maintained, as did their colleagues, that although Andrew remembered what he did, he was unaware at the time that in stabbing Nancy he was likely to cause her death. Andrew, they said, was acting like a zombie. But if Andrew knew that he had a knife in his hand and that he was plunging it into Nancy's body, the blood spurting over him as well as her, surely he must have been to some extent aware of his actions. "He registered," Ervin said, "clearly what he was doing."

But if he was aware of his actions, did he know what he was doing was wrong, both in terms of law and conscience? The defense argued that Andrew was in a dissociative state, so that his actions were automatic and involuntary. The dissociative state represents a "disorder of consciousness as a result of part of the nervous system shutting off," leading to a state of semi-automatism.

The concept of the dissociated state has long had an appeal for writers. It appears in the stories of Edgar Allan Poe and is classically depicted in R.L. Stevenson's *The Strange Case of Dr. Jekyll and Mr. Hyde*.

> It was [Dr. Jekyll exclaims] on the moral side, and in my own person, that I learned to recognise the thorough and primitive duality of man. I saw that of the two natures that contended in the field of my consciousness, even if I could rightly be said to be either, it was only because I was radically both.

"Every human being," George Beard wrote, "lives two lives, the voluntary, in which he acts more or less under the control of the will and the involuntary, in which he acts automatically, and over which the will has but limited power or none at all." According to Dr. Jensen:

> [I think Andrew] was aware of what he was doing but unable to stop what he was doing. . . . I think he was aware of the fact that he was striking out with a knife, and I think that he was following along cognitively what was taking place and it's as though he was outside of himself watching himself doing it.

"He described it," Orchard said, "almost like a third party...as though he were watching somebody else doing it. His mind and his conscience were in suspense. He was like a man watching a scene on television in which he happened to be the actor on the screen."

What the defense psychiatrist failed to take into account, however, is that dissociation, such as occurs in sleepwalking, a diabetic coma or an epileptic seizure, invariably involves amnesia, whereas Andrew had photographic recall of his actions, even in matters of detail such as noting the time on Nancy's television clock when he got up. The fact that Andrew remembered the events of that early morning argues strongly for believing that he knew at that time what he was doing.

In the last resort, Andrew's mental state has to be interpreted within the general context of his life and character, and the evidence in this respect certainly suggests that Andrew was no mere automaton at moments of crisis in his life, but possessed a degree of choice, and so of control, over what he did.

In his evidence Dr. Ervin admitted that Andrew "would be able to make choices." Chumak put the question:

> [as to whether] he could make choices — if something was attractive to him — in this case, if a woman was sexually attractive to him, would he be able to choose to make that choice, to be with her and to be with her in a violent way — to be close to her physically, sexually and in a violent way?

Ervin agreed that this was feasible but countered by stating that consciousness, observation and choice were all part of the primitive instinct. Yet if choice is part of the primitive crocodile brain, it is at least arguable that Andrew could have chosen not to murder Nancy.

"Andrew knows," the neurologist Dr. Anderson reported in 1983, "what he is doing during these temper outbursts." He was capable of making choices. Indeed in Andrew's previous so-called psychotic episodes there had nearly always been some occurrence, however low-key, which had acted as a trigger. These episodes were not inconsequential but activated within the environment. In Dr. Anderson's words, "he has an unpredictable temper, always seemingly provoked." His previous acts of violence represented an intelligible reaction to wrongs which he fancied he had suffered: neglect at home, rebukes at school, the rejection of his affection by his girlfriend at school and Lisa Orsatti. We do not know precisely what caused the incident at Andrew's uncle's house but it could easily have been teasing by the children, by the rebuke which his aunt was to administer to him, or even by something which had happened at school. His uncle's house and Nancy's apartment became, in his mind, outreaches of home rather than sanctuaries from it. His violence formed a coded message to the outside world but understandably the outside world could not decipher it. Children who find it difficult to articulate their feelings and who possess limited linguistic competence, frequently do "act out" their grievances rather than discuss them with their parents or others in authority whom they regard with hostility.

Andrew did over-react — that was part of his problem — but his reactions were, within the framework of his own patterns of thought, intelligible, even logical. What he did seems to have been rooted in a known situation of which he was aware, the consequences of which he may well have realized, even if he was unwilling to take them into account. It seems at least possible that what he did was sparked off by something he felt, which was neither wholly meaningless nor involuntary and that he chose to do what he did, because at the time that was what he wanted to do.

There is, moreover, a further point in relation to these earlier episodes which may have some bearing on Nancy's murder. It was pointed out that many of Andrew's actions were senseless because he was bound to be caught. But smartness is not a necessary or even a frequent component in criminal mentality; if it were so, far fewer criminals could be caught. The criminal has many of the attributes of the child; criminality, it has been said, is a combination of egoism, infantilism and sex. The child takes what he wants without considering the consequences. That Andrew was emotionally immature can hardly be doubted.

The earlier episodes were not senseless in that they lacked an objective, however bizarre the object may appear. There was a recurrent pattern of sorts. Many involved driving a car away from the city, which he had come to identify with failure and unhappiness. The country stood for peace, tranquility and joy, and in particular the family home in the Muskokas where he first met Nancy. Imprinted strongly in his mind was his affection for his grandfather John Osler, though he had died seven years earlier. Andrew continued to identify the Osler summer home with the harmony which escaped him but for which, in some muddled sense, he was looking. The Elysium which he sought was an illusion, but the pursuit of it was not wholly illusory. His last act as a free man was to drive Nancy's own car northwards.

The defense stressed that the violent episodes which recurred in Andrew's life were not merely pointless but that Andrew was himself acting as a sort of automaton with no rational control over his actions. Yet in fact there seems to have been a strong element of calculation and common sense. His motive was explicit enough. "I struck out against them [his parents] by getting myself in shit." When, in September

1981, he took his parents' car to his grandmother's summer home, he took care to sweep up the glass from the broken window through which he had entered. When history repeated itself two years later, Andrew had sufficient sense to get help to free the car from the snow when it skidded on the ice, and to use his father's credit card to buy gas. He held up the storekeeper at Balsam because he had run out of cigarettes. When he went berserk at the Jephcotts, Andrew chose *not* to shoot Amy and took care to destroy only his own possessions and left his aunt's untouched. "He took the desk drawer and was throwing things. I noticed that anything that was ours, he didn't break. . . . If he took a pencil out and he thought that it was ours, he did not break it." When Andrew was at Penetang, there was no recurrence of these violent episodes. After he stole Bill Jephcott's car and ran away from the police, Andrew went to the tennis club and phoned his parents, saying, "I guess you guys think you're pretty smart." After the murder he systematically stripped, showered and tried to wash away the blood from the soiled garments. Andrew exercised great care in tracing Nancy's signature before he forged the check. These episodes were threaded by a realistic common sense that one would not expect to find in someone in the grip of a so-called dissociative state.

Many of his peers, who found him an agreeable companion, refused to believe that Andrew was mad. "From all the time I've known him, he seemed to be okay," Wayne Erwin commented. "I know he's not nuts. . . He was just a normal guy." "He was a nice guy," said Gary Fox, who worked at Toby's. "He wasn't loud or anything, he was the type who would just sit down and shoot the shit. . . . When I found out about it, I couldn't believe it. It just blows you away. He was just a normal kid." "I was really shocked," was Lori McConnach's reaction. "He didn't seem like that kind of person. I couldn't believe that he just carried on normally like nothing happened." "I just know," was Noel Nault's comment, "that there's no way Andrew is insane."

In all of the earlier criminal episodes Andrew seems actually to have appreciated the nature and consequences of what he was doing and there seems to have been an element of free choice in his actions. What he appeared to lack was the moral responsibility. It was not so much that he could not control his impulses as that *he lacked the will to do so*. It was less a question of brain damage or a borderline personality problem than what in old-fashioned language might be described as conscience.

Why did Andrew kill Nancy? Was it so motiveless as it was made out to be? Dr. Orchard stressed that it was pointless. It was, he said, an incongruous act, since Nancy was one of the few people Andrew really liked and trusted, indeed loved insofar as he was capable of love. Dr. Ervin was somewhat more cautious in his judgment:

> I think this crime was pointless in the ordinary sense [but] it was not a matter of chance that he was in Nancy's apartment at the time when everything was going to hell... it is not a random killing. It is not a matter of chance that he murdered Nancy.... She's a kind of doomed target, as we look at the drama unfolding. Who else is he going to go to when he is at the limits? She is there and so she's the one who fell victim to this.

Not for the first time were there discrepancies in the opinions offered by the experts. The bucket of evidence produced by the defense was not without holes.

Why did the sight of Nancy's sleeping body release an impulse which led to her destruction? What triggered off Andrew that fatal Monday morning? Was there a motive? If the murder was motiveless, as the psychiatrists contended, then the defense's argument — that Andrew was so abnormal as to be insane — was immensely strengthened. But if Andrew had a motive for what he was doing, then it is plausible to suggest that his action was deliberate.

Paul Chumak argued strongly that there was a motive. He suggested this was plainly a sexual killing and/or a sadistic psychopathic murder. Prima facie, the evidence seemed to bear this out, so much so that at Andrew's interrogation at Bradford police station Sergeant Stewart had not even bothered to ask Andrew why he had killed Nancy. The crime had all the trappings of a conventional sex murder: a nearly naked body brutally stabbed and sexually assaulted. Andrew's own statement of what he had done that night seemed to bear out such an interpretation.

Surely there must have been some sexual undertones that previous evening. Dr. Ervin agreed that Andrew was capable of sexual drives but argued that his affection for Nancy would normally have kept such drives under control. Andrew said himself that he had had a "crush" on Nancy for several years, but that he had never had nor had suggested having sex with her.

Apart from Mrs. Eaton's and Kristi Morrison's conversations with Nancy over the phone, our knowledge of precisely what occurred that Sunday evening is limited. We do not know whether before Andrew retired to the sofa, he may have suggested to Nancy the possibility of sex.

The venue itself was in some respects highly inflammable: Andrew in an unstable state seeking a release from tensions which were becoming unbearable, sitting on Nancy's double bed with Nancy in her nightshirt. To suppose that a seventeen-year-old boy, highly strung, in close physical contact late at night with a twenty-three-year-old woman did not have sexual feelings is surely incomprehensible. It requires little effort of the imagination to wonder if at some stage he may not have suggested that he should sleep with Nancy or at least have sex with her. If the suggestion was made and Nancy dismissed it, Andrew would have experienced a humiliating rejection. If the suggestion was never made, then the thought remained in the unconscious in a state of suspended animation. Andrew was, as one of the psychiatrists observed, "a walking time bomb."

That there is a link between sexual activity and aggression seems most likely. Electrical stimulation of areas of the brain which elicit an immediate penile erection are within a millimetre of sites which produce a rage response, suggesting that the two are interactive.[6] Paul Chumak had tried to show that when Andrew woke Nancy, it was because he wanted to have sex with her. When she refused, his temper flared and he plunged the knife into her body. Dr. Orchard strongly rejected the suggestion, yet sex was surely the culminating act in this grim saga. "After I stabbed her I raped her. . . . I took off my pants and had sex with her and ejaculated into her. . . . She was dead when I raped her."

The defense strategy was to distance in time, as far as possible, the murder and the rape. This served two purposes. First, in Canadian law, a sexual assault resulting in death is automatically first-degree murder. If, however, the rape occurred *after* death, that is, if it was not a sexual murder, then, if the insanity plea failed, Andrew would be convicted of a lesser charge. Secondly, making the case that the rape was not part of the murder strengthened the defense's case that Andrew's actions were aberrant to the point of insanity, that he was in the grip of impulses over which his mind had no control.

But even if the rape did happen much later, it does not mean that Andrew was insane. Necrophilia, as Krafft-Ebing defined it, "is best comprehended as a fetishism with an admixture of sadism, in as much as in essence it is of mastering and possessing an absolutely defenseless object, a corpse. It is not an uncommon supplement to a sadistic killing nor is it, as a number of precedents illustrate, a mark of insanity." Necrophiliacs are, as a rule, found to be sane by the courts and are dealt with accordingly.

In one case which was brought before the Supreme Court of Victoria, Australia, in 1974, the accused, a married man with homosexual tendencies, induced a male friend to go up with him into the mountains, shot him through the head, stripped the body and buggered it. He then threw it down a mineshaft. When he returned home he carried on as if nothing had happened until the police caught up with him. "I was," he told them, "really excited inside me. I was mad with power and nothing could stop me." Although he pleaded insanity, he was sentenced to death, a sentence later commuted to fifty years imprisonment with a minimum sentence of forty years.

In Andrew's case, the evidence suggests that the rape probably occurred at the time of or soon after the murder. When Andrew went to cash the check at the Royal Bank at 11:00 A.M. he was wearing the black pants from which he had washed the bloodstains, but he had discarded the white shirt with the blue trim, stained with blood and semen, in the bathroom where earlier he had taken a shower.

In statements which he made to the psychiatrists some five months or more later, Andrew, however, seemed to modify what he had told the police upon his arrest, implying then that he had raped Nancy immediately after killing her. From what he told the psychiatrists much later it appeared that four or even six hours may have elapsed before he had intercourse with Nancy's dead body, indeed after he returned to Farnham Avenue from his errands downtown.

Andrew told Dr. Orchard that intercourse had occurred as he tried to lift the girl's body from the floor to the bed. It is not wholly inconceivable that Andrew's sexual desire could have been reawakened, a few hours after the murder, by the sight of Nancy's spreadeagled body, then an anonymous corpse, the face covered, reminding him of the feverish pleasure which he had experienced some hours previously. Yet sex, literally in cold blood, would seem an astonishing outcome of the morning's events, given that we are told that as Andrew returned to comparative normality his feeling was one of hopelessness. Dr. Ervin could only suggest that the psychotic episode waxed, waned and then was revived again some hours later, but this was only speculation. All in all, it seems more likely, especially as the pathological evidence points towards the earlier occasion, that the verisimilitude of Andrew's later statements to the psychiatrists must be doubted.

What, however, is incontrovertible is that rape occurred. Whether the murder was an involuntary act or a deliberate act in which the desire for sexual gratification was a leading ingredient, sex certainly entered into it in the form of rape. It is generally agreed that rape has three major components, all closely interrelated with each other: anger, provoked by a feeling of being rejected or by a desire for retribution for assumed wrongs; power, where rape is a means of denying deep feelings of inadequacy and insecurity; and sadism, where the rapist reaps the pleasure which the infliction of pain and suffering arouses. All three motive forces seem to have been involved in Andrew's onslaught on Nancy.

In some sense Nancy was all that Andrew was not. She had a loving mother, a good income, many close friends and a satisfying job. Andrew had undoubtedly become dependent on her, a blow to his self-esteem. She had, however kindly, "put him down," and she had shown that whatever sexual favors she might grant others they were not for him. She had tried not merely to give him advice, to help him, but to exert a measure of influence, even control over him. Nancy had told Andrew not to bring drugs or his dubious friends into her apartment. When he took her car away, she informed the police. After that incident Nancy told a neighbor, Paul Fitzgibbon, that she had "trusted him for the last time." Andrew could no longer take the use of her apartment for granted. "She had," she told Paul, "taken Andrew under her wing." She had become, as Andrew had once described his Aunt Amy, a surrogate mother, a role which because of his ambiguous relationship with his mother Sarah, was not without potential dangers.

When he went to Nancy's apartment that Sunday evening Andrew was in a more desperate state than ever, without a roof over his head, with inner fears, with deep feelings of despair and resentment at the way the world was treating him and with mounting desires which needed release. In a sense, though in which exact way it is difficult to say, Nancy failed him that night. Whether or not she had explicitly rejected any overtures that he may have made, anger simmered in his unconscious and, on waking, it turned into red rage. Nancy became the focal point for all the humiliations and despair that he had experienced. Andrew, it had been said, "is likely to demand and even to take by force what he wants." It was as if all his grievances against the world had been focused momentarily upon Nancy in a monstrous act of rage.

Murder [in Frederick Wertham's words] is a consequence of severe lapses of ego control which makes possible the open expressions of primitive violence born out of previous and now unconscious traumatic experiences. A violent action is the only solution to a profound central conflict whose real nature remains below the threshold of consciousness.

Andrew felt himself to be both inadequate and insecure. The insecure man wishes to keep his personal esteem inviolate. He repudiates any challenge to it. He may even interpret an act of kindness as an invasion of his private world, an intrusion which he resents because it makes him dependent on the goodwill of others. To strike at the person upon whom he had become dependent might serve to bring back the self-esteem which he had lost, and so provide a sense of self-fulfillment and achievement. In such circumstances the act of murder might be a means of compensation, even a self-fulfilling creative act. "The loner," as Dennis Nilsen observed, "has to achieve fulfillment within himself."[7]

Andrew was at an existential divide in his life. He had to assert himself, throw off his dependence on Nancy and his family and so demonstrate his own identity. This entailed bringing Nancy totally within his power. She had to offer up what still, in some sense, was unpossessed, her body. The loved one must deny him nothing. The victim was the scapegoat through whom the killer fulfilled his destiny.

In many religions the blood involved in the sacrifice of slaughtered animals is a fundamental ingredient for enhancing the life of the slayers. Even in Judaic and Christian rituals sacrificial blood as a life-giving force has a symbolic place. In primitive cultures priests offered their gods the still palpitating hearts of their victims and in some mysterious way the life force of the victim was transferred to the killer. The experience is a temporarily intoxicating one, for it casts into oblivion the existential burden of life and momentarily brings into being a trance-like state of ecstasy.

By the very act of murder and rape Andrew's impotence had been transformed into omnipotence. For one fleeting moment he had a crowning achievement. If the juggling with the eggs meant anything, it stood for exhilaration at the completion of the task.

There was a third aspect of the murder to which Paul Chumak had called attention, but which was strongly refuted by the defense. Chumak had pointed out that there were a number of superficial cuts on Nancy's chest which implied the likelihood of a sadistic assault on someone who had refused to comply with his sexual demands.

There can be little doubt that in many respects Andrew fits in well with the prototype of the sadistic murderer.[8] Such a man is normally an introspective and withdrawn person, to outward appearances quiet and uncommunicative. Ordinarily he is a loner who is often ill-at-ease in the company of family and friends. He usually adores his grandparents, as, for instance, Andrew did, but regards his mother alternatively with love and hatred. He gets on badly with his father who is punitive and authoritarian in character.

As a boy he is interested in games of war and scenes of violence. He will be frequently of good or at least moderate intelligence, but an indifferent worker. He will possess a deep sense of inferiority, so much so that any challenge to his self-esteem or threat to his masculinity will provoke a violent reaction.

It is the killing of the victim which affords the sadistic murderer the greatest satisfaction — that is his chief motive. If the victim resists his will, he becomes more determined and brutal. The sight of suffering itself arouses him further, his brutality heightened by the helplessness of the victim. He is so excited that he will use more force than is required merely to kill. His frenzy is such that the murder usually involves multiple stabbing, with injuries to the breast, the genitalia, the abdomen and the rectum. The subjection of the victim to his power is more important than either the infliction of pain or sexual intercourse. The deed done he will often leave his victim in the position in which the assault took place, making no attempt to rearrange the limbs but rather underlining the act of final degradation.

Immediately after the murder the sadistic killer feels a sense of relaxation and a release of tension. Emotionally he is flat. Were he not so, he could not be so insensible to the cruelties he has committed. He returns to normal life without difficulty, behaving in such a way that his friends find it impossible to believe that he could have committed such a savage crime.

Questioned about the murder, the sadistic killer seems relatively unperturbed, and remains so, calm, detached and almost bored throughout the subsequent trial. "He can detach himself from his killing, being aware of it but not emotionally involved." He may well describe himself as a victim of forces over which he had no control, "something inside me, other than myself, creating an influence over me." He may hear voices, the devil bidding him to do the deed, God forbidding him. In prison or in the institution to which he is sent, he usually proves cooperative and manageable, so much so that he may be released early, and sometimes kills again.

In many respects this portrait of the sadistic killer seems to be a profile of Andrew, in his personality, in his method of murder and in its aftermath. He, too, had been subject on at least one occasion to hallu-cinatory voices. The murder itself was of horrifying brutality. Nancy had certainly fought back, uncomprehendingly, destroyed by the extra-ordinary outcome of her own kindness. Clumps of her hair were found on the bed, indicating a violent struggle. "She tried," Andrew himself recalled, "to defend herself with her own hands." There were tell-tale cuts on his own hand, slight as they may have been, which had been made as she tried to wrench the weapon from her assailant. Nancy could have been killed by a single stab wound, but there were twenty-one, six at the back of the head, three to the upper back, three to the right hand, and nine in the chest area.

Once the impulse to kill Nancy was activated, Andrew was like a roller-coaster without a brake. "He was aware," the psychiatrist Dr. Fred Jensen commented at his trial, "of what he was doing, but unable to stop what he was doing. It was a blind rage to kill, the ultimate act of destruction."

> For whatever reason [Colin Wilson writes] man is capable of experiencing a morbid involvement in the act of destruction, as if some deep erotic nerve had been touched by a craving for violence. And, like the sexual impulse, this destructive impulse has the power to blind him to everything but its own satisfaction.[9]

What Andrew did was, of course, insensate, for it was self-destructive. Perhaps, in some obscure way, Andrew, who at least twice before had made half-hearted attempts at suicide, perceived that in killing Nancy he was also destroying himself. Many people have the capacity to kill but, however murderous their desires, they restrain them as a result of the moral discipline with which they have been indoctrinated and because of the punishment they would receive. But, if life seems void of meaning and purpose, such inhibitions may disappear and killing is less pointless, since it constitutes, in itself, a form of suicide.

In murdering Nancy Eaton, Andrew had brought down the curtain on his own wretched existence. He had, in effect, done away with Andrew Leyshon-Hughes.

But if this helps to explain why Andrew murdered Nancy, what made him a murderer, or rather what shaped a personality that was capable of murder? "Getting pleasure in causing pain to others," a Vermont psychologist commented, "is a peculiar personal idiosyncrasy that isn't achieved overnight. It is a process. You get there by pulling the wings off flies, then getting back at people by causing pain to them." Most youthful violence, another writer has suggested, is an interaction between "nature and nurture," an amalgam of psychological stress, biological or mental disorders, genetic factors and adverse social and intrafamilial conditions.

In a short, perspicacious study[10] Professor Elliott Leyton contended that the principal explanation for sporadic outrageous behavior, usually traced to mental disease, could be best understood and interpreted in the environment in which the child grew up and in the direct relationship of the family setting.

Each act of rage, each violent blow to person or property, represents an inarticulate but fundamental protest.

> Act is piled upon bizarre act [Leyton wrote] in an increasingly frenzied attempt to recover the lost object, the child's sense of worth and position, his or her social persona. . . . the child's attempt to recover the lost position often accelerates the process it wishes to curtail, for the bizarre acts, most often misinterpreted by family and society, speed up the cycle of alienation between adolescent and society. . . . This "senseless" displacement of rage . . . is a rational manner of communication . . . a metaphor through which the child tries to communicate with family and society. Regrettably the metaphor is destructive to all concerned.[11]

The psychopathic child finds it difficult, if not impossible, to explain his explosive conduct. "Maybe there's something the matter with me," said sixteen-year-old James, when he was asked to explain his acts of vandalism. "People bug me but I'm not hard to get along with," said fourteen-year-old Marie who terrorized her parents one day and was calm and normal the next. "I don't have a great amount of patience," Andrew admitted.

These non-explanations [Leyton comments] are merely sleights of hand, designed not to protect that adolescent from the severity of the law, but to protect himself from having to consider the central trauma in his life. Let there be no doubt that it is a major rupture in the child's social relationship that has pushed him or her in the direction of the judicial system.

Among the psychopathic children whom Leyton observed and interviewed at Hillview was Lucien Asprey.[12] Lucien "began throwing temper tantrums at the age of two." He did quite well at school until the age of twelve when his work and behavior deteriorated markedly.

"After a conflict in the home in the night," a social worker reported, "Lucien's behavior would correspondingly deteriorate the next day in school." He was suspended from school after he had told a nun "to go fuck herself." Lucien's father was a "very weak, frustrated individual," afraid to let anyone get too close to him; his mother, the stronger personality of the two, vacillated between blaming her husband and her son.

Lucien, feeling that his parents had rejected him, mixed with bad companions and began drinking heavily. The psychiatrist who examined him at Dartmouth in 1976 found no "disorders of his thought contents, no delusions and no hallucinations" but felt that he was probably reacting to his situation at home.

Admitted to Hillview, Lucien showed some signs of improvement, but as soon as he returned home he became violent, firing a .303 rifle through the ceiling. Readmitted to the institution, he became increasingly difficult, lashing out at all and sundry when he was thwarted, and even burying a case of dynamite in the nearby hills so that he could "blow the place up." Behind Lucien's explosive rages there lay desperation, stemming from "a childhood of rejection, a longing for love and support, and confusion and frustration regarding his father."

This, so Professor Leyton holds, is more often than not the key to much contemporary delinquency which can culminate in acts of terrifying violence. For what the child needs above all is a place in the social order, a sense of belonging. "All social actions," to quote Leyton again, "...take place inside society, and they constitute a kind of communiqué addressed to the social order." Where the child feels, albeit mistakenly or through his own fault, that he lacks a true identity in his family or school, he protests in an incoherent and inarticulate fashion, either against himself, leading to acts of would-be suicide, against his parents or in random and nihilistic attacks on people and property in the community at large.

This is illustrated by another case of murder, one which greatly shocked the state of Vermont in 1981, in part because the killers were both adolescents.[13] Two young girls, both twelve years old — Melissa Walbridge and Meghan O'Rourke — who were walking through the woods in the vicinity of their small hometown of Essex, were brutally set on and sexually assaulted by two youths, Jamie Savage, aged fifteen and Louie Hamlin, aged sixteen. Melissa was treated horrifically, evidently tortured before she died as the "teasing" incisions made with a knife on her chest suggested, suffering twenty-nine stab wounds in all. Meghan, left by the boys for dead, though in terrible agony, managed to crawl away, attracted attention and miraculously survived.

The two boys were high-school dropouts. They had a long history of delinquency, theft of cars and violence. They came from disadvantaged homes. "Hamlin's stunted moral development," the Vermont psychiatrist, Barry Nurcombe, said, "is a consequence of his having been raised in a family with chaotic child-rearing patterns, corrupt and brutalized patterns of sexuality, little affection and little capacity to appreciate the depth of his alienation." "By the time a Louie Hamlin or Jamie Savage kills," the author Peter Meyer sagely comments, "though barely pubescent, his mind is already woven into an intricate pattern of deviance."

Jamie Savage was still technically a juvenile and under existing state law would be freed on his eighteenth birthday. This caused such an uproar in the state that a special meeting of the legislature was summoned which changed the law. Henceforth there was to be no age limit for the prosecution of murder and for other serious crimes the age was lowered to ten. But the law could not be retroactive. After a period of detention in the Waterbury State Hospital where he spent most of the time watching television and doing some menial chores, Jamie was adjudged a delinquent and sent to a Pennsylvania psychiatric hospital for evaluation. In 1983, Jamie turned up in Arizona under the name of John W. Barber. When a local newspaper ferreted out the news, its head-line ran: "YOU CAN RAPE AND KILL AND THEN YOU CAN MOVE TO ARIZONA AND CHANGE YOUR NAME."

Louie Hamlin, Jamie's companion, the elder of the two, known as "The Hulk" because of his physique, was, according to the psychiatrist, "entirely selfish. He sees himself as an isolated person, feels no qualms of conscience about any of his behavior, has an extremely unpredictable and destructive under-current of rage." "He had," as someone put it more graphically, "a very short fucking temper." His attack on the two girls had taken place, Barry Nurcombe said, "in an emotional setting of smoldering rage." When the judge asked him what made him angry, he replied, "I don't know. It's just events that lead up to things. Just things in my everyday life. I get mad."

When as a boy his mother criticized him, Louie would rush from the house and walk the streets for hours. When he was only two, his aunt recalled, "he would throw himself on the floor, hit his head on the wall." A nun who had watched him at a catechism class expressed her fears that he was "going to kill somebody some time." "I had a reputation," he boasted, ". . . for not taking no shit from nobody."

Yet there was another side to Louie. "They wanted me," he said of his parents, "to act the way they thought I should act. . . . I'm a slow learner. It's a possibility I had brain damage when I had that tracheotomy." It came out that his father (a great collector of pornography), who was arrested for incest with Louie's sister shortly after Louie's own arrest, had sexually assaulted him when he was five. Louie excelled at swimming and, in spite of poor spelling and grammar, tried his hand at poetry which, with the help of a teacher who had befriended him, was actually turned into touching verse. The poems showed that at the back of Louis' chaotic mind, lay a yearning for tranquility. When his former teacher wrote to him in prison, he replied, professing love for her.

Neither Louie nor Jamie felt remorse for what they had done. Louie did, however, say that he was sorry and declared that he was now a born-again Christian; but "I didn't," he told the psychiatrist, "really feel it was wrong. I am only in prison because it is the law."

In his short life Louie had never managed to forge a genuine place for himself in society nor had he ever acquired a feeling of social obligation. He simply took what he wanted. He was, as Barry Nurcombe put it, "amoral rather than immoral, a-responsible rather than irresponsible." The question of insanity as a defense was discussed but rejected. Yet, given the nature of what he had done, it might seem that he had as much claim as Andrew to such consideration. Whilst his fellow killer Jamie escaped more or less scot-free, Louie was sentenced to forty-five years to life for murder and fifteen to twenty-five years for sexual assault.

These children, Jamie and Louie, were made what they were — young psychopaths — by their social environment and their family background. How does Andrew fit into this pattern? It was a striking feature of his life that some degree of contentment and an absence of explosive rage could be found only when he was away from the constricting influences of home. Even to some extent when he was under detention, at Penetang and in the Don Jail, incarceration provided a measure of harmony. If Andrew's psychotic episodes resulted from brain damage, surely there would have been occasions when such explosions found an outlet outside the home background. To the contrary, all of the major eruptions in his life were either home based or took place in what could be described as surrogate homes, his aunt's house, Nancy's apartment.

Andrew had been a troublesome child. On the one hand he had developed what may be described as a macho image of himself. He liked to bully other boys. His aunt suspected that he was bullying her children. He loved driving fast cars and motorbikes. His interest in war games pointed in the same direction. The cartoons that he drew for Dr. Carr were full of aggresive imagery. About some of his rampages there was an element of swagger, as when, after robbing the storekeeper at Balsam, he drove the snowmobile around and around. He even told one interviewer that he would like to become a cop. The tough-guy image he had of himself was fostered by hard drinking and occasional drug taking.

But behind this facade, there was a deeply unhappy boy, a non-achiever who lacked self-esteem, who seemed incapable of doing well at school or of holding down a job. Except for the certificates he had won for life saving at swimming, nearly everything Andrew had attempted seemed doomed to disaster: schools, camps, relations with his parents, his aunt and uncle, the girl at school and Lisa, his occasional employment.

Yet what was taking place was not occurring in a vacuum. The tantrums, the fits of rage, the violence which culminated in Nancy's murder were expressions of a fundamental reaction to the environment in which Andrew was living, possibly rooted in infancy. It was Andrew's constant refrain that his parents did not really love him and that he was neglected.

By his parents' own confession, the family home was often an unhappy one; there were constant rows between mother and father, between father and son, between mother and son. As Andrew expressed it to one of his many interviewers, "Things were lousy at home...there wasn't a good relationship." Dr. Solursh told Dr. Veeder (on 21 January 1983) of Andrew's "apparent resentment of his mother and father in particular.... There are obviously numerous factors in Andrew's resentment...his father's passive alcohol intake and his mother's overt aggression." In a bleak assessment of Andrew's home conditions, which she prepared for the Syl Apps Centre in August 1985, social worker Joy Freeman spoke of his parents' "decision to get married rather than to abort....":

> Andrew believes that his father had several affairs during his marriage. He also stated that his parents have attempted to separate at least once.... His relationship with his father appeared most problematic and hostile with Andrew expressing anger at his father's treatment (neglect) of his mother, his alcohol consumption and his inability to be available emotionally and be a "real" father. Essentially Andrew described his childhood as unhappy with a predominant sense of neglect and abandonment, even though he was privy to all the material trappings of a comfortable home.

To be fair to his family it is important to stress that such charges are founded on Andrew's word alone, and that Andrew — who clearly had an *idée fixé* in his mind about his parents — was a compulsive liar and fantasizer. This may well have been a part of his characteristic psychopathic makeup. His father told Dr. Veeder that, "Andrew lies and distorts." Unquestionably his parents did everything they conceivably could to help their errant son, but ultimately to no effect. Andrew grew up strangely isolated from emotional attachments at home. He was a lost soul.

In a significant study[14], Dr. Ken Magid and Carole A. McKelvey state that "if the proper bonding and subsequent attachment do not occur, usually between the child and the mother, the child will develop mistrust and a deep-seated rage. He becomes a child without a conscience." The bond of affection is normally forged in the first nine months of a child's life; by the first two years of his life the pattern of a child's future personality may have been already established. Daycare, nursery schools and others do not provide an effective substitute for mother care. The need for both parents to go out to work, in Magid's and McKelvey's estimation, accounts for the high increase in juvenile delinquency and the increase in the number of the psychopathic young in North America.

Dr. Foster Cline, a leading authority on disturbed children, stresses that thoughtful caring of the child is essential for trust in later life — trust of oneself, trust of others, and trust in humanity — and that the process actually starts with the feeding of the child at every fourth hour. "If," Cline writes "at any step things go wrong, lasting and severe psychopathology may result. The results of such trauma are not pretty, and they last a lifetime. . . . They warp the fabric of society."[15]

A child's needs are emotional as well as physical. "If children don't get sufficient love early in life," they may become psychopathic, a New York probation officer, Erica Manfred, commented. "If you're baking a cake and you forget to put the salt in while you're baking, you can't sprinkle it on top later. These kids never got salt in their cake. They've never been socialized." If a state of real trust between parents and child has been established, the child will be able to cope with crisis; but without that affectionate bond the child may be launched on a career which may, though not, of course, necessarily, end in violence. "The child to whom the mother is not accessible may learn that he cannot trust others and others will not care for him. Consequently he fails to learn to care for others and to develop a conscience."[16]

The authors of *High Risk* detail the characteristics of the unattached,[17] the future psychopaths, features which seem to fit Andrew like a glove: lack of ability to give and receive affection; self-destructive behavior; cruelty to others or to pets; stealing; extreme control problems; lack of long-term childhood friends; abnormalities in eye contact; parents seem unreasonably angry; preoccupation with blood and conflict; superficial attractiveness and friendliness with strangers; learning disorder; lying. Such children will display an explosive temper at apparently reasonable parental requests, as did Andrew. When they steal they do not actually need food or money but their action is brought on "by the terrible unexplained empty feeling inside." So Andrew told Natalie Wouk that he stole "to draw attention to himself." "Was he a liar to you — a persistent liar?" Chumak asked Andrew's mother. "He would," Sarah replied, "tell me what he thought I wanted to hear, and yes, he lied." Such children "can work a good con." They are manipulators who act so as to suit their needs at the time. One of the few occasions when Andrew showed annoyance at an interview was when he was accused of being a con artist. But his mother agreed that Andrew "would be manipulative if he wanted something." When, however, Chumak tried to ask Professor Ervin if Andrew "lied intentionally to manipulate the events of the murder," the judge disallowed the question.

The eyes of such children seem to undergo an intense change when they are in rage. One of their victims, Dorothy, a seventy-five-year-old woman raped by a young man, said of her assailant that he had the look of a "devil," an observation which Amy Jephcott had made of Andrew: "When finally I saw him, it was the most horrible face. It was like the devil looking out at me."

Such children seem to thrive on conflict. Toilet behavior is another feature of early life which can provide the theme for battles over control between a child and his parents, and leave behind, if unresolved, feelings of guilt and anger. They like to "get at" their mother, and their behavior may well imperil the marriage, as it is normal for the father to think that there is nothing very wrong with their child. These young psychopaths seem more or less impervious to control. In later life it is not surprising that, without close human attachment, they have a warped sense of sexuality and sex drives.

> What is it that is at the heart of the dark side of these individuals [Magid and McKelvey ask], the simmering volcano, that makes them so dangerous? At the core of the unattached is a deep-seated rage, far beyond normal anger.... The rage of psychopaths is that born of unfulfilled needs as infants. Incomprehensible pain is forever locked in their souls because of the abandonment they felt as infants.[18]

> The implication [Dr. Kegan writes of the psychopath] is that something has gone terribly wrong with the normal process of development at a highly conspicuous cost to those who are connected to the individual, but at an equally high, if less conspicuous cost to the individual himself.[19]

Ultimately, people like Andrew Leyshon-Hughes defy authoritative analysis. Their incomprehensible depravity escapes classification. They warn us, disturbingly, of the fundamental inscrutability of the human mind. "Every human being," Iris Murdoch writes in her novel, *The Philosopher's Pupil*, "is different, more absolutely different and peculiar than we can goad ourselves into conceiving.... We are in fact far more randomly made, more full of rough contingent rubble, than art or vulgar psycho-analysis lead us to imagine." We can search for conclusive explanations but, in the end, we can never find a single answer which will satisfy all the questions. The "rough contingent rubble" is always there to trip us up.

EPILOGUE

Brothers, I am sorry I have got no Morrison's Pill for curing
the maladies of Society.

THOMAS CARLYLE, *PAST AND PRESENT*

This disease is beyond my practice.

SHAKESPEARE, *MACBETH*

Yet we have gone on living,
Living and partly living.

T.S. ELIOT, *MURDER IN THE CATHEDRAL*

"IT IS AN ALL-TOO-FAMILIAR STORY", WRITE the authors of a recent
book:

> ...a psychopath with a pattern of criminal behavior is caught.
> His lawyer successfully argues that the psychopath's history
> shows he is a victim of madness and is not *legally* accountable
> for his crime. The judge orders the criminal to be confined to a
> mental hospital. Once evaluated at the hospital, however, the
> psychopath is found to be sane and competent. Diagnosis reveals
> no nervous or mental disease. The hospital is then *legally*

compelled to release him. This psychopath has fallen through
the cracks that exist in our legal and medical definitions of
insanity — because the *psychopath* does not meet the current
definitions of *insanity*.... Being neither legally sane nor insane
they fall through the cracks, continuing to commit crimes and
go free, leaving us a society at high risk.[1]

For the psychopath there is no cure. Oak Ridge, the high-security
wing of Penetang, the Hucker Report laments, has little in the way of
treatment to offer "patients diagnosed as psychopathic personalities...
[and is] at a loss as to what to do with them."[2] Within an institution
where tight control can be exercised, a psychopath may respond to
behavior modification therapy, only to revert to violent behavior in the
uncontrolled outside world.

> You cannot get rid of these nuisances and monsters [George
> Bernard Shaw wrote] by simply cataloguing them as subthyroidics
> and superadrenals or the like. At present you torment them for
> a fixed period, at the end of which they are set free to resume
> their operations with a savage grudge against the community
> which has tormented them. That is stupid. Releasing them is
> like releasing the tigers from the Zoo to find their next meal in
> the nearest children's playground.

Although the public may have an exaggerated view of psychopathic
criminals' propensity to commit crimes upon their release, there is a
sufficiently long list in Canada and the United States to testify that
such fears are not entirely unjustified. The psychopath Garry Trapnell,
the subject of Eliot Asinof's book, *The Fox is Crazy Too*, was arrested
twenty times but until he was imprisoned in 1973 for hijacking a
passenger jet (TWA 707 flying from Los Angeles to New York), he had
spent less than two years in prison because he had successfully masqueraded
as insane. "Either," Trapnell said, "a man falls under this antiquated
psychiatric scheme of things, or he doesn't. I can bullshit the hell out of
one of these psychiatrists in ten minutes."

In New York, another psychopath, George Fitzsimons, charged with
killing his parents, persuaded psychiatrists that he was no longer dangerous
and was released to live with his aunt and uncle, whom, he said he
loved "like his own mother." He later stabbed them both to death.

Gary Heidnik, the son of a retired Philadelphia city councilor, was sentenced in 1978 to detention in a psychiatric institution for kidnapping a mentally retarded woman and keeping her captive in a coal bunker. In 1981 he was released, made a small fortune but was then re-arrested on charges of murder, rape and torture — activities only revealed when the police found women kept as sex slaves, naked and chained to a sewer pipe in Heidnik's Philadelphia basement.

In 1974 a Canadian psychopath, James Odo, was charged with the murder of a fifteen-year-old boy but acquitted. Two years later he was sent to Dorchester Penitentiary for raping his five-year-old niece. In February 1980 he was released under mandatory supervision and moved in with a Mrs. Davidson. He offered to take her daughter, Darlene, to the local carnival and killed her on the way. As early as 1970, he was diagnosed as a latent schizophrenic living in a "borderline state," who could "go over the brink very easily." But Odo had escaped through the cracks in the system.

In 1971 another man, clearly psychopathic, was charged with violent assault, found not guilty by reason of insanity and sent under a lieutenant-governor's warrant for indefinite detention at Penetang. He was released four years later "because he had responded well to his therapy." He became a mental-health worker but could not overcome his compulsion to kill and stabbed a stranger to death. "I always had this aggression inside me," he said. "I don't know where it came from."

There have been a number of incidents where inmates have been sent from prison or a mental hospital to halfway houses, staging posts on the way to a full discharge, placed on "special trust," and subsequently committed another crime or killed. On 27 January 1988, thirty-two-year-old Melvin Glenn Stanton left Montgomery Centre in Toronto on an unescorted pass. Hours later he raped and stabbed to death twenty-five-year-old Tema Conter, while she lay sleeping in her apartment, ten blocks from the transition house.

That same week, another parolee, Patrick Mailloux, was convicted of murder. He had walked away from a Moncton, New Brunswick, halfway house, robbed a variety store and then shot the cashier, sixteen-year-old Laura Davis, to death.

Less than three months later, two diagnosed psychopaths, Robert Abel and Paul Cecil Gillis, were arrested in connection with the abduction, rape and attempted murder of a young girl. In 1976, Abel, from Chatham, Ontario, had murdered his wife Dianna, his two-year-old son, John, and his three-year-old daughter, Dawn. All three had been beaten on the head with a hammer and then strangled to death with a wire coat hanger. On the eve of the murders Abel told his mother, whose birthday it was the next day, that he was going to give her a birthday present she would never forget. In 1973, his friend, Paul Gillis strangled and raped Laverne Johnston and then threw her body into Georgian Bay. After his arrest he admitted to the murders of seventeen-year-old Barbara Statt in 1973 and fifteen-year-old Robin Gates in 1974.

Both Abel and Gillis, found to be insane and therefore not guilty of the six murders, were incarcerated on lieutenant-governor's warrants in the Penetanguishene Mental Health Centre. After spending four years at Penetang they were transferred to the medium-security wing of the St. Thomas Psychiatric Hospital and were subsequently allowed to leave on day passes. On 31 March 1988, the two men were alleged to have dragged a fourteen-year-old girl into their car in broad daylight while she was waiting at a bus stop in London, Ontario. The girl was taken to an abandoned warehouse in St. Thomas, where she was savagely beaten and raped. Then, while she was still unconscious, she was thrown from a bridge into a river and left for dead. Gillis and Abel, meanwhile, had returned to the psychiatric hospital in time for their 9:00 P.M. curfew.

Another psychopath, Allan George Foster of Vancouver, raped and murdered his eighteen-year-old sister-in-law in 1971. During his incarceration he attended psychotherapy sessions and by 1978 the experts agreed that Foster could be released into the community without risk. In support of his application for release, his case management officer wrote that, "Mr. Foster is a highly sensitive and intelligent person. He is one of the sanest people I have ever met." Foster managed to stay out of trouble for eight years until he was arrested in April 1986 for indecent exposure and placed in custody. He was released two months later after a psychologist came to the conclusion that, "Mr. Foster appears to have overcome the life stresses that caused him to flip out and take the life of another person."

Less than a year later, on 15 December 1987, the mutilated and partly clad body of Foster's common-law wife, Joan Pilling, was found in a pool of blood in Foster's Chilliwack, B.C., home. He had beaten her repeatedly with a hammer and then stabbed her in the chest eleven times with a carving knife. Pilling's twelve-year-old daughter, Linda, and Linda's friend, Megan, also twelve, lay in the next room, buried under a bloodstained mattress. Foster had beaten the two girls to death with a claw hammer and then raped their corpses.

"The evil part of me gives me the opportunity to give the right answers and to appear all right," Foster confessed to a psychiatrist hours after the three murders. "There is only one thing crazier than me, and that is the society that lets me do what I do."

The judge committed Andrew on a warrant from the lieutenant-governor to Oak Ridge, the high-security wing of Penetang, expressing the belief that he would not be freed until the authorities were assured that he was unlikely to put society at risk. His state is reviewed every year by a board chaired by a retired judge and four other people, two psychiatrists, a lawyer and a lay person. The average custodial period in Canada, for those held on warrants of the lieutenant-governor, ranges from 104 months in Saskatchewan to fourteen months in Nova Scotia. The Hucker Report states that at Oak Ridge, "the mean duration of stay... in the hospital is approximately three years... a small proportion leave in less than six months and... about half the patients in this group remain longer than two years."[3]

There is some evidence that Andrew may get an early release. He knows that it is to his advantage to conduct himself well, and has already won privileges which, within Oak Ridge's bleak confines, give him a relative degree of comfort. Whether or not Andrew is mad or bad or both, it is practically impossible to predict future dangerousness. Sufferers with behavioral problems like Andrew's do not easily respond to treatment or medication, nor is there any sure way of predicting whether a patient, whose institutional record has been good, will revert to violent behavior once he is at large in society again. "The present W.L.G. [warrant of the lieutenant-governor] system," the Hucker Report admitted, "relies on this kind of prediction and yet there is no evidence that mental-health professionals can accurately predict dangerousness; Oak Ridge itself amply confirms this position."[4] Little comment is needed beyond that of the chief psychiatrist at Broadmoor who stated that he was certain he could discharge half his patients into the community without risk — the trouble was that he did not know which half.

So while the outlook may look relatively good for Andrew himself, his release might be ominous for society. "I know how to play the game," Andrew said in an interview at Penetang in October 1986. "I won't be in here for long. Don't even need to be here. All I need is a week up at my cottage and I'll be fine."

Nancy's grave is a garden of roses, azaleas and lilies. On her marker, under her name and dates, Mrs. Eaton inscribed, "I held tight loosely." She visits her daughter's grave nearly every day.

It has not been a good three years for Mrs. Eaton and it does not get better. "My whole life," she said, "has been devoted to Tiger. Heaven knows where the new focus will be."

Before her death Nancy bought her mother a present, *Helen Reddy's Greatest Hits*. One of the songs on the tape, "You and Me Against the World," soon became their favorite:

> . . . You and me against the world
> Sometimes it feels like you and me against the world
> And for all the times we've cried
> I always felt the odds were on our side
> And when one of us is gone
> And one is left alone to carry on
> Well then remembering will have to do
> Our memories alone will get us through
> Think about the days of me and you
> Of you and me against the world.

It seemed an appropriate description of their life together after they left Edward. But it assumed a horrific irony after Nancy's murder, and still, when things are really bad, Mrs. Eaton puts on the tape and sings the words at the top of her lungs.

———————— ENDNOTES ————————

CHAPTER II

1. Quoted from Peter C. Newman, *The Canadian Establishment* (Toronto: 1975), 275.
2. Ibid., 275.
3. See Claude Bissell's penetrating biography, *The Imperial Canadian: Vincent Massey in Office* (Toronto: 1986).
4. Ibid., 306-7.

CHAPTER IX

1. Brian Masters, *Killing for Company* (London: 1985), 279.
2. See e.g. D.T. Lunde, *Murder and Madness* (New York: 1979); N. Morris *Madness and the Criminal Law* (Oxford: 1982); H. Prins, *Dangerous Behaviour: The Law and Mental Disorder* (London: 1986).
3. R. Partridge, *Broadmoor* (London: 1953), 28-29.
4. There is a growing literature on Sutcliffe: Michael Nicholson, *The Yorkshire Ripper* (London: 1979); David Yallop's brilliant study, *Deliver Us From Evil* (London: 1981); John Beattie, *The Yorkshire Ripper Story* (London: 1981); J. Cross, *The Yorkshire Ripper: The In-Depth Study of a Mass Killer and his Methods* (London: 1981); Gordon Burn, *Somebody's Husband, Somebody's Son* (London: 1984); N. Jouve Ward, *The Streetcleaner: The Yorkshire Ripper Case on Trial* (London: 1986).
5. For a graphic account, Lincoln Caplan, *The Insanity Defense and the Trial of John W. Hinckley, Jr.* (New York: 1987).
6. Elliott Leyton, *Hunting Humans: The Rise of the Modern Multiple Killer* (Toronto: 1986).
7. James M. Reinhardt, *The Murderous Trial of Charles Starkweather* (Springfield, Il: 1960); William Allen, *Charles Starkweather* (Boston: 1976).
8. Leyton, *Hunting Humans*, 281.
9. Jack Levin and James Fox, *Mass Murder: America's Growing Menace.* (New York: 1985), 208.
10. Ibid., 208.

CHAPTER XI

1. The term *psychopath* is synonymous with both sociopath and antisocial personality, but should not be confused with psychotic.

2. P. Gallwey, "The Psychodynamic of Borderline Personality," in *Aggression and Dangerousness*, ed. D.P. Farringdon and J. Gunn (Chichester, UK: 1985), 133.

3. Levin and Fox, *Mass Murder*, 209-210.

4. Peter Clyne, *Guilty But Insane: Anglo-American Attitudes to Insanity and Criminal Guilt* (London: 1973), 145-6.

5. Magid and McKelvey, *High Risk*, 21.

6. C. Turnbull, *The Mountain People* (New York: 1972).

7. For an incisive and telling study, see Magid and McKelvey, *High Risk*.

8. Experiments with young rhesus monkeys have shown that those that have been separated from their parents become asocial and aggressive.

9. Manfred S. Guttmacher, *The Mind of the Murderer* (New York: 1960).

10. Foster Kennedy, Harry R. Hoffman and William H. Haines, "A Study of William Heirens." *American Journal of Psychiatry* 104 (1947); J.M. Reinhardt, *Sex Perversions and Sex Crimes* (Springfield, Il: 1957).

11. There is abundant literature on Bundy, but the most useful book is Stephen C. Michaud and Hugh Aynesworth, *The Only Living Witness* (New York: 1983). There are other studies by Steven Winn and David Merrill, and Richard W. Larsen, and his case is perspicaciously summarized by Elliott Leyton, *Hunting Humans*, 68-111.

12. A useful survey in Colin Wilson, *A Criminal History of Mankind* (London: 1985).

13. Sydney Brock, *The Life and Death of Neville Heath* (London: 1947); Gerald Byrne, *Borstal Boy, Neville Heath* (London: 1949); M. Critchley, ed., *The Trial of Neville George Heath* (London: 1951); Pauli Hill, *Portrait of a Sadist* (London: 1960); C. Phillips, *For Murderer's Moon* (London: 1956) has essays on Heath, Christie and Haigh.

14. Gerald Byrne, *John George Haigh* (London: 1950); Lord Dunboyne, ed., *The Trial of John George Haigh* (London: 1953); Samuel Jackson, *John George Haigh* (London: 1953); Molly Lefebure, *Murder with a Difference: Studies of Haigh and Christie* (London: 1985); A.J. La Bern, *Haigh: The Mind of a Murderer* (London: 1974).

15. Ludovic Kennedy, *Ten Rillington Place* (London: 1971).

16. On Nilsen, see Brian Masters, *Killing for Company*, a well-researched and penetrating analysis.

17. R. Lloyd and S. Williamson, *Born to Trouble: Portrait of a Psychopath* (London: 1967).

CHAPTER XII

1. Mark Nichols et al., "Engineers of the Mind." *Maclean's*, vol. 101, number 16, 44.
2. V.H. Mark and F.R. Ervin, *Violence and the Brain* (New York: 1970), 97-108.
3. John C. Gunn, *Violence in Human Society* (Newton Abbot, UK: 1973), 109.
4. Alpinists were known to become excessively irritable and even aggressive as a result of lack of oxygen at great heights.
5. Dr. Ervin refers in his book to the case of a young girl, Jeannie, who had murdered her two stepsisters, one of them while she was babysitting, because the child cried. Neurological and psychological tests were inconclusive, but brain-wave recordings were stimulated by playing a tape of a baby crying.
6. Robert Prentky, "The Neurochemistry and Neuroendocrinology of Sexual Aggression," in *Aggression and Dangerousness*, 7-55.
7. Masters, *Killing for Company*, 242.
8. See the authoritative article by Dr. Robert Brittain, "Sadistic Murderer," in *Medicine, Science and the Law*, the official journal of the British Academy of Forensic Sciences, X (1970), 198-207.
9. Colin Wilson, *Order of Assassins* (London: 1972), 21.
10. Elliott Leyton, *The Myth of Delinquency: An Anatomy of Juvenile Nihilism* (Toronto: 1979).
11. Ibid., 15, 26.
12. Ibid., 112-130.
13. Peter Meyer, *Death of Innocence: A Case of Murder in Vermont* (New York: 1985).
14. Magid and McKelvey, *High Risk*, 3.
15. Foster Cline, *Understanding and Treating the Severely Disturbed Child* (Evergreen, Col: 1979).
16. Magid and McKelvey, *High Risk*, 61.
17. Ibid., 71-99.
18. Ibid., 26.
19. R.G. Kegan in *Unmasking the Psychopath*, ed. W.H. Reid et al. (New York: 1986).

EPILOGUE

1. Magid and McKelvey, *High Risk*, 195.
2. Stephen J. Hucker et al., *Oak Ridge: A Review and an Alternative* (Toronto: 1986), 10.
3. Hucker, *Oak Ridge*, 35. The custodial period varies from 104 months in Saskatchewan to eighty-six months in B.C., seventy-five months in Ontario, forty months in Quebec and fourteen months in Nova Scotia.
4. Ibid., 110.